NEW AND REVISED EDITION

SOUL

★ ★ ★ ★ OF A ★ ★ ★ ★

CITIZEN

LIVING WITH CONVICTION IN CHALLENGING TIMES

"I stayed up half the night reading *Soul of a Citizen*, finding it a beautiful and morally transcendent work. Paul Loeb is a personal hero of mine who gives decency and generosity a political character, in the humblest of ways. The new edition is magnificent." —JONATHAN KOZOL

PAUL ROGAT LOEB

"The voices Loeb finds demonstrate that courage can be another name for love."
—Alice Walker

"Loeb can pierce a cynic's armor with his practical examination of social change."
—*San Jose Mercury News*

"Thoughtful and encouraging, Loeb offers a rich spirituality of citizenship for both experienced activists and those just wondering where to begin."
—Jim Wallis, editor, *Sojourners*

"Paul Loeb brings hope for a better world in a time when we so urgently need it."
—Millard Fuller, founder, Habitat for Humanity

"*Soul* has inspired thousands of people, of widely differing perspectives, to take a stand. It teaches them how to get past the barriers to act, and shows why their actions matter. The new edition is a powerful personal guide to get people involved."
—Hans Riemer, former political director of Rock the Vote

"When my daughter asked from college how to be an effective grassroots citizen, I gave her Paul's book. The new edition is even more powerful."
—Josette Sheeran, executive director, United Nations World Food Program

"You are part of what's good about this world and I admire your work very much."
—Bill Moyers

"Loeb writes very powerfully."
—*Chicago Tribune*

"*Soul of a Citizen* has been a powerful resource to get thousands of students involved in their communities, giving them the opportunity to apply their learning in meaningful ways. This updated edition is both timely and exceptionally useful to campuses that want to reclaim higher education's central role in educating responsible, democratic citizens."
—Carol Geary Schneider, president, Association of American Colleges and Universities

"This wonderful book teaches us the value of taking chances and not being afraid to fail. It reminds us that the more we help others build productive lives, the better our own lives will be."

—Bob Chase, president, National Education Association

"Reveals that the spiritual resources of patience and hope are essential ingredients of soulful citizenship." —*The Lutheran*

"A much-needed call for community involvement."

—Art Levine, president, Teachers College, Columbia University

"An antidote for spirits sullen with cynicism."

—Sean Gonsalves, *Oakland Tribune*

"Recounts what's preventing regular folks from working in a more committed fashion beyond writing the odd check in these cynical times." —*Toronto Globe & Mail*

"A highly personable story of integrity and commitment that reminds all of us that we have often-unrealized abilities to live lives worthy of our convictions." —*Steelabor,* United Steelworkers

"Loeb has amassed a powerful arsenal for his assault on cynicism, [gathering] hundreds of stories of ordinary people who are changing the world one step at a time." —*The Oregonian*

"Loeb believes in commitment and believes in it passionately."

—*Columbus Dispatch*

"A lot of smart people who have some influence on the course of history will read and admire you—and learn from you."

— Kurt Vonnegut

"Paul Loeb is one of the finest spokespeople I know for a spiritually based citizen activism. A must-read for people seeking to heal our country and the world." —Marianne Williamson

"A new spirit of responsibility for the planet and those who inhabit it. We begin to sense what it might mean to treat the world as a sacred gift."

—Bishop Thomas Gumbleton, president emeritus of Pax Christi

"Wonderful stories and powerful lessons. Schools throughout the country are using this book as a core resource for study and discussion." —Youth Service America

"Like few other chroniclers today, Paul Loeb uncannily captures the thoughts and hopes, inchoate though they may be, of America. Loeb is a natural." —Studs Terkel

"Should be placed in the hands of every cynic who sees societal problems and then retreats to their private sanctuary and says 'there's nothing we can do.'" — *Public Citizen*

"*Soul of a Citizen* helps teach us what to do." —David Brower, founder, Friends of the Earth

"Skillfully erases the seams between the political and the personal. Loeb's eyes are wide open and his feet planted as he examines the roots of disengagement from community." —John Sweeney, president, AFL-CIO

"It will inspire people new to activism, and deals with cynicism and burnout in a good way for movement veterans. Altogether, a wonderful job, rich with specific experience." —Howard Zinn

"Convincingly affirms the human ability to create change." —American Library Association *Booklist*

"An important and inspiring book." —Michael Brown, founder, City Year

"Hopeful, fascinating, and admirable." —Robert McAfee Brown, Stanford chaplain emeritus

"Like Livy's history, this is a text that constantly seeks to elicit a moral response from its readers by the presentation of exemplary paradigms. . . . I was edified and stirred." —*America Magazine*, the Jesuit weekly

"Answers the most basic questions of what it takes to maintain hope and commitment: to act and keep on acting for humane social visions in an often resistant time."
—*Working America,* United Food & Commercial Workers

"Loeb's extensive personal interviews and traveling to campuses gives his work authenticity. The style of his writing makes his discoveries accessible."
—Henry Louis Gates, on Loeb's *Generation at the Crossroads*

"A tour de force of engaged spirituality." —*Yoga Journal*

"A call to get involved in ways that are both realistic and idealistic, that balance private and public needs, that encourage small steps that can lead to great impacts."
—*Thought & Action,* National Education Association

"Few recent books have inspired more college students, faculty, and staff to get involved in critical public issues than *Soul of a Citizen.*"
—Gwen Dungy, executive director,
National Association of Student Personnel Administrators

"For anyone worn down, a bracing double cappuccino!"
—Barbara Ehrenreich on *The Impossible Will Take a Little While*

"I assigned *Soul of a Citizen* to my class on race and ethnic identity. When faced with perplexing social issues, students, like many of us, often express cynicism and feelings of powerlessness. Loeb uses stories of ordinary citizens such as Rosa Parks to show that one doesn't have to be a 'great' man or woman to have a social impact. He also clearly demonstrates that sometimes great results are achieved by someone who just takes action. *Soul of a Citizen* is an inspirational book."
—Larry Zimmerman, University of Iowa, in *Phi Beta Kappa* magazine

"Every now and then a book comes along that seems to speak to you at the time you need to hear it the most. That is the case with *Soul of a Citizen.*" —*The Clarion-Ledger* (Jackson, Mississippi)

SOUL

OF A

CITIZEN

SOUL

OF A

CITIZEN

Living with Conviction in
Challenging Times

PAUL ROGAT LOEB

ST. MARTIN'S GRIFFIN
New York

www.stmartins.com

Library of Congress Cataloging-in-Publication Data

Loeb, Paul Rogat, 1952–
    Soul of a citizen : living with conviction in challenging times / Paul Rogat Loeb.—Rev. and updated ed.
        p.   cm.
    Includes index.
    ISBN 978-0-312-59537-1
    1. Social action—United States.   2. Social participation—United States.   3. Community organization—United States.   I. Title.
    HN65.L58 2010
    361.20973—dc22

                                                        2009041658

20   19   18   17   16   15   14   13   12   11

CONTENTS

SOUL

OF A

CITIZEN

Introduction to the New Edition

If I am not for myself, who will be for me? And if I am only for myself, what am I?

—*RABBI HILLEL*

We can learn a lot from the tales we tell about our heroes. I once had the privilege of appearing on a CNN show with Rosa Parks. "We're very honored to have her," said the host. "Rosa Parks was the woman who wouldn't go to the back of the bus. She wouldn't get up and give her seat in the white section to a white person. That set in motion the year-long bus boycott in Montgomery. It earned Rosa Parks the title of 'mother of the civil rights movement.'"

I was excited to hear Parks's voice even though I didn't actually meet her, since we were being interviewed from different studios. Then it struck me that the host's description—the story's standard rendition—stripped the Montgomery boycott of its context. Before the day Parks refused to give up her bus seat, she had spent twelve years involved with her local NAACP chapter, along with E. D. Nixon, an activist in the Brotherhood of Sleeping Car Porters union who was the head of the chapter; local teachers; and other members of Montgomery's African American community. The summer before, Parks had attended a ten-day training session at Tennessee's labor and civil rights organizing school, the Highlander Center, where she'd met an older generation of civil rights activists and discussed the Supreme Court's recent decision banning "separate but equal" schools. In the process, Parks also became familiar with previous challenges to segregation: Another Montgomery bus boycott, fifty years earlier, had successfully eased some restrictions; and a bus boycott in Baton Rouge had won limited gains two years before. The previous spring, a young Montgomery woman had also refused to move to the back of the bus, causing the NAACP to consider making her the centerpiece of a legal challenge—until it turned out that she was pregnant and unmarried, and therefore a problematic symbol for a campaign.

In short, Parks's decision didn't come out of nowhere. Nor did she single-handedly give birth to the civil rights movement. Rather, she was part of a longstanding effort to create change, when success was far from certain and setbacks were routine. That in no way diminishes the personal courage, moral force, and historical importance of her refusal to surrender her seat. But the full story of Rosa Parks reminds us that her tremendously consequential act, along with everything that followed, depended on all the humble, frustrating work that she and others had undertaken earlier, and on the vibrant, engaged community they had developed in the face of continual hardship and opposition. Her actions that day also weren't accidental—the product of her feet being tired, as we've so often heard—but rather a deliberate effort to challenge injustice. What's more, the full story underscores the value of persistence; had she given up in year three or seven or ten we'd never have heard of her. Finally, it reminds us that Parks's first step toward involvement—attending a local NAACP meeting—was as critical to altering history as her famed stand on the bus.

Heroes like Parks shape our images of social commitment—of how change actually takes place. Yet when I speak throughout the country, most of those who hear my talks don't know the full story of her involvement. In this instance, the conventional portrayal may actually make it harder for us to get involved. It suggests that engaged citizens emerge fully developed and socially adept, to take bold and visionary stands. It implies that we act with the greatest effect when we act alone, at least initially. It assumes that change is instantaneous, as opposed to a series of incremental and often-invisible actions that gradually—and taken together—gather momentum and influence events. Depicting Parks as a lone pioneer reinforces the romantic but ultimately false myth that anyone who takes a committed public stand, or at least a fruitful one, has to be a larger-than-life figure—someone with more time, energy, courage, vision, or knowledge than any normal person could ever possess.

By elevating Parks to superhero status, the myth also obscures the story's most powerful lessons of hope—that when we begin to act on our beliefs, we set out on a journey whose rewards we can't anticipate, that seemingly modest initial steps can lead to powerful results, and that any of us can contribute to bringing about change, in small or large ways. Parks's story also reminds us that as we do tackle common problems, we can discover and develop strengths and passions we never knew we had. We can begin to reconnect with our fellow human beings, with our wisest and most humane instincts, and with the core of who we are, which we call our soul.

GATED COMMUNITY OF THE HEART

In the personal realm, most Americans are thoughtful, caring, generous. We try to do our best by family and friends. At times we'll even stop to help another driver stranded by a roadside breakdown, or give some spare change to a stranger. But too often, a wall separates each of us from the world outside, and from others who've likewise taken refuge in their own private sanctuaries—what we might call the gated community of the heart. We've all but forgotten that public participation is the very soul of democratic citizenship, and that it can profoundly enrich our lives.

The reason many of us retreat from social involvement is not, I believe, that we think all is well with the world, certainly not in these challenging times. I live in Seattle, a city that until recently had a seemingly unstoppable economy. Yet every time I'd go downtown I'd see men and women with signs saying "I'll work for food" or

"Homeless vet. Please help." Their suffering stood in stark contrast to the unprecedented wealth all around them. And it diminished me as a human being. Because I travel extensively, I also witness what's happening in other U.S. states. Even before the crash of 2008, people in all but the most affluent of enclaves kept saying, "Things are hard here," and explaining how America's economic boom had passed them by.

Now, in far more difficult times, many more people feel precarious, with a sense that their lives could be upended in an instant, if they haven't been already. We struggle to get by on meager paychecks—or none at all. We worry about layoffs, overwork, the rising costs of health care and education. We wonder if we'll ever be able to retire. Whether minimum wage workers with two jobs, college students working thirty hours a week, or white-collar professionals sending work-related e-mails at midnight, simply trying to survive from one day to the next feels daunting enough. Trying to change the world, or even a small part of it, seems a luxury.

To be sure, the issues we now face are complex and often overwhelming. One day while revising this book, I picked up my local paper (which itself went under a few months later, after 135 years of publication). The world's most respected scientists were warning of catastrophic climate change if we didn't reverse course, but the catastrophes were already occurring. Runaway wildfires scorched Australia, the legacy of a dozen years of drought. Argentina's once immensely productive agriculture belt was being decimated by drought as well. And California farmers were being threatened with the cutoff of their water supply. Meanwhile, China was spending $14 billion to respond to its most recent extreme weather events, and Kentucky ice storms had left nearly a million people without power. Add to this disturbing litany melting ice caps, which the summer before had created the first open Arctic water passage in human history.

How can we comprehend the consequences of such wholesale, reckless toying with the habitability of the earth? More important, how will we redress them? How can we make sense of a world where Nike pays Michael Jordan more to appear in its ads than it pays all the workers at its Indonesian shoe factories combined? Or where the planet's 500 richest people control more wealth than the bottom 3 billion, half of the human population? Or where financial speculation has become so omnipresent it can threaten the entire global economy? Is it possible even to grasp the process that led to these crises, and all the others we face?

Yet what leaves too many of us sitting on the sidelines is not only the complexities of the world or the scope of its problems. It's not only uncertainty about which issues to address or how to do so. Certainly we need to decide for ourselves whether particular causes are wise or foolish—be they efforts to build a stable, equitable, and sustainable economy; to address the cycles of desperation that breed war and global terrorism; or to reverse the environmental damage that we've caused. We need to identify and connect with worthy groups that take on these issues and others, whether locally or globally. But first we need to believe that our individual involvement is worthwhile, that what we might do in the public sphere will not be in vain.

This means we face a challenge that is as much psychological as political. As the Ethiopian proverb says, "He who conceals his disease cannot be cured." If we're to heal our society and heal our souls—which, in my view, go hand-in-hand—we need to understand our cultural diseases of callousness, shortsightedness, and denial of difficult challenges. But even more fundamentally, we need to acknowledge and confront the pervasive sense of powerlessness that afflicts our society. How did so many of us become convinced that we can do nothing to affect our common future? And, by contrast, how have others managed to remove the cataracts from their eyes and muster the confidence to work powerfully for change? These are the questions this book attempts to answer.

YOU MAKE YOUR LIFE COUNT

When we do take a stand, we grow psychologically and spiritually. Pete Knutson is one of my oldest friends. During his thirty-five years as a commercial fisherman in Washington and Alaska, he's been forced, time and again, to respond to the steady degradation of salmon spawning grounds. "You'd have a hard time spawning, too, if you had a bulldozer in your bedroom," he says, explaining the destruction of once-rich salmon habitat by commercial development and timber industry clear-cutting. Pete could have simply accepted the degradation as inevitable, focusing on getting a maximum share of dwindling fish populations. Instead, he's gradually built an alliance between Washington State fishermen, environmentalists, and Native American tribes, persuading them to work collectively to demand that habitat be preserved and restored and to use the example of the salmon runs to highlight larger issues like global climate change.

The cooperation Pete created didn't come easily: Washington's fishermen were historically individualistic and politically mistrustful, more inclined, in Pete's judgment, "to grumble or blame the Indians than to act." Now, with their new allies, they began to push for cleaner spawning streams, rigorous enforcement of the Endangered Species Act, and an increased flow of water over major regional dams to help boost salmon runs. But large industrial interests, such as the aluminum companies, feared that these measures would raise their electricity costs or restrict their opportunities for development. So they bankrolled a statewide initiative to regulate fishing nets in a way that would eliminate small family fishing operations.

"I think we may be toast," said Pete, when Initiative 640 first surfaced. In an Orwellian twist, its backers even presented the measure as environmentally friendly, to mislead casual voters. It was called "Save Our Sealife," although fishermen and environmentalists soon rechristened it "Save Our Smelters." At first, those opposing 640 thought they had no chance of success: They were outspent, outstaffed, outgunned. Similar initiatives had already passed in Florida, Louisiana, and Texas, backed by similar industrial interests. I remember Pete sitting in a Seattle tavern with two fisherman friends, laughing bitterly and saying, "The three of us are going to take on the aluminum companies? We're going to beat Reynolds and Kaiser?"

But they refused to give up. Instead, Pete and his coworkers systematically enlisted the region's major environmental groups to campaign against the initiative. They brought in the Native American tribes, with whom they'd painstakingly built coalitions. A fisherman who was a member of the highly conservative Assemblies of God church persuaded his minister to send a letter to each of their congregations in the state.

Pete's group also worked with the media to explain the larger issues at stake. And they focused public attention on the measure's powerful financial backers, and their self-serving stake in its outcome. On Election Night, remarkably, Initiative 640 was defeated throughout the state. White fishermen, Pentacostals, Native American activists, and Friends of the Earth staffers threw their arms around each other in victory. "I'm really proud of you, Dad," Pete's twelve-year-old son kept repeating. Pete was stunned.

"Everyone felt it was hopeless," Pete said, looking back. "But if we were going to lose, I wanted at least to put up a good fight. And we won because of all the earlier work we'd done, year after year, to build our environmental relationships, get some credibility, and show that we weren't just in it for ourselves."

We often think of social involvement as noble but impractical. Yet as Pete's story attests, it can serve enlightened self-interest and the common interest simultaneously, while giving us a sense of connection and purpose nearly impossible to find in a life devoted purely to private pursuits. "It takes energy to act," said Pete. "But it's more draining to bury your anger, convince yourself you're powerless, and swallow whatever's handed to you. The times I've compromised my integrity and accepted something I shouldn't, the ghosts of my choices have haunted me. When you get involved in something meaningful, you make your life count. It blows my mind that we beat Initiative 640 starting out with just a small group of people who felt it was wrong to tell lies."

In fighting to save both their environment and their economic livelihood, Pete and the volunteers he enlisted strengthened their own souls—as did Rosa Parks during her long journey. By risking taking a stand, they shifted history in small but significant ways.

How the rest of us might achieve something similar is not always clear. We often don't know where to start. Most of us would like to see people treated more justly, the earth taken care of properly, and wise and creative solutions applied to the vast problems of our communities, our country, and our planet. But we find it hard to imagine playing a meaningful role in this process. We lack faith in our ability to make a difference. The magnitude of the issues at hand, coupled with this sense of powerlessness, have led far too many of us to conclude that social involvement isn't worth the cost.

Such resignation isn't an innate human trait. Rather, it's what psychologists call learned helplessness. Society has systematically taught us to ignore the ills we see, and leave them to others to handle. Understandably, we find it unsettling just to contemplate crises as profound in their implications as global climate change, species extinction, or the destruction of the rainforests. Or the slide of so many once-comfortable individuals and communities toward the economic abyss. We're led to believe that if we can't instantly solve every one of these problems, we shouldn't bother to become socially active at all—an outlook that's helped create the difficult situation we now face. We're also taught to doubt our voice. We feel we lack the time to properly comprehend the issues we care about, and fear that no one will listen to what we say. To become socially involved, we believe, requires almost saint-like judgment, confidence, and character—a standard we can never meet. Whatever impulses toward involvement we might naturally feel are thwarted by a culture that demeans idealism, enshrines cynicism, and makes us feel naïve for caring about our fellow human beings or the planet we inhabit.

THE DREAM OF PRIVATE SANCTUARY

When I grew up, in the fifties and sixties, I believed in my government. Most Americans did. Gradually, as the Vietnam War ground on, many of us recognized how often our leaders were lying to us.

In the wake of this massive betrayal of trust, and much work by peace and justice activists, many Americans began to question the confidence they vested in our leaders, and started to challenge official policies.

This skepticism was healthy, but it also had a downside. After Vietnam and Watergate, people began assuming that all politicians lie, an outlook reinforced by government abuses and scandals in presidential administrations from Ronald Reagan and Bill Clinton through George W. Bush. Indeed, we now tend to believe that deception is the defining characteristic of political life, and we take it for granted that wealthy and powerful interests will always buy and sell politicians like so many trading cards. By assuming that the public realm will inevitably be debased in this way, thus conceding defeat before engaging in the battle, we risk passing on a world that's meaner, more polarized, more desperate, and unquestionably more corrupt. Working to change things doesn't guarantee that our lives or our society will improve. But hopelessness and cynicism become self-fulfilling prophecies.

In the chapters to follow, I'm going to try to convince you that our most serious problems—both the public ones and those that seem most personal—are in large part common problems, which can be solved only through common efforts. The dream of private sanctuary is an illusion. It erodes our souls by undermining our sense of larger connection, whether to our fellow human beings or to that force many of us call God. The walls we're building around ourselves, around those closest to us, and ultimately around our hearts may provide a temporary feeling of security. But they can't prevent the world from affecting us. Quite the opposite. The more we construct such barriers, the more private life, for most of us, will grow insecure.

Think about why we spend more and more time at work, and why most families need two incomes to make ends meet—assuming they can even find one job. The reasons vary, but basically our average wages buy less than they used to. We worry about paying the bills when we or our children get sick. We wouldn't if the United

States provided affordable universal health care coverage. Students struggle with staggering burdens of debt, unthinkable in any other advanced industrial country. They wouldn't if student financial aid hadn't been systematically shifted from grants to loans during the Reagan years. We used to hope for solid pensions funded by our employers. Now we rely on melting IRAs and 401(k)s, and spend hours trying to make the right gambles in a tilt-a-whirl casino economy. Surely there's a more hopeful way to live.

I've written *Soul of a Citizen* because I'm certain this more hopeful way is possible. I'm certain because I've witnessed it—again and again, under every imaginable set of circumstances, and among people as diverse as America itself. For much of the past forty years, I've watched ordinary citizens get involved, find their voice, and take a stand. I've seen them embark on that passage from a purely private life, in which we leave the destiny of our communities to others, to one that joins private and public.

THE POWER OF THEIR ACTIONS

My experience leads me to believe that the main distinction between those who participate fully in their communities and those who withdraw into private life doesn't rest in the active citizens' grasp of complex issues, or their innate moral strength. Instead, those who get involved view their place in the world very differently. They have learned specific lessons about approaching social change: that they don't need to wait for the perfect circumstances, the perfect cause, or the perfect level of knowledge to take a stand; that they can proceed step by step, so that they don't get overwhelmed before they start. They savor the journey of engagement and draw strength from its challenges. Taking the long view, they come to trust that the fruits of their efforts will ripple outward, in ways they can rarely anticipate.

I've also come to believe that the lessons of human courage are transferable: When we read or hear about someone working for justice halfway across the globe or fifty years ago, we can draw inspiration to fuel our own actions. And when we enter almost any social justice movement, it will lead us to others, because the issues and participants intertwine.

Valuable books exist on the nuts and bolts of social involvement: lobbying Congress, pulling a rally together, coordinating an e-mail list, and generally mobilizing our communities. I've listed some in my online Resource Guide, which I describe at the end of the book, in Continuing the Journey. But *Soul of a Citizen* is less about these important strategies and tactics than about the equally critical question of how we, as individuals, can learn to heed our deepest convictions, to act—together with others—toward shaping a better world, and to continue doing so throughout our lives. In particular, I'd like this book to be an antidote to the sense of powerlessness that too many people feel, a meditation on what it means to fight for a more humane world in a challenging and sometimes overwhelming era.

Along the way, I hope to dispel the notion that people who take social stands and those who don't represent different species, separated by impassable barriers: A marginal few, according to this myth, leap from the womb holding protest signs; the rest of us, who are "normal," view our political withdrawal as almost a genetic trait that can't be modified, and rarely concern ourselves with issues that we believe we can't control. I'll do my best to challenge these mistaken assumptions, analyzing the barriers we face and describing ways to overcome them.

Community involvement, like any challenging personal path, offers no instant miracle cures: "Save the earth in thirty days. Ask me how." But when I talk with people who've been active for years, few regret their decisions, despite the difficult tasks they've taken on. In addition to the satisfaction they may derive from succeeding in their causes, they say that they've enriched their personal lives as well. Social activism gives them a sense of purpose, pride, and service; teaches them new skills; shows them how to confront daunting obstacles; and lets them experience new worlds. It offers camaraderie and helps them build powerful friendships, partnerships, and sometimes romances. Even many who've withdrawn from the public arena and now watch from the sidelines wistfully recall their experiences of shared commitment, standing shoulder to shoulder with people similarly concerned. There's no greater antidote to powerlessness than joining with others in common cause.

The 2008 election was an example of this. Whatever you may think of Barack Obama's performance as president, and I have my own mixed feelings, his victory depended on citizen involvement. Without massive numbers of citizens involving themselves in new ways to register voters, convince the undecided, and get supporters to the polls, Obama would never have advanced beyond the primaries, much less beaten John McCain. His campaign deliberately encouraged unprecedented levels of individual participation from the campaign's very start, blending conventional electoral approaches with grassroots citizen outreach. Drawing on campaign resources and their own initiative, supporters registered voters at football games and student centers, at libraries and post offices, and by canvassing door-to-door. They made countless phone calls, emailed, texted, and networked on Facebook, lobbied relatives and friends, slept on couches in battleground states, and turned virtual networks into on-the-ground organizing. A record 3.2 million people contributed money, and an unprecedented 13 million signed up for the campaign email list.

Those who participated felt the strength of their actions, a powerful sense of being part of something larger than themselves, and a newfound voice and strength. They recognized that their own efforts, even if small, mattered precisely because of being matched by the actions of many others. Taking a leap of faith, they staked their time, money, and hopes on an improbable candidacy, exposed themselves to ridicule or rejection by going public with their preference (as did equally committed volunteers for McCain, Clinton, and all the other candidates), and ultimately helped carry Obama from a long shot to the presidency.

At least for Obama supporters, involvement has declined sharply since that campaign, risking a vicious cycle of disappointment and withdrawal. Meanwhile those who opposed him have found new energy. One election can change only so much, however high the hopes people vest in any given candidate. The changes it can make possible depend on the continuing actions of ordinary citizens, of whatever perspectives, from publicly voicing their convictions to voting. Shortly after Obama assumed office, I visited a University of Alabama class where students were reading an earlier edition of this book. I asked them for their sense of the national mood. "It's an anxious time, a vulnerable time," said one young woman. "Everyone's unsure of what's going to happen in so many areas, so we're waiting to watch and see."

She caught the mood wonderfully, but her conclusion, however accurate, left me troubled. It's understandable to want to watch and wait, but it's also a trap. Relying too much on any political leader, no matter how noble their stated aims or exalted their rhetoric, is a form of passivity. And to revert to passivity is to squander our chance to shape history. In particular, it surrenders our chance to counterbalance the entrenched and powerful interests that have helped create many of our most critical problems to begin with, interests whose destructive influence can be curtailed only through common action. Watching from the sidelines eliminates our chance to find out what we truly believe and value, which happens only by working for it through actions large and small. More important, it ignores a historical moment when the potential for much-needed change is greater than it's been in a long time. Precisely because so many old approaches seem not to work any longer, and so many American citizens are hungry for new ways of doing things, we have a chance to begin solving some long-festering problems. It won't happen overnight, to be sure, but maybe we'll finally wean ourselves off fossil fuels, rebuild a sustainable economy and decent social safety net, and begin to address the roots of global war and terrorism. The crises we face are accompanied by huge risks, certainly, but they also represent opportunities for progress—as long as enough ordinary citizens get involved. You might therefore view this book as an invitation to act on these opportunities—and to do so even if you have hesitations and doubts.

A NEW EDITION FOR A NEW WORLD

Soul of a Citizen first came out in 1999, at the tail end of the Clinton years. I'd been involved in citizen movements since I was a high school student in the late 1960s, and had written three earlier books, on the psychology of nuclear weapons workers, on grassroots peace activists, and on engagement and withdrawal in the generation that the media labeled Gen X. As I traveled the country to speak on these books, people kept asking how they might surmount the barriers to involvement, take a stand, and keep on taking stands, despite the inevitable obstacles. I wrote *Soul* in response.

The book took a while to find its audience. Nearly thirty publishers rejected it before St. Martin's responded. Most bookstores carried only a single copy each, buried in the back stacks. *Soul* seemed doomed to oblivion. Somehow, though, people began to find out about it, and to pass the word to friends. College faculty assigned it in their classes, from first-year readings to graduate seminars, and students of all political perspectives began e-mailing me, describing how it had changed their lives. I remember checking my suitcase at an airport when the skycap, an older African American man, asked, "Do you have your books in there?" He'd been reading *Soul,* he said, in his church social justice group, and people were really inspired by it. Enough readers found their way to it that the first edition moved 100,000 copies.

Now, over a decade after its initial release, it seemed time to update *Soul* for a new world. I've gone through every page, paragraph, and sentence, adding fresh stories and perspectives, dropping or changing others, working to create a book that speaks to all our new challenges and opportunities.

You may wonder whether the book covers all forms of community involvement, or only those congruent with my own particular perspective, shaped by the peace, justice, and environmental movements in which I've participated. I considered including more citizens associated with the political right. Their movements are important subjects of inquiry. Their rank-and-file participants are sincere and often admirably passionate in their convictions.

But this isn't an encyclopedia of social activism. We all have our perspectives, and this is the reflection of one human being on what it means to live a life of commitment. So I've drawn my examples from a variety of people who inspire me. Not all consider themselves driven by explicit political visions—left, right, or whatever. Many are just trying to help their communities. Others have taken strong committed stands with which I wholly disagree—and then acted on other issues in ways I found powerfully encouraging. I've profiled, for instance, how the communications director of the highly conservative Christian Coalition became friends with the founder of the liberal organization MoveOn, then joined in working to keep the Internet accessible to all. I've also recounted how the vice president of the National Association of Evangelicals shifted his prime focus from lobbying against abortion and same-sex marriage (questions that still concern him) to working on the need to address global climate change; as he put it, the issue "shook my theology to its core."

Whatever your political viewpoint, I suspect that *Soul* will offer significant parallels with your personal dilemmas and decisions, and hope it will serve as a useful guide to acting on your convictions and values. I also believe you'll find yourself respecting—and, in some cases, admiring—many of the people whose stories I describe, even if their perspectives differ from yours. If you disagree with some of their arguments and causes (or mine), that's fine. You may even get involved on the other side. But I suspect you'll discover some unexpected common ground. No one political group or viewpoint has a corner on idealism or an inside track on what works, and when we listen to those who seem to be our opponets, our responses can sometimes unexpectedly converge.

I've already mentioned a couple of the people I profile in this book. Here are some others: A self-described "drunken party girl" at Virginia Tech got involved in global climate change and went on to create a powerful campus sustainability plan. A Maine housewife helped lead a path-breaking campaign finance reform initiative "so my kids won't grow up in a cynical world." After an elderly neighbor died of cold because no one would repair her house, a middle-aged Latina with an eighth-grade education got involved in a local community organization in San Antonio—and eventually testified before the U.S. Senate. An African American man who had served seventeen years in the California prison system initiated a pioneering drug rehabilitation effort based on trying to give people, as he said, "the support they need, in a language they can understand." A Seattle environmental activist who had just celebrated her hundredth birthday concluded that, after speaking out all her life, "You do what you can. And then you do some more."

Inevitably, the causes that stir our hearts will differ. Our conscience may be shaped by widely divergent worldviews, our judgment informed by disparate experiences. Whether we view ourselves as religious or secular may lead us to frame our language and metaphors in dissimilar ways, or provide a differing basis for what we believe. But regardless of these differences, those of us who become socially engaged seem to follow parallel routes to involvement. And those of us who hold back seem to encounter parallel obstacles. Whatever our passions and commitments may be, we all face similar questions about how to cross the threshold from passivity to participation, have our voices heard, make our actions count, and reawaken and sustain our faith in the future.

In keeping with my belief that common solutions emerge best from common discussion, I've woven the voices and perspectives of dozens of people into this book—individuals from diverse backgrounds, situations, and belief systems—whose efforts to heal the world have given me hope. You might want to envision this book as a walk in the woods with this varied group, a chance to engage them in a passionate conversation about the state of the world, the state of our souls, our role as citizens, and the legacies we'll leave to our children.

WORTHY OF OUR CONVICTIONS

None of us has the final answers to the most urgent questions of our time. But as you listen to this wide-ranging conversation, keep in mind that we're talking about the common problems of our society, and their potential common solutions. No individual citizen is solely to blame for climate change, homelessness, or the hollowing out of our economy. At the same time, however, we must remember that individuals shape institutions and societies, and that anything done on behalf of a group is also done on behalf of its members. As Rabbi Abraham Heschel said: "In regard to cruelties committed in the name of a free society, some are guilty, while all are responsible." If I were forced to use one word to describe what this book is about—the soul of *Soul,* so to speak—I'd say responsibility, and I'd have in mind all of its manifestations, all the ways in which we as individuals and as citizens can be responsive to and responsible for the world in which we live.

On a more practical level, I'd like *Soul* to speak to that part of ourselves that isn't apathetic or uncaring, but feels slightly overwhelmed and wonders whether our actions can matter. Many of us are already involved in worthy public concerns. Because we feel our causes are crucial, we assume others will join with us once they receive the information they need. But people are spurred to action not so much by knowing the right facts and numbers as by hearing stories that affirm human worth and purposefulness, and embody a worldview that makes sense of the confusion and contradictions in their lives. We forget this basic lesson when we get lost in what Trappist monk Thomas Merton called "the contagion of [our] own obsessions." If we want to change people's minds, we need to know why they resist even the most urgent social causes.

Those of us who've made social activism a focus of our lives also need to develop the steadfastness that will enable us to persist in the face of the inevitable frustrations. In spite of our passionate engagement, we all experience moments of bleakness. I'd like to offer some perspectives to sustain our spirits for the long haul, to help us savor the journey, and to help us find hope when progress seems elusive.

Many of us have joined various movements, then burned out and left. We may have spoken out against wars from Vietnam to Iraq, worked to protect the environment, sought to improve the future of our communities, and to build a just economy. Then we hit walls of indifference or seemingly immovable political obstacles, became overloaded, or felt let down by our fellow activists, our fellow citizens, or leaders we once supported. After a while, we concluded sadly that meaningful action was impossible, and retreated to our private sanctuaries, exhausted and disillusioned.

Most of us who've withdrawn in this fashion remain concerned about the future, uneasy about our silence. With our political voice muted, guilt about our inaction and memories of frustrated hopes may actually make it harder to recommit ourselves than it would be to get started had we never gotten involved to begin with. We find it easier to remain disgruntled spectators. Turning our attention toward easier tasks, we become what political theorist Hannah Arendt called "inner immigrants," privately outraged at our society's directions, but publicly silent. I hope this book will help those of us with this history to rekindle our concern and rediscover the visions of human dignity that originally stirred our passions. I want to challenge the notion that if we don't find the perfect solution, the approach that will instantly change the world, our efforts are worthless. If we can reconnect with our conscience and regain a sense of hope, our voices can be powerful once more.

Finally, even more of us would like to be involved but have never taken the first steps. Maybe we've been psychologically intimidated, or have focused on other priorities, such as work, school, family responsibilities, or personal growth. Maybe the time and circumstances never seemed right. Lacking previous experience, we may feel even more overwhelmed at the thought of beginning, more uncertain of our voice, more doubtful that our choices can matter. Working for social change may indeed take us into a new country, expose us to new vulnerabilities, call on strengths that we may not yet know we have. Yet there are ways to avoid exhaustion and overload. We can learn as we go—from the people we'll meet and from the impact we'll have—ways to make our journey of commitment less daunting. If you are just beginning to consider social involvement seriously, I'd suggest that you think about how much it can give back, both to yourself and to the world. I'd argue that nothing compares to this satisfaction.

If you embark on this journey, I hope *Soul of a Citizen* will give you strength. I hope it will offer ways to keep your commitment alive, tap wellsprings of creativity and optimism, and remind you of the potential power of your actions. As Rabbi Hillel asked 2,000 years ago, if we are not for ourselves, who will be for us? And if we are only for ourselves, what are we? Whoever we are, and whatever paths we follow, we can all lead lives worthy of our convictions.

CHAPTER ONE

Making Our Lives Count

Souls are like athletes that need opponents worthy of them if they are to be tried and extended and pushed to the full use of their powers.
—*THOMAS MERTON*

We're often taught to view our lives as a zero-sum game. With all the pressures we face, we barely have time for family and friends. How could we possibly take on some demanding cause?

Yet for all the frustration we expect, when we do get involved, we get a lot back: new relationships, fresh skills, a sense of empowerment, pride in accomplishment. "A rich life," writes philosopher and theologian Cornel West, is fundamentally a life of serving others, "trying to leave the world a little better than you found it. . . . This is true at the personal level . . . [but there's also] a political version of this. It has to do with what you see when you get up in the morning and look in the mirror and ask yourself whether you are simply wasting time on the planet or spending time in an enriching manner."

Again and again, I've heard active citizens say that what motivates them the most is the desire to respect what they see in the mirror. The exercise isn't about vanity, but about values, about taking stock of ourselves and comparing the convictions we say we hold with the lives we actually lead. It's about seeing ourselves from the viewpoint of our communities, the earth, maybe even God. If eyes are windows to the soul, and faces reflections of character, looking in the mirror lets us step back from the flux of our lives and hold ourselves accountable.

Sound a bit daunting? It can be. As the saying goes, not one among us is without fault. But such self-examination can also be enormously rewarding. For it's equally true that not one among us lacks a heart, which is the wellspring of courage (the word is derived from *coeur,* French for "heart"). At the core of our being lie resources many of us never dream we possess, much less imagine we can draw on.

I NEVER KNEW I HAD IT

Virginia Ramirez, of San Antonio, Texas, could easily have lived out her days without ever discovering her hidden inner strength. She left school after eighth grade to get married. "That was what most Hispanic women in my generation did. My husband went to work after sixth grade." Although dropping out seemed normal at the time, she felt frustrated when she couldn't help her children with their homework, and she dreamed of resuming her education someday. Virginia wasn't completely detached from her community: She was active in the PTA, "not running the meetings, but making the cookies and punch, carrying out the tasks." She'd babysit for her neighbors, help in whatever ways she could, "doing basic community work without realizing it." Mostly, though, she focused on private life, raising her five children while her husband worked for a taxi company.

When Virginia was forty-five, she realized that an elderly neighbor was getting sick every winter. The neighbor was a widow who lived in a house so dilapidated that it couldn't retain heat. "She was one of those people who always paid her taxes on time, always faithfully making out her little money orders. But she couldn't afford to repair her house, and everyone around here was just as poor. So I went with her to city agencies trying to get help. They kept sending us from place to place, from department to department. Finally she died of pneumonia. The paramedics said she'd never have died if her house hadn't been so freezing cold.

"I was very angry," Virginia recalls. "I'd never been so angry in my life. This woman had done everything she was supposed to, and now she was dead because no one could help her fix her house. Someone said there's this community organization called COPS, and maybe they could help. I'd heard of them before, but thought they were too radical, a bunch of nuts."

At that time, in the early 1980s, the largely volunteer-based Communities Organized for Public Service (COPS) had been around for eight years. The organization grew out of a network called The Industrial Areas Foundation, established by the late Saul Alinsky, the godfather of modern community organizing (who also inspired the community organization that Barack Obama worked for in Chicago). COPS began by working through churches to organize San Antonio's desperately poor Latino population. The group successfully pushed for municipal investments in storm sewers, parks, and schools in the town's long-neglected *barrios,* and got major downtown businesses to hire their residents. COPS eventually secured over a billion dollars of public and private resources for their community through a combination of grassroots organizing and innovative protests. During one series of protests to get downtown businesses to hire more Latino workers, lines of COPS members endlessly exchanged pennies to tie up traffic at local banks, and sympathetic nuns tried on bridal gowns at local department stores to put pressure on their staff. But Virginia had paid the organization little heed.

So it was with some hesitation that she attended a COPS meeting at her church, where she raised her hand and said, "I have this problem. This neighbor lady of mine died because it was cold and they wouldn't fix her house. I want someone to do something about it."

"What are *you* going to do about it?" the COPS organizer asked. But Virginia didn't know what to do. That was why she'd come to the meeting in the first place. "I thought you people were supposed to be able to help," she said, and walked out of the meeting in anger.

A few days later, a COPS organizer knocked on Virginia's door. She was a nun, and that was the only reason Virginia let her in. "All I want to know is why you were so angry," asked the nun. Virginia was angry, she said, because she'd tried to help the old lady and failed. But that wasn't all. She also was upset because her kids weren't getting properly educated in school. Because she'd given up on her own education and dreams. Because she'd had to watch her father, whom she'd adored, be humiliated again and again by police and store owners when they drove from state to state to pick crops. She was upset because no one seemed to care about her community.

The nun didn't advise Virginia to do anything in particular. She just asked if they could talk again. When she returned, she suggested that Virginia hold a house meeting, to see if her neighbors had concerns, too.

Nine people came. Virginia had never conducted a meeting. Her stomach felt hollow and clenched. Her legs shook so much she almost fell over. She could barely open the door. But gradually people began to talk of their problems and experiences. Their neighborhood had been thrown together at the cheapest possible cost, built for workers at the nearby slaughterhouses, which were now closed down. It lacked sidewalks and adequate sewers. Most of the houses were crumbling. As she listened, Virginia realized that more was at stake than the needless death of her neighbor; this was about the future of her community.

Convinced that the neighborhood hadn't received its share of public funds, Virginia and other COPS members painstakingly researched documents at City Hall. And they were right: The city had built a street in a more affluent area with money actually earmarked to repair homes in their *barrio*. The next step—testifying before the City Council—took even more courage. When Virginia walked to the podium to protest the diversion of funds, she was so nervous she forgot what she was going to say. "I didn't remember my speech. I barely remembered my name. Then I turned around, saw the sixty people who'd come with me, and realized I was just telling the story of our community. So I told it, and we got our money back.

"It was hard to stand up to politicians and tell them what we wanted, because it's been imbedded in my mind to be nice to everybody. It seemed rude at first. But I began to understand the importance of holding people accountable for what they promise."

As they did with other newly energized community members, COPS trainers helped Virginia reflect on each step she took in every campaign, and acquire the skills to research, negotiate, articulate a point of view, analyze people's needs, and channel her anger. They also introduced her to a new community of people who were similarly involved. One of these new colleagues, a sixty-eight-year-old widow, became her inspiration. "Even though she didn't know English and couldn't read or write," Virginia recalls, "she spoke out and stood up for her beliefs. She talked to other families. And she kept telling me, 'Go back to school.' She always said, 'You have to represent us.' "

Even with this support and inspiration, Virginia's journey into public life wasn't easy. She often prayed over whether her newfound path was right, asking God for guidance, "like what am I doing with these crazy people and where is it going to lead?" Yet her involvement also strengthened her faith, giving new meaning to biblical lessons that had once seemed more remote and abstract. "Suddenly you read these stories about injustice from thousands of years ago," Virginia says, "and it seems like they're talking about today. You feel like you have a chance to be one of God's instruments, to do His work by helping your community. You feel closer to Him in the process."

Yet Virginia's choices still raised difficult tensions, particularly in her family. At first her husband was critical of her involvement, saying "That's not your role" and telling her she was neglecting her household. "My kids were mostly grown, but Hispanic women weren't supposed to do these things. It was hard for him to understand that I was becoming a totally different person—going out of the house, going to meetings, wanting to talk about the things I was doing. Then my mother would call every day and say, 'This is not for you. What are you doing to your family?' It was like twenty-four-hour guilt. You're torn between your home and your desire to grow as a person."

Eventually, Virginia returned to school and acquired her GED. Then she enrolled at a community college. Studying for a college test—her first test in over forty years—Virginia was sitting with books spread across the kitchen table, and no supper ready, when her husband came home. He ran his finger over the furniture to show her the accumulated dust. "Look at this house!" he yelled. "It's going to ruin. You're not taking care of anything."

"I'm preparing my future," she responded, her voice trembling. "If you don't like it, that's too bad, because I'm going to do it."

She'd never talked to him that way, and he was shocked. "I'm sorry," Virginia said, "but this is a priority." It took her husband a long time to get used to her new attitude and concerns, "to realize," as Virginia says, "that I was going to keep on going to school and to my meetings." But he slowly accepted Virginia's transformation and even took pride in it. "I'd begun to think of myself as a person. I'm Virginia Ramirez, not just someone's wife, mother, or daughter. My husband realized I was getting involved for both of us."

College gave Virginia the credentials to secure a new job, training and supervising over 300 volunteers who do health education outreach in low-income neighborhoods. During more than twenty years with COPS, she's moved up in the organization, first training people in her parish, then working with other local churches to develop their members' leadership skills as well. She's focused particularly on women like herself—working to inspire them, as others had spurred her to action. Using her own unexpected journey as an example, she's taught them to find their own voice and speak out for their communities, despite any doubts or hesitations they might have, and even over the initial resistance of their husbands. "At first all the men in the neighborhood said they had a lot of respect for me, 'but just don't get my wife involved.' After a while they began to come around."

Virginia has also negotiated with the mayor and bank presidents on major community development projects, pressured local corporations for decent jobs, and worked on after-school literacy projects. "We have a new business incubator and a teen center so kids have someplace to hang out besides the streets. The city gave people money to fix up the crumbling houses. Now they take so much pride in it. We're still a poor neighborhood but we finally have hope."

Virginia realized how far she'd come when she went to Washington, D.C., to testify before the U.S. Senate on an innovative job-training program that she and other COPS members had helped develop. The night before, she "prayed to God that I wouldn't make a complete fool of myself," but was far more afraid, she said, "talking to my neighbors the first time, and speaking at that first City Council meeting. By the time I got to the U.S. Senate I was used to it." Afterwards, she thought "about how this process had changed me, developed potential I'd never dreamed of. I tell people I learned all my talents and confidence at the University of COPS. The people there found some spark in me. I never knew I had it."

STRETCHING THE SOUL

"Heart," "spark," "spirit"—whatever word we use for the mysterious force that animates us, its full potential cannot be realized in isolation. Indeed, according to developmental psychologists, individual growth is possible only through interaction with the human and natural world, and through experiences that challenge us. "Souls are like athletes," wrote the Trappist monk Thomas Merton, "that need opponents worthy of them if they are to be tried and extended and pushed to the full use of their powers."

Many of us may already know the value of stretching our souls in personal life. We know the virtue of learning to voice our needs, fight for our choices, recover from psychological intimidation. This process may require acknowledging painful truths, withstanding conflict, standing firm on what seems like shaky ground. We may need to question familiar habits, overcome self-doubt, and begin to separate who we really are from the roles we've been taught. Jungian analysts like James Hillman would say that by taking these steps we reconnect with what the Greeks called the *daimon,* the "acorn" of character at the core of our being. Psychiatrist M. Scott Peck described spiritual healing as "an ongoing process of becoming increasingly conscious."

We are slower to attempt such transformations in the public sphere. Self-assertion there requires us not only to modify our outlook and behavior but also to confront a bewildering and often disorienting maze of institutions and individuals, powers and principalities. So we stay silent in the face of common choices that we know are unwise or morally troubling. We keep our opinions to ourselves, because we doubt our voices will be heard, mistrust our right to speak, or fear the consequences if we do speak out. We feel we lack essential political skills. Like Virginia before she attended her first COPS meeting, or Rosa Parks before her first NAACP meeting, we simply do not know we have it in us.

Yet coming out of one's cocoon in the public sphere is just as necessary to self-realization as it is in the private. I once told a young Puerto Rican activist about the notion, common among many of his fellow students, that they'd lose their identity by getting involved— find themselves "swallowed up" by the movements they joined. He laughed and said the reverse was true. "You learn things you never knew about yourself. You get pushed to your limits. You meet people who make you think and push you further. You don't lose your identity. You begin to find out who you really are. I feel sad for people who will never have this experience."

You begin to find out who you really are. The implication is clear enough: We become human only in the company of other human beings. And this involves both opening our hearts and giving voice to our deepest convictions. The biblical vision of *shalom* describes this process with its concept of "right relationships" with our fellow humans, and with all of God's creation. The turning point for the Buddha, writes James Hillman, came only "when he left his protected palace gardens to enter the street. There the sick,

the dead, the poor, and the old drew his soul down into the question of how to live life in the world." As Hillman stresses, the Buddha became who he was precisely by leaving the cloistered life. A
doctor I know works in a low-income clinic because, she says, "seeing the struggles of others helps me be true to myself. It helps me
find out how people in very different circumstances live out their
humanity." Community involvement, in other words, is the mirror
that best reflects our individual choices, our strengths and weak-
nesses, our accomplishments and failures. It allows our lives to
count for something.

THE COSTS OF SILENCE

Twenty years after Harvard Law School hired him as its first full-
time African American professor, Derrick Bell took an unpaid protest leave, refusing to teach until the school hired a minority woman
to its faculty. It was not a decision made in haste. Bell had long campaigned for this. But each time a new position opened, the Law
School somehow could find not a single minority female candidate
in the world who was worthy enough to hire. The school's resistance
continued despite Bell's stand. After three years, the school forced
him to resign. His conscience had cost him a tenured job at the most
prestigious law school in America.

Yet Bell didn't feel defeated. Quite the opposite. His public
stance had preserved his core identity and integrity. "It is the determination to protect our sense of who we are," he writes, "that leads
us to risk criticism, alienation, and serious loss while most others,
similarly harmed, remain silent."

What Bell means is that silence is more costly than speaking out,
because it requires the ultimate sacrifice—the erosion of our spirit.
The toll we pay for stifling our emotions in personal life is fairly
obvious. Swallowed words act like caustic acids, eating at our gut.
If the condition persists and the sentiments are sufficiently intense,
we grow numb, detached, dead to the world around us. When,

however, we take steps to redress our private losses and sorrows, we often feel a renewed sense of strength and joy, of reconnecting with life.

A similar process occurs when we want to address public issues but stay silent. It takes energy to mute our voices while the environment is ravaged, greed runs rampant, and families sleep in the streets. It takes energy to distort our words and actions because we fear the consequences of speaking out. It takes energy, in other words, to sustain what the psychiatrist Robert Jay Lifton calls "the broken connection," splitting our lives from our values. Like autistic children, we can blank out the voices of our fellow human beings. But if we do, we risk the decay of our humanity. When we shrink from the world, our souls shrink, too.

Social involvement reverses this process, releasing our choked-off energy, overcoming the psychic paralysis that so many of us feel, reintegrating mind and heart, body and soul, so that we can speak in one voice—our own—and mean what we say. There's even a physical corollary to this integration. In *The Healing Power of Doing Good,* Allan Luks describes various studies that confirm what he calls the "helper's high": People who volunteer in their communities experience significantly greater physical pleasure and well-being in the process of their work, a general sense of increased energy, and in some cases an easing of chronic pain. A Harvard School of Public Health study found that African Americans who challenged repeated discrimination had lower blood pressure than those who did not. So taking stands for what we believe may help us save more than our souls.

Sociologist Parker Palmer describes the resulting unleashing of truth, vision, and strength in the lives of people like Rosa Parks, Vaclav Havel, Nelson Mandela, and Dorothy Day, who've acted on their deepest beliefs. "These people," he wrote, "have understood that no punishment could be worse than the one we inflict on ourselves by living a divided life." And nothing could be more powerful than the decision to heal that rift, "to stop acting differently on the outside from what they knew to be true inside."

LEARNED HELPLESSNESS

America's predominant culture insists that little we do can matter. It teaches us not to get involved in shaping the world we'll pass on to our children. It encourages us to leave such important decisions to others—whether they be corporate and government leaders, or social activists whose lifestyles seem impossibly selfless or foreign. Sadly, and ironically, in a country born of a democratic political revolution, to be American in recent years is too often to be apolitical. For many, civic withdrawal has become the norm. The 2008 presidential campaign challenged this trend by inspiring vast numbers of previously disengaged citizens to volunteer in ways that shifted not only the presidential race, but also close races for the Senate, the House, and state governorships. But even then over a third of potentially eligible Americans ended up staying home. And despite all the passionate volunteers, far more citizens did little beyond casting their vote. Absent a highly contested election, it's easier still to sit on the sidelines and simply hope our leaders will take care of things.

Overcoming our instinctive civic withdrawal requires courage. It requires learning the skills and developing the confidence to participate—as Virginia Ramirez did in the process of finding her voice. It also requires creating a renewed definition of ourselves as citizens—something closer to the nation of active stakeholders that leaders like Thomas Jefferson had in mind.

The importance of citizens' direct participation in a democracy was expressed thousands of years ago, by the ancient Greeks. In fact, they used the word "idiot" for people incapable of involving themselves in civic life. Now, the very word "political" has become so debased in our culture that we use it to describe either trivial office power plays or leaders who serve largely personal ambitions. We've lost sight of its original roots in the Greek notion of the *polis:* the democratic sphere in which citizens, acting in concert, determine the character and direction of their society. "All persons alike," wrote Aristotle, should share "in the government to the utmost."

Reclaiming this political voice requires more than just identifying problems, which itself can feed our sense of overload. I think of an Arthur Miller play, *Broken Glass,* whose heroine obsesses while Hitler steadily consolidates his power. From her safe home in Brooklyn, she reads newspaper articles about *Kristallnacht:* synagogues smashed and looted; old men forced to scrub streets with toothbrushes while storm troopers laugh at them; and finally, children shipped off to the camps in cattle cars. Her concern contrasts with the approach of her family and friends, who insist, despite the mounting evidence, that such horrors are exaggerated. Yet she does nothing to address the situation publicly, except to grow more anxious. Eventually she becomes psychosomatically paralyzed.

The approach Miller's protagonist takes toward the horrors of Nazism echoes that of far too many people who spend hours following every twist and turn of the twenty-four-hour news cycle, yet never take action that might address them. It also resembles the condition of learned helplessness. People who suffer from severe depression, psychologist Martin Seligman found, do so less as a result of particular unpleasant experiences than because of their "explanatory style"—the story they tell themselves about how the world works. Depressed people have become convinced that the causes of their difficulties are permanent and pervasive, inextricably linked to their personal failings. There's nothing to be done because nothing can be done. This master narrative of their lives excuses inaction; it provides a rationale for remaining helpless. In contrast, individuals who function with high effectiveness tend to believe that the problems they face result from factors that are specific, temporary, and therefore changeable. The story they live by empowers them.

This is not to say that change is easy, nor that everyone is in an equal position to bring it about. Some individuals and groups in America possess far more material and organizational resources than others. This reflects our deep social and economic inequities. But as *Tikkun* magazine founder Rabbi Michael Lerner has observed, we often fail to use the resources we do have, which may be of a different kind. "Most of us," Lerner says, "have been subjected to a set of experiences in our childhood and adult lives that makes us feel that we do not deserve to have power." Consequently, we can't imagine changing the direction of our society. We decide that things are worse than they actually are—a condition Lerner refers to as "surplus powerlessness." Think again of Virginia Ramirez's accomplishments, when she joined forces with other once-powerless people in fighting for their community.

The illusion of powerlessness can just as easily afflict the fortunate among us. I know many people who are confident and successful in their work and have loving personal relationships, yet can hardly conceive of trying to work toward a more humane society. Materially comfortable and professionally accomplished, they could make important social contributions. Instead they restrict their search for meaning and integrity to their private lives. Their sense of shared fate extends only to their immediate families and friends. Despite their many advantages, they, too, have been taught an "explanatory style" that precludes participation in public life, except to promote the most narrow self-interest.

Whatever our situations, we all face a choice. We can ignore the problems that lie just beyond our front doors; we can allow decisions to be made in our names that lead to a meaner and more desperate world. We can yell at the TV newscasters and complain about how bad things are, using our bitterness as a hedge against involvement. Or we can work, as well as we can, to shape a more generous common future.

THE RENT WE PAY FOR LIVING

Paradoxically, one effect of overcoming learned helplessness is recognizing the extent to which others have helped us, and the extent to which our lives are bound together. Despite the myth of the rugged individualist, none of our lives is entirely of our own making. Small wonder, then, that those who participate in public life talk so much about the need to repay the blessings they've received. For some, this stems from a specific sense of good fortune, of living in comfort while others are hungry and desperate. But I've heard the

same sentiment expressed by people from the poorest of surroundings, recalling key friends, relatives, or mentors who offered them
inspiration, hope, or a helping hand. In fact, the poorest fifth of
Americans contribute twice as high a percentage of their income to
charity as do the wealthiest fifth. As Children's Defense Fund founder
Marian Wright Edelman writes, social involvement may simply be
"the rent we pay for living." A Seattle massage therapist, reflecting
after getting involved with children's issues, echoes the sentiment:
"Before, I felt I was living happily in my own small nucleus while the
rest of the world decayed around me. I now feel more empowered,
with less of a sense of despair about everything that's wrong."

When we work shoulder to shoulder with others for a greater
common good, we gain a powerful sense of human solidarity. We see
this phenomenon in other contexts all the time. People become inspired and expansive when they pull together to face a storm, flooded
river, or other natural disaster. Whatever soldiers have thought about
the wars they fought in, a similar feeling makes them look back to
their combat experiences as a time of profound meaning and unparalleled camaraderie.

Rarely does social involvement place us in the path of destructive
natural forces or armed opponents, but it does involve risk. At the
very least, it requires us to make ourselves psychologically vulnerable. It impels us to overcome distracting habits and petty concerns,
to challenge internal fears, and to face criticism from those who will
call our efforts fruitless, foolish, or a waste of scarce time.

In return, social involvement converts us from detached spectators into active participants. We develop new competencies and
strengths. We form strong bonds with coworkers of courage and vision. Our lives become charged with purpose. Yvon Chouinard, the
founder of the Patagonia outdoor clothing company, once told me
about the challenges he faced while mountaineering, surfing, and
building a successful corporation. By the tone of his voice, he communicated the sense of accomplishment these activities had given
him. But his enthusiasm grew even stronger when he described helping organize Japanese surfers to clean up their beaches and switching Patagonia's buying patterns to phase out environmentally

destructive nonorganic cottons. Chouinard's participation in environmental activism was even more deeply gratifying than his corporate success, because it produced results well beyond what he could achieve personally.

IT SHOOK MY THEOLOGY TO ITS CORE

When we do get involved, we never know where the process will lead—for ourselves, or the issues we take on. As vice president for governmental affairs of the National Association of Evangelicals (NAE), Rich Cizik represented 4,500 congregations serving 30 million members. Considering himself a "Reagan conservative" and a strong initial supporter of George W. Bush, Cizik had been with the organization since 1980, serving as its key advocate before Congress, the Office of the President, and the Supreme Court on issues like opposition to abortion and gay marriage. During the Clinton era, he had begun to expand the organization's agenda by tackling such issues as human trafficking and global poverty, working with groups across the political aisle. Later he'd convinced the organization to take a stand against torture. But he thought little about climate change until 2002, when he attended a conference on the subject and heard a leading British climate scientist, Sir James Houghton, who was also a prominent evangelical. "You could only call the process a conversion," Cizik said. "I reluctantly went to the conference, saying 'I'll go, but don't expect me to be signing on to any statements.' Then, for three days in Oxford, England, Houghton walked us through the science and our biblical responsibility. He talked about droughts, shrinking ice caps, increasing hurricane intensity, temperatures tracked for millennia through ice-core data. He made clear that you could believe in the science and remain a faithful biblical Christian. All I can say is that my heart was changed. For years I'd thought, 'Well, one side says this, the other side says that. There's no reason to get involved.' But the science has become too compelling. I could no longer sit on the sidelines. I didn't want to be like the evangelicals who avoided getting involved during the civil rights movement and in the process discredited the gospel and themselves."

One day during the conference, Houghton took Cizik on a walk in the gardens of Blenheim Palace, Winston Churchill's ancestral home. It was a lovely day, sunny and bright. Houghton said, "Richard, if God has convinced you of the reality of the science and the Scriptures on the subject then you must speak out."

"Let me think about it," Cizik responded. He knew he'd meet resistance from his colleagues and board. But Houghton convinced him that the world couldn't solve the issue without serious American participation, and that the Republican Party was the major political force blocking action in the United States, in contrast to Europe, where conservative parties had helped take the lead on the issue. "As evangelicals, we're forty percent of the Republican base, so if we could convince the evangelical community to speak out, it could make the key difference," Cizik said. American evangelicals, Houghton told him, might literally hold the fate of the planet in their hands.

After leaving the conference, Cizik began reading and learning. Flying over the Sahara, he got a sense of the "tens of thousands of acres that are lost to climate-related desertification each year," which in turn leads to major refugee migrations and potential wars over water. He coordinated a retreat with key evangelical leaders, like Rick Warren, and major scientists, like Houghton and Harvard's E. O. Wilson. Then he took a similar group to Alaska to witness the melting glaciers and permafrost, the disruption of native communities, the spruce trees dying because the bark beetles now survived the warmer winters. They visited Shishmaref, a native village that is being forced to relocate because the permafrost has crumbled beneath it and the sea ice that once served as a storm buffer is gone. "Our first night there, we saw a lunar eclipse, shooting stars, and the Northern Lights." It reminded him of the phrase in the psalm, "Creation pours forth its praise to its creator. . . . The heavens give witness to God's glory."

His Alaska group, said Cizik, "included those who believe life on earth was created by God, and those who believe it evolved over three-and-a-half billion years. What became obvious to both groups is that this earth is sacred and that we ought to protect it. God isn't going to ask you how he created the earth. He already knows. He's going to ask, 'What did you do with what I created?' If we're leaving a footprint that destroys the earth, we've failed to be good stewards."

The more Cizik learned, the more it challenged him to "treat caring for God's creation as a moral principle," and to continue enlisting others. In 2004, Cizik convinced the NAE to release a paper called "For the Health of the Nation," which urged its members to live in conformity with sustainable principles, talked of "creation care," and stated, "Because clean air, pure water and adequate resources are crucial to public health and civic order, government has an obligation to protect its citizens from the effects of environmental degradation." Two years later, he helped organize the Evangelical Climate Initiative, a major statement from eighty-six key evangelical leaders, including major megachurch pastors like Warren, the presidents of thirty-nine Christian colleges, and the national commander of the Salvation Army. The statement described climate change as an urgent moral issue for Christians and called for the government to act on it.

As Cizik expected, not everyone was happy with his taking environmental stands. "I had people on my board who said, 'Don't touch the issue. If you do, we'll make your life very difficult.'" Twenty-two evangelical leaders signed a letter urging the NAE not to take a position on global climate change. James Dobson, founder of Focus on the Family, and major conservative activists like Heritage Foundation founder Paul Weyrich and the Family Research Council's Gary Bauer called for Cizik's firing.

Some of this Cizik attributed to "simple ignorance of the science" and some to "bad theology—people who believe the earth is going to be destroyed anyway, so why bother." But he also wondered how much came from people "afraid they'll lose their power, influence, capacity to raise money, what they perceive to be their priorities. They're afraid that they'll offend political allies."

But Cizik and the others persisted. Although they never quite convinced the NAE to take an official stand on climate change, the organization reaffirmed the moral importance of "creation care," a core perspective that encouraged further dialogue.

"The issue shook my theology to its core," Cizik told me. "It changed me as much as my being born again thirty years before. This threatens the whole planet, so it raises a basic issue of who we are as people. Climate change isn't just a scientific question. It's a moral, a religious, a cosmological question. It involves everything we are and what we have a right to do."

Whatever propels us beyond the merely personal—be it awe at the power and mystery of nature, religious belief, outrage at the sight of another person suffering, concern about the crises of the planet, or simply a sense that we can do better than we have—we each need to take that all-important step of bringing our private convictions into the larger public arena. Because that's where we'll find our common humanity. As my friend the fisherman Pete Knutson says, "You get a lot back when you're with a good group of people taking a stand on something that matters."

Religious traditions stress the importance of listening to the spirit within, to guide our personal choices. This same voice can guide our public action. In fact, the connection between soul and acting rightly in the world lies at the core of these traditions. The ancient Jews spoke of *ruah,* the spark of life or breath of God, which gave insight, understanding, and physical sustenance. The obligation to love others and love God was the essence of right living, they said, of being truly human, as opposed to pursuing false gods and living a life of estrangement. We achieve redemption through engagement, not isolation. The more we exercise compassion for our fellow human beings, the closer we get to God.

Whether we frame the world in religious or secular terms, we don't have to be passive creatures of our circumstances, condemned to watch from the sidelines. Psychologist Jean Houston urges us to overcome detachment and ineffectiveness by joining "local life to great life." Cornel West talks of redeeming "life's epic significance." And we do both when we extend caring and generosity to a larger social domain.

Mary Oliver describes the resulting gain in her poem "When Death Comes":

When it's over, I don't want to wonder
if I have made of my life something particular, and real.
I don't want to find myself sighing and frightened,
or full of argument.
I don't want to end up simply having visited this world.

Oliver's images go to the heart of the matter. Will we remain mere visitors, planetary tourists? Or will we recognize that the earth is our home, and create a common future with our fellow inhabitants? Only by choosing the latter course will we realize, in the words of a young Atlanta activist, Sonya Vetra Tinsley, "that you can shape the world as much as it shapes you."

HOLDING TO THE DIFFICULT

Social involvement isn't all sweetness and light, and successes rarely come easily or instantly. It often feels hard just to raise public issues. Unless our acquaintances, colleagues, or friends are already politically engaged, it's awkward to ask them to act or even care about climate change, homelessness, or Darfur. It feels as if we're intruding on their private liberty, their right to be left alone by the claims and afflictions of the world. Our culture makes us feel that raising our beliefs in public is like parading some disreputable personal passion. "Are you talking politics again?" our acquaintances may moan, as if the whole subject is just too strange to mention.

The more we challenge institutional power, the more heat we'll take. As Sister Helen Prejean writes in *Dead Man Walking*, her memoir of working with death-row inmates, "Get involved with poor people, and controversy follows you like a hungry dog." When Martin Luther King challenged the Vietnam War, he found himself attacked by *The New York Times*, *The Washington Post*, even the NAACP. "Many who have listened to him with respect will never again accord him the same confidence," wrote the *Post*. "He has diminished his usefulness to his cause, to his country, and to his people."

Participation in public life often requires us to confront blindness, shortsightedness, greed, and the will to dominion that theologians call evil. Taking on larger causes sets us up for repeated heartbreak and for anger and frustration when people we hope will respond spurn the most basic appeals to human solidarity. Like any true path of psychological or spiritual inquiry, social commitment invites us to confront issues and forces we'd just as soon leave undisturbed. It can bring us face to face with more cruelty and suffering than we ever thought possible.

Yet here as elsewhere, the most challenging experiences may teach the most valuable lessons. Someone once asked the Dalai Lama how he responded to the continued brutal occupation of his country by the Chinese. "Because of the difficult situation," he explained, "this Dalai Lama became more realistic, closer to reality. If things are good, it's easy to pretend. When things become desperate, we cannot pretend. We have to accept the reality." The poet Rainer Maria Rilke explained: "We must always hold to the difficult; then that which now still seems to us the most alien will become what we most trust and find most faithful."

I ENJOYED THAT DAY

As Rilke and the Dalai Lama suggest, satisfaction can be found even amid the most testing of situations. Legendary boxer Muhammad Ali recalls how good it felt to decide finally to resist the Vietnam-era draft. He lost his world boxing championship, was publicly reviled, and was sentenced to five years in prison (though the sentence was eventually overturned on a technicality). If he quietly submitted, Ali was assured, he'd never face combat. But he could not live with supporting a war he felt was morally wrong and "leading more boys to death."

"That day in Houston in '67 when I went to the induction center, I felt happy," he says, "because people didn't think I had the nerve to buck the draft board of the government. And I almost ran there, hurried. . . . The world was watching, the blacks mainly, looking to see if I had the nerve to buck Uncle Sam, and I just couldn't wait for the man to call my name, so I wouldn't step forward. I enjoyed that day."

CHAPTER TWO

We Don't Have to Be Saints

We can make ourselves whole only by accepting our partiality, by living within our limits, by being human—not by trying to be gods.

—*WENDELL BERRY*

I believe many of us want to pursue something more than relentless self-interest—what Thomas Moore calls "a national persona of hype, ambition, narcissism, and materialism." We would like to find ways to connect with each other, express our compassion, and experience a sense of purpose impossible to attain through private pursuits alone. When we don't find ways to voice this larger self, our most generous impulses have nowhere to go.

Chief among the obstacles to acting on these impulses is the mistaken belief that anyone who takes a committed public stand, or at least an effective one, has to be a larger-than-life figure—someone with more time, energy, courage, vision, or knowledge than a normal person could ever possess. As we've seen with Rosa Parks, even our most noted historic figures often started their involvement in modest ways, and had as many failures as successes. Mahatma Gandhi's grandson, Arun Gandhi, tells the story of how his grandfather's family mortgaged everything they had—their land, their jewelry, everything of value—to send Gandhi to law school. Gandhi graduated and passed the bar, but was so shy that when he stood up in court all he could do was stammer. He couldn't get a sentence out in defense of his clients. As a result, he lost every one of his cases. Gandhi was a total failure as a lawyer. His family didn't know what to do. Finally, they sent him off to South Africa, where he literally and metaphorically found his voice by challenging the country's racial segregation.

I like viewing Gandhi not as the master strategist of social change that he later became, but as someone who at first was literally tongue-tied—shyer and more intimidated than almost anyone we can imagine. Given where he ended up on his subsequent journey, who knows what might be possible for the rest of us.

But most of us never get the chance to be inspired by the stories of those who've acted for change—because we don't encounter them. For too many of us, the past is a foreign country. The very stories that might remind us of our potential impact and strength are ignored, caricatured, or otherwise dismissed by our cultural gatekeepers. As a result, apart from a handful of famous names largely detached from their contexts, most of us know next to nothing of how ordinary men and women have fought to preserve freedom, expand the sphere of democracy, and create a more just society. Of the abolitionist and civil rights movements, we at best recall a few key leaders—and often, as with Rosa Parks, we don't know their actual stories. We know even less about the turn-of-the-century populists who challenged entrenched economic interests and fought for a "cooperative commonwealth." These days, who can describe how the union movement ended eighty-hour workweeks at near-starvation wages? Who knows about the citizen efforts that first pushed through Social Security? How did the women's suffrage movement spread to hundreds of communities, and gather enough strength to prevail?

A student from West Virginia eloquently described the problem. "We learn the conclusions," he said. "But we don't learn the process. We learn that Lincoln freed the slaves, women got the vote, and some unions were organized. We learn that Martin Luther King said 'I have a dream,' that people cheered him on, and that the president signed a Civil Rights Bill. But we have no sense of how any of that actually happened, what the participants experienced, or how change occurred. If we did, it would help us with the issues we face now."

We're equally detached from more contemporary examples of engagement. Apart from scattered pictures, sound bites, or brief media stories, most of us have a minimal sense of the actual process of social change—with all its passion, frustration, difficult perseverance, and feeling of consequence and purpose.

In fact, we're often left with unflattering stereotypes. As Taylor Branch wrote in *Parting the Waters*, the first volume of his epic history of the civil rights movement, we're taught to view social activists as people who shout loudly and rudely in a hushed museum, as grandstanders, as "zealots, people who oversimplify the world into good and evil without room for the murky truth, who lack the quality of self-effacement in their enthusiasm for their own views."

Many have remarked on America's historical amnesia, but its implications are hard to appreciate without recognizing how much the absence of memory erodes our ability to understand who we are, individually and as a nation. In our collective amnesia, we lose the mechanisms through which grassroots social movements of the past successfully shifted public sentiment and challenged entrenched institutional power. Equally lost are the means by which their participants managed to keep on, sustaining their hope, and eventually prevailing in circumstances at least as difficult as those we face today. As the novelist Milan Kundera writes, "The struggle of man against power is the struggle of memory against forgetting."

Think again about the different ways one can frame Rosa Parks's historic action. In the prevailing myth, Parks decides to act almost on a whim, in isolation. She's a virgin to politics, a holy innocent. The lesson seems to be that if any of us suddenly got the urge to do something equally heroic, that would be great. Of course most of us don't, so we wait our entire lives to find the ideal moment.

Parks's real story conveys a far more empowering moral. She begins with modest steps. She attends a meeting, then another, helping build the community that in turn supported her path. Hesitant at first, she slowly gains confidence as she speaks out. She continues despite an unpredictable and hostile context, as she and others act as best they can to challenge deeply entrenched injustices, with frequent setbacks and little certainty of success. Her story suggests that change is the product of deliberate, incremental action, whereby we join together to try to shape a better world. Sometimes our struggles will fail, as did many earlier efforts by Parks, her peers, and their predecessors. Other times they may bear modest fruit. And at times they will trigger a miraculous outpouring of collective courage and heart—as happened with Parks's arrest and all that followed. We can never know beforehand the consequences of our actions.

THE PERFECT STANDARD

"I think it does us all a disservice," says Atlanta activist Sonya Vetra Tinsley, "when people who work for social change are presented as saints—so much more noble than the rest of us. We get a false sense that from the moment they were born they were called to act, never had doubts, were bathed in a circle of light. But I'm much more inspired learning how people succeeded despite their failings and uncertainties. It's a much less intimidating image. It makes me feel like I have a shot at changing things, too."

Sonya had attended a talk by one of Martin Luther King's Morehouse professors, in which he mentioned how much King had struggled when he first came to college, getting only a C, for example, in his first philosophy course. "I found that very inspiring, when I heard it," Sonya said, "given all that King achieved."

I was similarly inspired to learn that when Montgomery NAACP head E. D. Nixon bailed Rosa Parks out of jail and then called Martin Luther King to help lead the bus boycott, King initially resisted. He was new in town. People were just getting to know him. Since he was only twenty-six, he was reluctant to take the lead. He had all sorts of understandable reasons to demur. But Nixon persisted and when he called him back, King responded, "Brother Nixon, I can go along with you on this." Had Nixon not approached him, King might never have taken his own first steps toward deeper involvement, on a stage that ended up making him a national figure.

King's hesitation matters, because once we enshrine our heroes on impossibly high pedestals, it becomes hard for mere mortals to measure up in our eyes. However individuals speak out, and for whatever cause, we can always find some reason to dismiss their motives, knowledge, and tactics. We fault them for not being in command of every fact and figure, for not being able to answer every question put to them, or for the smallest inconsistencies in how they act or live. We can't imagine how an ordinary human being with ordinary flaws might make a critical difference in a worthy social cause.

As a result of such images, many of us have developed what I call the perfect standard: Before we will allow ourselves to take action on an issue, we must be convinced not only that the issue is the world's most important, but that we understand it perfectly, will be able to express our views with perfect eloquence, and that we ourselves have perfect moral character.

The perfect standard assumes many forms. At Minnesota's St. Olaf College, a half-dozen students were sleeping in makeshift cardboard shelters to dramatize the plight of America's homeless. As one participant recalled, "Lots who passed by treated us like a slumber party. They told us we were cute. But when we kept on for a couple days they began to get annoyed. One girl yelled, 'Homeless people don't have blankets. You're being hypocritical.' I was half asleep but I said, 'Yes they do. They have blankets and friends. They just don't have homes.' She looked like she'd be satisfied only if we got soaked in the freezing rain."

In effect, the activists were ridiculed for not being pious enough. Yet even had they demonstrated their commitment by standing in the rain until they became hypothermic, or by launching a hunger strike, odds are the critics still wouldn't have been satisfied. They would have turned their argument around and accused the activists of trying to be martyrs, of taking things too seriously. Whatever the critique, the approach is the same: Identify a perceived flaw, large or small, then use it to write off an entire effort.

To hear others invoke the perfect standard against us is damaging enough. It's worse to subject ourselves to it. As a result, for instance, we often refrain from tackling environmental issues because they're so technically complex that we decide only credentialed scientists should address them. We don't speak out on homelessness because we aren't homeless ourselves. Though outraged when moneyed interests corrupt our political system, we believe we lack the authority to insist campaign financing be reformed. Whatever the issue, whatever the approach, we never feel we have enough knowledge or standing. If we do speak out, someone might challenge us, might find an error in our thinking or an inconsistency—what they might call a hypocrisy—in our lives. As spiritual writer Marianne Williamson says, "We have insidiously convinced ourselves that our wisdom is not wisdom, our common sense is not common sense, and our conscience is not conscience."

The very proliferation of issues can also be daunting, as we wait—and wait—for the perfect cause. I remember one young woman who wanted to get involved in addressing child poverty. "But I'd think of all the related issues," she said, "gangs and drugs, inadequate schools, poor health care, parents working too many hours at low-paying jobs. By the time I thought about how to take on each of them, I was so exhausted I couldn't do anything."

It's also tempting to lose ourselves in endless information. We can spend our lives trying to gather ever more facts and arguments from every conceivable Web site, blog, Facebook posting, or twenty-four-hour cable news source. Just as our culture has no notion of economic sufficiency, so the perfect standard leaves us with a permanent insufficiency of knowledge—and a convenient way to dismiss anyone who dares take a public stand. As everything that can be known continues to increase, the effort to know everything grows increasingly doomed. Yet we don't dare speak out unless we feel prepared to debate Bill O'Reilly on national network news.

ACT AND THE WORDS WILL FOLLOW

Eloquence is desirable, to be sure, but it's not as important as kindness, concern, and a straightforward declaration of belief, for starters. Dr. Rachel Naomi Remen tells the story of a woman she knew who got cancer. A male psychiatrist who was the woman's longtime running partner began avoiding her, even when she called. Finally the woman beat her cancer back into remission. Shortly afterward, she ran into the psychiatrist, and told him how hurt she was that he hadn't returned her calls. "I'm sorry," he said, "I simply did not know the right thing to say." Remen asked the cancer survivor what she would have wanted to hear. She smiled sadly. "Oh, something like, 'I heard it's been a hard year. How are you doing?' Some simple human thing like that."

Trusting our direct emotional responses may give us a way out of the perfect standard's trap. Will Campbell has been a Baptist preacher, a civil rights activist, a farmer, a writer, and a volunteer cook for his friends, musicians Waylon Jennings and Willie Nelson. As described in his memoir, *Forty Acres and a Goat,* one day Will was invited to participate in a student conference on capital punishment. Only at the last minute did he discover that he was supposed to formally debate an erudite scholar. Will's opponent delivered a long philosophical argument in favor of the death penalty as a means for buttressing the legitimacy of the state. Then Will got up to present the case against it. Nothing equally weighty came to mind, so he said, slowly and deliberately, "I just think it's tacky," and sat down.

The audience laughed. "Tacky?" the moderator asked. "Yessir," Will repeated. "I just think it's tacky."

The moderator asked him to expound, and Will repeated his statement.

"Now, come on, Will," the moderator said. "'Tacky' is an old Southern word, and it means uncouth, ugly, lack of class."

"Yessir, I know what it means," said Will. "And if a thing is ugly; well, ugly means there's no beauty there. And if there is no beauty in it, there is no truth in it. And if there is no truth in it, there is no good in it. Not for the victim of the crime. Certainly not for the one being executed. Not for the executioner, the jury, the judge, the state. For no one. And we were enjoined by a well-known Jewish prophet to love them all."

Not everyone will agree with Will's position on capital punishment, though I personally find it convincing. And I'm not lobbying, nor would Will, for disdaining reasoned arguments. But we should never be completely seduced by them into laying aside our core values. Most of us know it's tacky for families to sleep on the street, for children to attend crumbling and underfunded schools, for corporations to clear-cut 1,000-year-old forests, and for politicians to sell their favors to the highest bidder. Merely by virtue of its complexity and sophistication, modern society makes moral engagement more difficult. We don't need to compound the problem by demanding perfection of expression. As Will Campbell's testimony shows, simplicity can still be forceful and eloquent. The larger point is that social change *always* proceeds one way or another in the absence of absolute knowledge, as long as people are willing to follow their convictions, to act despite their doubts, and to speak even at the risk of making mistakes. As the philosopher and poet Rabindranath Tagore once wrote: "If you shut your door to all errors, truth will be shut out."

GOOD-ENOUGH ACTIVISTS

No one is immune to the crippling effects of the perfect standard. In this time of immense technological and economic change, many of us who've been active in social causes before feel daunted by both the size and array of contemporary problems. Even when we know better, we sometimes feel we have to tackle everything at once. If our efforts don't instantly achieve dramatic results, we are quick to criticize ourselves, and doubt that our efforts can matter.

In the 1960s, psychoanalyst D. W. Winnicott developed the now-accepted concept of "the good-enough mother." Winnicott argued that the goal of errorless child-rearing is a destructive and impossible standard that produces guilt and recrimination. As Jon and Myla Kabat-Zinn explain in their book about parenting, *Everyday Blessings,* "There is no question about doing a perfect job, or always 'getting it right.' 'Perfect' is simply not relevant, whatever that would mean. . . . What is important is that we be authentic, and that we honor our children and ourselves as best we can." In this vein, maybe we should also aspire to become "good-enough activists," realizing that although we may never win the Nobel Peace Prize, our contribution can still make a difference.

In *Dead Man Walking,* Sister Helen Prejean stresses the same point: "Better to help ten real hurting people—or nine, or one," she concluded, "than to be overwhelmed and withdraw and do nothing." We can pick one issue or another, this or that tactical style. As long as we act thoughtfully and generously, and don't trample people's lives in the pursuit of our causes, our efforts can help, whether or not we're certain about every facet of each issue. It's like the process that occurs when religious people pray: Even if they don't feel the presence of God with them at a particular moment, the act of praying still has meaning.

According to another version of the perfect standard, we shouldn't begin working for social change until the time is ideal—say, when our kids are grown or we ourselves are out of school, when our job is more secure, or when we retire. We wait for when our courage and wisdom will be greatest, the issues clearest, and our supporters and allies most steadfast. Such hesitation is reasonable. We are subject to real pressures and constraints. Yet when in life will we not be subject to pressures, of one kind or another? When will public participation not require a shift from familiar and comfortable habits? What's more, the issues that most need our attention will probably always be complex, forbidding, and difficult to address effectively. As Rachel Naomi Remen reminds us, "Being brave does not mean being unafraid. It often means being afraid and doing it anyway."

If we trust our convictions, we can take stands with whatever formal credentials we have. As David Halberstam describes in his wonderful book *The Children,* the group that led the pivotal Nashville civil rights sit-ins, former Student Nonviolent Coordinating Committee (SNCC) head John Lewis (now a Georgia Congressman) began as the most unsophisticated person imaginable. Lewis was so "country," his friends from the rural South said he made *them* feel like city boys. Stuttering when he talked, preaching to the chickens because he had no other audience (and presiding over chicken births, baptisms, weddings, and funerals), Lewis was the last person one would have expected to change history.

Involvement also knows no age barriers. Adam Werbach was eight years old when he first saw timber clear-cuts from an airplane, and "wondered what kind of monster created them. They were great slashes and gaps, like Martian footprints in the forest." Shortly afterward a Sierra Club petition came in the mail demanding the resignation of James Watt, Reagan's Secretary of the Interior. Adam took it to his third-grade class and his neighbors. People laughed, but at week's end, Adam had 500 signatures.

As a child, Adam spent many hours in a nature preserve in the Santa Monica Mountains, close to his house in the San Fernando Valley of Los Angeles. His parents camped and hiked and wrote checks to the Sierra Club, Amnesty International, and the ACLU. In seventh grade, Adam started an animal rights club that focused on needless cosmetic testing. His science teacher opposed the organization, calling its meetings an inappropriate use of school time, and many of his fellow students mocked Adam. But the head of the school offered encouragement, as did other teachers, his rabbi, and his highly religious grandfather, who ran a clothing store and had helped found a local temple. Adam was elated when companies such as Clairol and Gillette gave in to a national boycott and reduced their animal testing.

After Adam wrote about the difficulties and successes of the animal rights group for a national newsletter, teenagers concerned with environmental issues started calling him from around the country. With his parents subsidizing his phone bill, he pulled together a large informal network. In high school, he attended a Vermont environmental camp called the Mountain School. "We hiked, camped, and studied writers like Aldo Leopold, John McPhee, Bill McKibben, and Henry David Thoreau," he says. "People were always saying that we were too young to understand the issues. So I felt I had to know them better than anyone else."

A few months later, Adam returned to L.A. and stopped by the local campaign office of Big Green, a statewide environmental initiative. "Who's organizing high school students?" he asked. "Well, *you* are," responded the staffer in the office.

Within days, Adam had enlisted 500 student volunteers by calling every active student he knew, then approaching high school environmental clubs, student government associations, YMCAs, Scout troops, and every other group he could find. The students canvassed, answered phones, and "did everything imaginable," Adam says. "Almost universally, they'd say 'I wish someone had called me before.' If I hadn't happened along, if I'd gone to a Dodgers game instead, none of them would have ever gotten involved."

The initiative was narrowly defeated by its lavishly funded opposition. But Adam was struck by the enthusiasm of his young volunteers, and wondered how many more he could involve if only he had the resources to reach them. Of all the national environmental groups, the Sierra Club seemed to have the broadest grassroots base, so he started the Sierra Student Coalition (SSC).

Given the degree to which his peers were stereotyped as apathetic and passive, Adam figured that the Sierra Club's national board would be wary of investing time or money. So he first approached the Southern California chapter, where he already knew some active members. The chapter donated seed money that Adam used to conduct a weeklong training camp, modeled on the Mountain School, for a racially diverse group of high school and college activists who then launched SSC through their friendship networks and the newsletters and phone banks of local Sierra Club chapters. The group sponsored cleanups at local rivers and beaches, circulated petitions on key national legislation, and distributed black snow cones to dramatize opposition to oil drilling in the Alaska National Wildlife Refuge.

By September 1992, when Adam presented the SSC project to the national Sierra Club board, it had 25,000 members. Hesitant at first, the board finally gave the group official status. Then, acting on the encouragement of David Brower, the then eighty-three-year-old environmental legend, Adam ran for the national board himself and, at twenty-one, became its youngest member ever.

Adam had begun with his third-grade petition. Now he was helping set policy for one of the largest grassroots environmental groups
in America. At every point, he had ample reason to hold back, to
lower his expectations, to decide that he was simply too young and
inexperienced, or that the challenges he took on were impossible. Instead, he acted despite his doubts, and each step opened up new possibilities.

SAFER IN RETROSPECT

While we wait for the ideal time to arrive, weeks, months, and years
pass by. We squander repeated opportunities to involve ourselves in
the larger community for causes whose justification may be imperfect and whose outcome is far from certain—in other words, causes
that are real. The perfect standard promotes endless deferral.

In part, that's because social justice battles always look safer and
more clear-cut in retrospect. I once joined a civil disobedience protest during a Seattle fund-raising visit by then-Vice President George
H. W. Bush. One of those taken into custody for sitting down in front
of the doors was the head of a local alternative school who had
worked with Martin Luther King in the South. The arraigning judge
asked him a routine question about previous arrests.

"I was arrested in Birmingham," my friend explained. "I was arrested in Selma." And he reeled off a succession of civil rights battles.
"No," said the judge, getting testy, because those were the "good"
arrests, "I mean recently." "Yes," my friend said with an enormous
grin. "I have lots of those, too."

Sometimes we're called to take moral stands not only when the
time seems less than ideal but also when we're extremely vulnerable. When Alice Walker was a poor and relatively unknown writer,
a major magazine commissioned her to write an autobiographical
piece about growing up in the Deep South. Over lunch at a fancy
New York restaurant, the magazine editors insisted on changes that
Walker felt would make the piece more pleasant and sunny, but also
wholly inaccurate. She argued and resisted. Finally, one of the editors

said, "Listen to us, Alice. If you want us to publish your article, you *have* to make these changes." Walker needed the money and exposure. She was far from being able to call her own shots, but she gathered her manuscript and turned to leave. "Listen to me," she said. "All I *have* to do in life is save my soul."

Contrary to stereotype, we're most effective when we realize that there is no perfect time to get involved in social causes, no ideal circumstances for voicing our convictions. What each of us faces instead is a lifelong series of imperfect moments in which we must decide what to stand for. Choices may at times be thrust upon us, as Alice Walker's and Virginia Ramirez's were on them. More often we'll have to seek them out consciously, in contexts that don't always encourage them and sometimes when we don't feel ready. The wonder is that when we do begin to act, we often gain the knowledge, confidence, and strength that we need to continue.

THAT KIND OF PERSON

Sonya Vetra Tinsley, whom I mentioned earlier in this chapter, grew up with a sense that change had to come from ordinary people, like those she grew up with in a small town in rural Georgia. Sonya's grandparents had worked there as sharecroppers. Her father, co-principal of the local high school, died of cancer when Sonya was six. Her mother taught reading and math, but received only a paraprofessional salary, which left the family economically struggling. "Girl Scouts, the church, and the PTA were different in our African American community than in suburbia," says Sonya. "You weren't doing things just for yourself or for fun. You were also shaping the next generation, trying to prepare kids to swim upstream. You couldn't leave it up to some distant heroes."

Given Sonya's influences, it seemed natural, when she went off to college at Atlanta's Emory University, to start a black women's group, serve on an official committee exploring campus racial issues, and create interracial coalitions to address hunger and homelessness. When she graduated, she ran a youth program in Atlanta's

desperately poor Summerhill neighborhood and started a multiracial circle of young feminists, humorously called Amazon Salon. She
also organized a series of concerts that brought together hip-hop
and R & B groups (to reach young black audiences), socially concerned rock bands and acoustic musicians (with their mainly white
following), and local community activists.

Sonya called her music project Serious Fun, and she hoped it
would reduce Atlanta's racial divisions by bringing people together
across racial lines and by offering a broadly inclusive vision of justice. Promoted by local radio stations, the project had a powerful
impact. At one event a representative of a welfare mothers' support
group gave an address. On other occasions, audiences heard from
a homeless people's advocacy group, a project to unionize day labor-
ers, and organizations spearheading efforts to register minority and
low-income voters. Sonya moved the concerts around the city so
people from different neighborhoods could attend and in the process
develop a stake in the project. Her goal, she said, was to "slowly
make people comfortable about going outside their familiar turf. We
wanted to bring together diverse communities who'd probably otherwise never meet."

Serious Fun also nurtured an interracial community of local
musicians, bringing them into Atlanta schools to perform and discuss
issues like violence, teen pregnancy, racism, and images of women.
The organization ran workshops on youth and student organizing,
and on the role of the arts—continually linking music to a larger
social vision.

"So many of the things I believe," says Sonya, "I was taught as a
child. Maybe I believed them on a deeper level than anyone intended.
But I heard every word about equality and freedom and people having the chance to be who they are. I learned that it is not just bad or
lazy people who have hard times. I was also taught to take seriously
the biblical message about Jesus Christ living as a human being, with
human doubts and frailties. It isn't just a footnote to the story. All
of this taught me that your actions could matter even if you weren't
famous enough to name a highway after."

Sonya's community involvement led her "to meet so many people who inspired me, people I wouldn't have met in any other way. They were regular people. They didn't have some mythic level of courage or idealism, but they were full of hope and hadn't given up." These encounters, Sonya says, strengthened her homegrown faith that "life doesn't have to be just a series of things that happen to you. And we're not damned and doomed to the world as it is."

Sonya's perspective challenges the notion that some individuals are simply destined for greatness, while the rest of us are not. In contrast with countless people who've told me that they'd like to do more but are just not "the kind of person who gets involved," her story suggests that the ability to make a difference in our communities is not something innate, but a learned skill—even if it helps to begin learning it as a child, as Sonya did. Similarly, theories of developmental psychology argue that there are no natural leaders or followers, nor people who by virtue of superior genes become activists—only individuals who through circumstances or habit have had their voice and vision encouraged. "The essential and democratic finding," writes the essayist Carol Bly, in *Changing the Bully Who Rules the World*, "is that what were once loosely called 'leadership qualities' are part of the formula for every member of the species."

In fact, on some occasions, seemingly powerless people are in a better position to change history than their more fortunate counterparts. At a conference on spirituality and nonviolence convened by the Dalai Lama and fellow Nobel Peace Prize winners from Guatemala and East Timor, the Dalai Lama commented that small countries like theirs had "taught much to the world." East Timorese Nobel laureate Jose Ramos-Horta agreed, speaking of how independent Norwegian organizations brokered key peace accords in Guatemala and in the Middle East. More powerful individuals, institutions, and nations, he said, are too often blinded by their strength. It is left to those more vulnerable to promote compassion and justice.

A similar idea underlies what liberation theologians call the "preferential option for the poor." This is the belief that people who seemingly occupy history's margins can transform the world in unexpected, even profound ways. Born in humble circumstances and, as radical existentialist Albert Camus once said, keenly aware that all is not well under the sun, they may offer richer perspectives on suffering and sacrifice, and truer visions of the human condition, than those who from birth are told the world is theirs to command.

The roster of ordinary people who through practice and perseverance have transformed themselves and their communities is long indeed. Nobel Peace Prize winner Lech Walesa was a shipyard electrician before events thrust him into the forefront of Poland's Solidarity movement. Luiz Inácio Lula da Silva dropped out of school after the fourth grade, shining shoes and working as a street vendor before he became a lathe operator. He later joined and then led the steel workers union, helped found the Brazilian Workers' Party, and eventually was elected president of his country. Jody Williams taught English as a Second Language and worked with various citizens' groups before joining the International Campaign to Ban Landmines and winning the Nobel Peace Prize five years later, in 1997. These people were not fulfilling some preordained destiny. They were developing character—their own unique character—by taking the risk of speaking out for what they believed. As the eighteenth-century Hasidic Rabbi Susya once put it: "God will not ask me why I was not Moses, He will ask me why I was not Susya."

If participation in public life is not the inevitable realization of intrinsic personality traits, but instead a process through which our personalities evolve, then taking action is also an experiment in self-education. Sociologist Todd Gitlin argues that such learning often takes place precisely when we enter "that difficult, rugged, sometimes impassable territory where arguments are made, points weighed, counters considered, contradictions faced, and where honest disputants have to consider the possibility of learning something that might change their minds." Social activism, in other words, is as much a matter of learning how to listen, and especially to those who disagree with us, as of learning how to voice our beliefs.

Viewing our involvement as a process of learning helps us respond to a legitimate question: Might it just make things worse to stand up for our beliefs? To be sure, not all grassroots campaigns or acts of conviction are benign. We need to sort out for ourselves the true causes from the false, and the institutional changes that build human dignity from those that erode it. We need to distinguish humane social visions from scapegoating, from projection, from manipulated "reforms" that destroy our communities to save them, and from well-intentioned ideas whose consequences have gone awry.

To begin with, we need to set some limits on our means, so they're consistent with our ends. Whatever our beliefs, bombing animal research facilities, abortion clinics, or military recruiting centers clearly crosses the line by risking human injury. Our actions may inevitably conflict with the interests of some individuals and institutions, but even leaving aside the costs of any political backlash we might create, no cause can justify the chance of casually hurting or killing other people.

We can also do our best to be honest in our own political speech. That doesn't mean telling our employer our every thought if we're trying to organize a union, or telegraphing our game plan to a corporation whose toxic dumping we're trying to challenge. It does mean that when we speak for a cause, we represent it as accurately as possible. If we play fast and loose with the facts of the issues we take on, we'll taint those issues in the process. Manipulating the truth is different from not knowing every answer.

But even if we act with all the goodwill and thoughtfulness in the world, how do we know the changes we're promoting will do more good than harm? I'll talk more about this later on, but it helps to constantly test our assumptions, perceptions, and desires against the complex truths we encounter. It matters if we listen to our "opponents," are open-minded about our assumptions, and don't get too self-righteous about our vision. It's also natural for our views to evolve, even while we hold true to basic principles of fairness and justice.

I experienced such an evolution in my own political journey concerning the Vietnam War. In 1964, when I was twelve, I passed out literature for Lyndon Johnson, who said he wasn't going to send American boys to fight in a war that Asian boys should fight for themselves. The next spring, in a debate in my seventh-grade social studies class, I argued that we had to trust our president's decision that the Communist threat in Vietnam was serious, and had to be stopped. My opponent said that we had "a tiger by the tail" and ought to stay out. "If we don't take a stand now," I answered, "they'll be landing on the beaches of California." That dire warning was a cliché of the time. Since I was living in West Los Angeles, where kids spent their weekends swimming and body surfing on the beaches, the image hit home. Just about all my classmates backed my position.

Then the myths buttressing the war began to crumble. Exposed to critical perspectives that became steadily more convincing, I joined that small but growing number of Americans who mistrusted the government line. I came to feel that the war was unequivocally wrong and that my previous rationalizations were nothing but official lies. I soon attended my first candlelight vigil, then organized antiwar activities at my high school and later at Stanford University. This paved the way for the questions I've been asking ever since—about how citizens might fulfill the promise of democracy.

Was I wrong when I spoke out in support of the Vietnam War? Should I have kept my views to myself until I learned all the facts? I don't believe so. Had I not acquired the habit of voicing my beliefs, I might never have taken a stand for *or* against the war. The lesson I learned—and it helped to discover this early on—was the importance of remaining open to other points of view and letting new arguments, information, and perspectives change my mind. I'm not saying that we should abdicate judgment and switch positions at the first sign of inconsistency or error. We should remain faithful to causes that make sense, and stir our hearts. But a mind that admits no new light eventually withers. A heart that remains closed inevitably grows rigid. Sometimes those who oppose us have the most to teach us.

LIVING WITH AMBIGUITY

People often say that they're hesitant to take action because they're uncertain about the relevant issues or how they can best address them. Sometimes we do need to think things through before we jump in. But uncertainty can be a blessing. "Sometimes we are most open to conversion and transformation when we don't get it," writes Sister Mary Smith, of Portland's Franciscan Renewal Center, "when we cannot figure it out. We have to give it over. It is beyond our control, beyond our fixing, beyond our repair. The fact that we don't get it could be the best news of all. Because in not getting it we are opened up to a new way of seeing, a new way of hearing, and possibly a new way of living."

Smith isn't endorsing passivity, just reminding us that heartfelt social involvement inevitably leads us into new spiritual terrain. Theologian George Johnson amplifies this point in *Beyond Guilt and Powerlessness*. "Most of us," he says, "are more comfortable with answers than with questions. When faced with a problem we generally approach it with the assumption that information, insights, and proper action will bring satisfactory solutions. We want to fix things right now."

But as Johnson explains, "the reality of a broken world" often leads to ambiguity rather than certainty. "What we thought, believed, assumed, or followed is suddenly brought into question. . . . Receiving more information unsettles us rather than making things clear and easy. . . . It should not surprise us that our journey into the lives of those who cry for help will be discomforting."

It's also important to realize that those of us who work for social justice often have no choice but to pursue our fundamental goals by means that are sometimes unclear, ad hoc, and seemingly contradictory. I remember one Vietnam-era demonstration that focused on the role of major oil companies in promoting the war. With no ready alternative, my friends and I drove 35 miles to the demonstration in San Francisco. As we stopped to fill up at a gas station, it dawned on us that we were financially supporting one of the same companies we would soon be vocally opposing. We felt more than a little absurd. I experience a similar disjunction when flying across the country to give climate change talks or attend related conferences, in the process helping increase the very greenhouse gases I'm aiming to reduce. But often we can only act effectively in ways that seem paradoxical. So we do the best we can, and acknowledge the ironies of the situation.

We're familiar with such contradictions in our personal lives. We love family and friends despite their flaws and missteps. A lonely few wait indefinitely for partners who match their romantic ideal in every possible way, but most of us take the leap of falling in love with people who, like ourselves, fall well short of faultlessness; then we do our best to love them for who they are. Anyone who has children knows that they are the very embodiment of unpredictability. We can influence, but surely not control them. To all those who are dear to us we can only respond, moment by moment, as lovingly and mindfully as possible, improvising as we go. We embrace these necessarily uncertain human bonds, because the alternative is a life of isolation.

Public involvement demands a similar tolerance for mixed feelings, doubts, and contradictory motives. When we do act, others may view us as heroic knights riding in to save the day, but we're more like knights on rickety tricycles, clutching our fears and hesitations along the way. Gandhi called his efforts "experiments in truth," because successful results could be discovered only through trial and error. We take action despite our fears and less-than-perfect preparation.

How, then, shall we characterize those who participate in our society as active citizens? They are people of imperfect character, acting on the basis of imperfect knowledge, for causes that may be imperfect as well. I could be mistaken, but I think that's a profile any of us could match, given a willingness to live with ambiguity and all it implies, including some inevitable failure and frustration. That kind of imperfection may not be saintly, but living with it in the service of justice is a virtue.

WOUNDED HEALERS

I once took a workshop that psychologist Joanna Macy called "Despair and Empowerment." We used various exercises and rituals to

voice our bleakest feelings about the state of the earth and humanity, and then to work through them to find hope. Participants spoke
about everything from the erosion of topsoil, to the destructiveness
of current wars, to one man's outrage about the rape of his sister. At
one point Macy herself broke down, saying, "I do these damn
workshops. People vent and cry. But nothing changes." Then she
returned to being a steadfast guide.

Although mock vulnerability can be used to manipulate others,
Macy's genuine moment of doubt gave me much more respect for her
than if she had remained unequivocally in command, untouched by
the emotional vulnerabilities she'd called forth. She reminded me that
when the people we look to as leaders acknowledge their own uncertainties, their visions become all the more human and accessible.

Taking a stand neither requires nor confers moral perfection. At
best, in Catholic theologian Henri Nouwen's words, we're "wounded
healers." Acknowledging this can help us put our lives in perspective, nurture compassion, and make us more patient with human
frailty. As farmer and essayist Wendell Berry writes, "We can make
ourselves whole only by accepting our partiality, by living within
our limits, by being human—not by trying to be gods." Virginia
Ramirez's strong Catholic faith spoke to the value of proceeding
despite our inevitable human flaws. "Sometimes this work is very
hard," she said, "and I get tired. But I can talk with God if I have a
bad day and think about what to do. I can look at other people and
not judge them so harshly, because they have good qualities and
weak qualities, just like me. If I make a mistake—like not listening
to somebody, or talking to them rudely and hurting them—I can
remember that human beings make mistakes and it's okay to make
a wrong step. When I know God forgives me, I'm less afraid to fail."

Acknowledging our vulnerability doesn't lessen the practical
challenges, like learning how to build coalitions and apply political,
cultural, and economic pressure to force major institutions to act
more humanely. But pragmatic approaches work best when we're
honest about our own limitations, and when we're willing to learn
from uncertain contexts. As novelist Madeleine L'Engle once wrote:
"Only machines have glib answers for everything."

Of course, vulnerability isn't always a strength. Some people are so personally besieged that it's all they can do to get by. They may have been raised, in the words of anthropologist Mary Catherine Bateson, "to believe messages of disdain and derogation," to feel that their words and thoughts don't matter. They may have so little confidence that they can barely find their private voices, much less take difficult public stands.

Even those of us who feel reasonably strong face periods when personal cataclysms overwhelm us. If we or our family members are ill, if we're going through a divorce, if we've been laid off and are struggling to find work, or if a loved one dies, we may be able to deal with little else. When a close friend contracted throat cancer partway through the revision of this book, I cut back on my work to help him get through the treatments; I did the same when my father suffered through a health crisis a couple months later. Sometimes we have no choice but to focus on more private concerns.

If at times some people feel so individually overwhelmed that they must temporarily withdraw from the world, who can blame them? But meanwhile the rest of us can use their vulnerability, and our own, to appreciate more fully why compassion matters, and to understand how seemingly personal troubles often have social and economic roots.

Children's Defense Fund founder Marian Wright Edelman, who worked briefly with Martin Luther King when she was a young civil rights lawyer, is yet another person who found more to admire in him than rousing speeches and stalwart action. King was, she says, "someone able to admit how often he was afraid and unsure about his next step. . . . It was his human vulnerability and his ability to rise above it that I most remember. He didn't pretend to be a great powerful know-it-all. I remember him discussing openly his gloom, depression, his fears, admitting that he didn't know what the next step was. He would then say: 'Take the first step in faith. You don't have to see the whole staircase, just take the first step.' "

CHAPTER THREE

One Step at a Time

People say, what is the sense of our small effort. They cannot see that we must lay one brick at a time.

—*DOROTHY DAY*

The journey of a thousand miles begins with one step.

—*LAO TZU*

When we think about the problems of the world, it's easy to feel overwhelmed and to become paralyzed. The way to avoid this, as Martin Luther King suggested, is to proceed at our own pace, step by step, breaking down our goals into manageable tasks and not worrying too much about the precise political impact of every choice we make. Nothing gets accomplished when we try to do everything at once. Given how easily our hopes for a better world can be dashed, this approach lets us fight for what we believe with reasonable expectations, patience, and a sense of balance. To borrow the classic Alcoholics Anonymous maxim, the best way to get involved in social change is "one day at a time."

This incremental process doesn't have to lead to dramatic public controversy. And it doesn't always produce immediately visible results. But invariably it alters those involved, in ways that can't be foreseen. As feminist writer Gloria Steinem says, "As for who we will be, the answer is: We don't know. . . . But we do know that growth comes from saying yes to the unknown."

French theologian Phillipe Vernier offers a similar perspective on conducting a life of spiritual purpose: "Do not wait for great strength before setting out," he cautions, "for immobility will weaken you further. Do not wait to see very clearly before starting: one has to walk toward the light. Have you strength enough to take this first step? . . . You will be astonished to feel that the effort accomplished, instead of having exhausted your strength, has doubled it—and that you already see more clearly what you have to do next."

As Steinem and Vernier suggest, social involvement challenges us to create our own narratives as we join with others to build a community garden, organize our workplace, or encourage our neighbors to speak out on a key public issue. There is no preordained plot, no characters free of contradiction and confusion, no tidy ending. As Alice Walker says, "It's a practice, like any other. You never get it completely." But since it's a story of your own making, you can start anywhere you wish.

African American activist Julius Davis began under circumstances many would consider discouraging. As a teenager he'd spent most of his time doing drugs and committing petty crimes. Scorning everything about high school except sports, he was forced to repeat tenth grade, and barely graduated. Afterward he worked as an unskilled construction laborer and telemarketer. Mostly, he spent his time smoking pot, hanging out, and partying.

One day Julius was getting stoned at his cousin's apartment in the Bronx, dejected because he'd just broken up with a woman he'd hoped to marry. Idly leafing through a stack of music, he came upon the seminal Malcolm X speech "The Ballot or the Bullet," and played it. He'd never read or heard anything like it. Ten minutes into the speech, he no longer felt high. Instead, he was transfixed by Malcolm's words, "like how he talked about all the wars we fight, when we won't fight racism and poverty, and how if you fight for justice here, you'll know what you're fighting for."

Julius thought about how he'd gotten where he was and what

he wanted to do. He started reading intensely—everything on Malcolm; Carter Woodson's *The Mis-Education of the Negro;* Saul Alinsky's *Rules for Radicals;* and a self-help book that was a gift from his uncle, David Schwartz's *The Magic of Thinking Big.* Feeling for the first time that learning had meaning, he enrolled in Buffalo's Erie Community College. There he began participating first in black nationalist politics, then in multiracial coalitions with New York's state student association. Julius eventually became the second African American president of the national federation of student governments, the U.S. Student Association. Later he worked for the Children's Defense Fund, for an Atlanta community foundation, and for Public Allies, an organization that places young, socially concerned men and women in community service and advocacy programs, and whose Chicago office Michelle Obama would end up running. Each step led to another. Each opened up new possibilities. Julius's picture of himself and his vision of what the world could be emerged as he acted.

BEYOND THE COMFORT ZONE

When I ran cross-country years ago, our coach always urged us to get beyond our comfort zone—that pace at which we could run forever but would never win a race. That's what Julius did; he left his comfort zone, an often painful and difficult process that Cornel West describes as "stepping out on nothing, hoping to land on something."

Psychologist James Prochaska has studied how people do and don't manage to quit smoking, lose weight, or overcome alcoholism. If we're contemplating such changes, he says, we first need to acknowledge what we gain from the self-destructive behavior—for instance, the ease of familiar patterns and the safety of having a shield against the world. The same is true of social involvement. Before we take the first step, it helps to consider elements of our lives that have previously held us back—our particular roots of inaction. It's difficult to overcome barriers of which we're unaware. But by bringing them to light, we can better gauge the effort that we'll need to overcome them, and that effort can in turn strengthen our resolve.

I'm not suggesting that social movements can prevail solely by sheer determination. But success is unlikely if we fail to develop the will to change, and if we do not acquire, however slowly and incrementally, confidence that change is possible. At the peak of the Reagan-era Cold War, a West Los Angeles housewife named Suzy Marks and her husband, a real estate agent, were invited by their rabbi to come to a meeting on the nuclear arms race. Apart from voting, the couple had never participated in political activities. They'd paid little attention to the Vietnam War, concentrating instead on raising their kids. But since the rabbi had specifically asked them, Suzy went to the meeting and then attended an interfaith conference, during which a nun invited her to participate in a peace vigil on a major boulevard. Suzy was hesitant but went anyway, she says, because the arms race seemed "an ultimate issue that threatened all of us and all of our children." Standing on the street corner, she covered her face with her placard, showed herself briefly, then hid again, terrified that a friend might pass by and recognize her. Over and over she peeked out around the sign, then darted back again, like a rabbit in a carnival shooting gallery. After a dozen rounds of this, the nun laughed and asked, "Having problems?" Suzy admitted, yes, she guessed she was. But she ducked out a little more from behind her sign.

Since that first vigil, Suzy went on to help spearhead a statewide initiative aimed at converting military facilities to other uses, to be arrested in a demonstration at the Nevada nuclear test site, to organize against an anti-immigrant referendum, and to work on fundraising and educational outreach for a community-based foundation that supports grassroots organizing.

"Looking back," Suzy remembers, "my standing out holding the sign was a turning point. It was okay that I was scared. I think understanding my own ambivalence and hesitation makes it easier to reach out to people who are also reluctant to make themselves vulnerable by taking a stand. It's better to hold a sign in front of your face, put a scarf over your head so your friends don't recognize you, or do whatever you have to, than never get involved at all."

Writer Frances Moore Lappe says the arts of democratic participation comprise skills and confidences that can be learned in only one way—by practice. Think of kids learning to walk. They pull themselves up with the help of a chair, take a step, stumble, fall flat, then get up, and try again. They're not deterred by failure, even as we hover over them. They keep trying until they succeed. To be sure, social activism is a more complex process than figuring out how to walk. It can take us on to new and seemingly treacherous ground, where we know neither the language nor the rules. But the principle is the same. Each step, no matter how awkward or hesitant, prepares us for the next. "Once you get involved," says fisherman Pete Knutson, "you start paying attention to things in a different way. You see new opportunities."

Political psychologist Ervin Staub has explored how human destructiveness builds on itself. Torturers, concentration camp guards, and death squad members, he says, generally undertake a series of increasingly brutalizing acts, each of which further dehumanizes their victims and strengthens a sense that these victims have earned their suffering by their actions or character. Each step confirms the perpetrators' sense that their actions are justified.

Conversely, Staub finds, those who take powerful humanitarian actions also learn incrementally. And when bystanders take relatively small actions to challenge injustice, this can trigger more significant responses on the part of others. Rescuers of Jews in Nazi-occupied Europe often responded first to the need of a friend or acquaintance, then went on to help strangers. Children who teach a younger child, write letters to people in the hospital, or make toys for poor kids develop more receptiveness to helping people in need than those who don't share such experiences. Humane morality, Staub concludes, "is learned through moral action."

BRINGING OUT THE BEST IN US

I saw this process of sequential engagement in the life of a Connecticut housewife named Alison Smith. While she was raising her kids in a small rural town, a developer arrived one Thanksgiving weekend, when no one was around, and cut a canal to drain the water from a large marsh that adjoined her backyard. "He was slimy and greedy," she says, "doing things on the sly. He filled in the land and built new houses. Gradually it dawned on me that we had wetland regulations, that he'd broken the rules, and that no one was doing anything about it. So I went to a town meeting of a couple hundred people, and waited for someone to say something. Nobody did. So even though I didn't know that much about the issues, I voiced my opinions as best I could—red-faced, hesitant, and embarrassed. And I found that all these other people were thinking the same thing. They'd say it to each other, but not in public. It was really hard for me to speak out, but it was also really neat."

Shortly afterward, a neighbor suggested that she join the League of Women Voters. "I told her I wasn't much of a joiner, but she kept asking me to different meetings and said I could bring my three-year-old daughter." Gradually Alison got involved, working mostly on wetland problems and recycling programs. "I was hesitant at first. I don't have a college degree. I'm more of a behind-the-scenes person. But I've always felt like someone who cares, even if I didn't always know what to do about it."

When Alison moved to Maine, she joined the League's Portland affiliate, focusing on clean-air issues and transportation alternatives. She helped organize a broad coalition to pass a new state law on waste-oil recycling. "The more I did, the more confident I became. The more I felt I had something to contribute." By the fall of 1995, when she was asked to collect signatures to get a new campaign reform measure on the ballot, Alison jumped at the chance.

"We've become so used to being disgusted with elections and politicians," she said. "We assume that almost anyone who gets in will be corrupt. But the decisions they make in our name matter hugely, often leaving us with even less power. I didn't know whether the initiative would pass, but I didn't want cynicism to rule my life. I'd like to see politics bring out the best in us, not the worst. I get tired when people complain all the time but never do anything to change things."

Maine's Clean Elections Act offered candidates for state office an alternative to the degrading and often corrupting process of financing their campaigns. Under its provisions, they could choose a Clean Election Option, pledging not to take private funding or spend their own money (apart from modest initial seed funds), and raising a designated number of $5 contributions in their district to demonstrate their grassroots support. In return, they would receive enough public money to mount a full-scale campaign; if privately funded opponents or outside political committees out-spent them, they'd get enough additional money to stay competitive. The initiative also included other reforms, including tightened limits on individual and corporate spending.

In a single day, 1,100 volunteers qualified the measure by staffing tables outside polling stations. "I just sat at a table with a sign saying 'Do you want to take big money out of politics?'" recalls Alison. "Almost everyone who came over responded and signed."

The campaign worked closely with members of an allied research project that publicized in-state contributions from such sources as the tobacco and trucking industries. It was especially effective in inviting the press to film a $100-a-plate event that industry lobbyists held for the chair of the banking and insurance committee in the state legislature. These stories, says Alison, "helped us talk about the issue not only in speculative terms, but in terms of how wealthy interests were buying and selling our government. People felt they didn't have to accept this as the way things always had to be."

As she got more deeply involved, Alison met with newspaper editorial boards and spoke wherever anyone would have her. "I felt nervous when the League asked me to do new things like speak at press conferences. 'Why on earth would they want me to do it,' I asked, 'instead of some expert?' But I also found that as an ordinary person I had more credibility than the political professionals. The more I talked with people, the more I began to understand the issues. When people asked why I was involved, I'd tell them about the cynicism that seems to be destroying the very core of our democracy. I'd repeat over and over how if we could just break the links between money and politics, we'd begin to have a solution."

The initiative passed with 56 percent of the vote, and it changed Maine's politics. One Republican legislator said that before the Act's passage, he always had to listen to his donors first; now he was finally free to vote on his and his constituents' beliefs. By 2008, three-quarters of the candidates in the state were participating. Although the Clean Elections Act couldn't legally affect federal races, its popularity among voters helped persuade Maine's two Republican U.S. senators to buck party leadership and back serious campaign finance reform efforts in Congress. Citizen efforts have since led to statewide public financing legislation in Arizona, Connecticut, and Vermont.

The success of the Maine initiative also changed Alison personally. "It gave me a sense that I really can do something just by showing up to further a cause—this fundamental cause of democracy that affects everything I care about."

Without Alison's efforts and those of other grassroots volunteers, the campaign measure probably wouldn't have passed. But nothing about her involvement was inevitable. Years earlier, when she noticed the developer's bulldozer, she could have said to herself, "I'm not the kind of person who gets involved." But by taking an initial step, responding to what was happening in her own backyard, she said, in effect, "I'm going to find out what kind of person I can be."

THE PATCHWORK CITIZEN

It's important to recognize that Alison's transformation did not represent a departure from her core values, the notions of responsibility and fair play that she learned when she was a child. Instead, she simply was applying them in new arenas. When Alison nervously attended that first town meeting, she already possessed everything she needed to take her first step into the unknown. The same is true of almost all social activists. Even those from apolitical backgrounds often credit their parents with providing a basic ethical framework. Families with strong ties to friends and neighbors may instill in their children an appreciation of community. Parents with strong faith traditions often transmit a powerful sense of the importance of caring and compassion. Whatever our backgrounds, they can provide us with ethics as relevant to the actions of society as they are to our personal lives.

Family experience, of course, is only one of many influences on character development. "We know," psychologist Lillian Rubin writes, "that there are shifts and changes in identity as we take on new roles and adapt to different life stages. Each passage—from single to married to parenthood, for example, or from youth to midlife to old age—calls upon a heretofore unrealized part of the self. [Each part], when consolidated and internalized, leaves us with a new and different sense of who we are. But each new definition of self doesn't wipe out the last one. Rather, it is layered over all that came before, each successive self-image becoming part of the complex and often conflicting patchwork that defines the self."

Similarly, social involvement builds on who we already are, even as it changes us in unexpected and lasting ways. I saw this in Virginia Ramirez. For all the newness of her public commitments, she also built on longstanding beliefs, like her strong Christian faith. "When people ask me to do something I've never done before," she said, "I tell myself, I'm going to do the very best that I can, and God is going to give me the strength that I need. Fear can cripple you if you let it, but I always feel God's presence, so I say, okay, let's take that step, let's see what happens."

In fact, Virginia and other grassroots COPS leaders often used biblical passages in their training sessions, to make connections with participants' core moral frameworks. "We'll work from our personal stories, and from the Scriptures, all those sections that talk about justice. We'll look at our city, how divided it is between rich and poor. The Bible talks about that, too, and how it's wrong. It gives us strength, and puts things in perspective. I've read it all my life, but I'm reading it differently now," says Virginia.

We often patch together our models of activism from the social or cultural traditions at hand. We choose what inspires us, what we can stitch to our previous experience, what those we admire recommend by their example. The process reflects a more general need to sort through our familial and cultural legacies, as we craft an evolving sense of self. We "compose" lives of commitment, to use the term of Mary Catherine Bateson, by continually asking what we believe in, then devising ways to participate in public life that mesh our convictions with our circumstances.

If we speak to people's passions, they're more likely to get involved in social causes. At the University of Michigan, for example, a fraternity- and sorority-organizing group called Greeks for Peace kept trying to get two art majors involved. Although the young women said that they liked the group's social-justice ideals, they never came to meetings or events. Then someone asked them to make a banner for a march. They threw themselves into the task with all their energy and creativity, and volunteered their services for subsequent projects. They had found their niche through their art.

I've mentioned psychologist James Hillman's concept of the *daimon*, the "acorn" of character that propels us toward a specific vocation or a calling. In *The Soul's Code*, Hillman explores ways we can use this concept to look beyond our routine daily concerns and ask why we were put here on earth. It's a common belief that social activism is itself such a distinct calling—okay for some, unsuitable for most. Hillman himself, however, rejects this idea. He told me it was "simply nonsense" to consider public engagement a separate path, appropriate only for the select few. Rather, he stressed, any true calling impels us toward service to the community, even as our particular passions, strengths, and gifts will determine the shape of our service.

Think again of Pete Knutson, and the unlikely coalitions he organized to restore the salmon runs. His social activism wasn't a substitute for fishing, but an outgrowth of it. It was an extension of feeling called to a vocation he considered challenging, worthwhile, and intimately connected with the health of the natural world.

Some people have computer skills. Others play music, perform theater, or cook great food. Others are effective networkers who like nothing better than to pull people together for common projects they believe in, or persuasive speakers who can charm opponent and friend alike. Not every private passion can be joined to the common good, of course. But social activism that is in some measure an outgrowth of our deepest beliefs and values, of that patchwork creation we call the self, is most likely to endure.

THE JOURNEY OF A THOUSAND MILES

Taoist philosopher Lao Tzu said, "The journey of a thousand miles begins with one step." I've mentioned my defense of the Vietnam War in seventh grade. Actually, my small steps toward involvement began the year before, when I was eleven. I'd recently transferred to a West Los Angeles elementary school that held an annual Christmas pageant, although most of the students were Jewish. We were supposed to sing Christian songs, pretty innocuous ones like the "Little Drummer Boy." But I said, "I don't want to sing these songs. It's fine if other kids sing them, but these aren't my songs. They're Christian songs, and I'm Jewish."

"You have to," said the teacher. "That's what the class is doing." When I continued to refuse, she took me to the principal, who repeated that I had no choice, "because," as he explained, "everyone else is singing and you have to, too." When the principal called my parents, they told me, "Don't make trouble. You can always stand in the back and just mouth the words."

I really wasn't looking to cause a scene, but it felt like a violation of who I was to sing a song expressing adherence to a belief that wasn't mine, so I continued to refuse. Eventually the principal said, "Okay, you can sit in a room by yourself and not have fun when everybody else is having fun." "Fine," I responded, "I will. I'll read a book."

As an adult, I can sit in a Christian church and appreciate the majesty of the singing, sermons, and prayers, as ways of explaining our connection with those awe-inspiring forces that move the world. As a child, however, I heard only the requirement to name myself as something that I wasn't. I didn't think of demanding that the other Jewish children withdraw. Nor did my refusal to abide by an unreasonable school policy alter that policy, or at least not that year. But by standing up for my integrity, I discovered the power of conviction, taking my first small step toward a lifetime of engagement.

I WOULDN'T BE HERE NOW

Whatever our age when we first venture into the public arena, our inaugural steps will almost certainly seem modest, even inconsequential. And our goals may often seem improbable. As the familiar adage counsels, we can't run without first learning how to walk, and we can't walk without first learning how to crawl. That's true even when we're trying to act on the largest national or global stage.

Two years after environmentalist David Brower convinced Adam Werbach to run for the national Sierra Club board, Brower backed Adam again, this time to become the Club's national president, at age twenty-three. "I think he saw me as the club's future," Adam said. "I obviously had some trepidation as to whether I had the skills to do it. Here I was barely balancing my checkbook, having gotten through college by working as a handyman and doing office temp work. I'd been accepted to Columbia film school, was singing in a rock band, and trying to write a novel. Suddenly I'm thinking about applying to run a national organization with six hundred thousand members, a fifty million-dollar annual budget, and a staff of three hundred. College doesn't exactly prepare you for that. But I also felt I had something to offer. I decided, 'Why not run?' "

To Adam's surprise, the board elected him. During his two terms, the Club grew in members and donations, shifted $4 million in annual spending from D.C. lobbying to local grassroots organizing, and spearheaded boycotts of major corporations with problematic environmental records. It also reached out to a new generation through MTV, Adam's syndicated college newspaper column, and partnerships with musicians like the Beastie Boys, eventually lowering the average age of members by ten years. Meanwhile, Adam led the Sierra Club into new alliances with hunters, farmers, religious groups, and low-income and minority communities.

"I've learned that going ahead and doing the best you can is better than waiting until you have all the answers," Adam told me just after being reelected for his second term. "I learned that at the very beginning, when I was foolish enough to think anyone would even listen to a third-grader gathering signatures. If I hadn't started back then, I wouldn't be here now."

WE'D FOLLOW UP AGAIN

Like Adam, Meredith Segal took on an immensely daunting challenge when she launched Students for Barack Obama on Facebook. It was July 2006, eight months before Obama officially launched his campaign. At the time, conventional wisdom suggested Obama had only a remote chance of winning the Democratic nomination, much less the presidency. But his Democratic Convention speech two years earlier had inspired Meredith, and she checked out *Dreams from My Father* and *The Audacity of Hope*. "I just felt so excited that someone was talking about issues like the Iraq war and making college affordable. I admired Obama's intelligence and clarity." She decided to try to demonstrate enough support from students to help convince him to run, and to convince others to support him. Facebook seemed the perfect outreach medium, "because," as she explained, "you can see whether something is just a crazy notion or whether a significant number of people are interested."

Meredith grew up near Portland, Maine, "in a town with more cows than people." She started her community involvement at age eight, "volunteering at a pre-school, reading to the kids." In middle school and high school she built houses with Habitat for Humanity and brought together two rival high schools for a hockey tournament that raised $4,000 for the Make-a-Wish Foundation, to fulfill the dreams of children with life-threatening diseases.

But she also began to question the limits of volunteerism. "It was exciting to help a family that never had a house of their own. But I'd also wonder why a country as wealthy as ours would let people be homeless to begin with. I'd get frustrated that, with all this effort,

I was only helping one family or one child. The more I got involved, the more I started thinking about broader solutions."

When Meredith started at nearby Bowdoin College in 2004, she volunteered to do campus voter registration for the John Kerry campaign, and within a week, she was in charge of the effort. When her group went door-to-door, some students responded that "they were too busy or that their vote wouldn't really matter, but we'd follow up again and again until they'd finally vote just to get some peace in their lives." Their effort turned out almost every supporter on the campus, and Kerry took Maine. But of course, it wasn't enough to make a difference at the national level. "Lots of us were crying," Meredith said, "and I kept thinking, if only someone had been able to execute a similar program on the huge Ohio campuses, we could have had a very different outcome. I felt our efforts could either end with this disappointment or be channeled into the future."

With the election over, Meredith shifted her attention to studies and a program that matched Bowdoin students with special needs kids. Concerned about the Iraq war, she also started Bowdoin Students for Peace and helped launch similar groups at other Maine schools. Meredith admitted that she has "a propensity to get involved in things—maybe too many." But what made this possible—besides being organized, energetic, and able to stay up multitasking until 3:00 a.m.—was her willingness to jump in and learn as she went along without knowing how a particular project would turn out. Even when progress was elusive, as in the case of challenging America's involvement in Iraq, or when she lost, as with the Kerry campaign, she trusted that her efforts would still help build something useful. She embodied that core leap of faith that Reverend Jim Wallis, editor of the wonderful radical evangelical magazine, *Sojourners,* describes as "believing despite the evidence and then watching the evidence change."

Her Obama project built on everything she'd done so far. She began by inviting her friends, asked them to reach out to others, then systematically searched out Facebook members who'd mentioned Obama or his books and invited them as well. When she posted a request for a Web designer, a freshman from George Washington

University named Tobin Van Ostern responded. At that point, Tobin didn't have a definite candidate preference, but he was impressed by the size and enthusiasm of Meredith's group. Soon he was co-chairing the effort.

Meredith and Tobin spent the fall of 2006 building a chapter structure and working to enlist anyone who showed interest. They had over seventy chapters by the following January, when a senior Obama staffer called. Meredith asked if the candidate could speak to a group of students, and they agreed on a February event at Virginia's George Mason University. Meredith and Tobin's group would produce the audience and handle the logistics, while the campaign would cover the costs. Obama's staff told him that the rally was organized on "something called Facebook," and maybe 300 people would be there. Instead, 3,500 students showed up, from campuses as far away as Michigan and Florida. Many carried signs that said, "I drove all night to see you." Meredith and Tobin introduced Obama, who quoted Martin Luther King's statement that "the arc of the moral universe is long, but it bends to justice," and challenged young people "to grab hold of that arc."

A week later, Obama formally launched his campaign, and Meredith and Tobin were invited to make their group the official student wing. After meeting with key staff in Chicago, they returned to school, continuing to reach out to new campuses while juggling classes, labs, and papers. With a half-dozen core volunteers, they created teams on each campus, focusing on sophomores and juniors, who likely would still be in school during the general election. Their conference calls generally began at 1:00 a.m. because, as Meredith said, "that's when students are free." And they continued to reach out on Facebook, drawing on a new feature where "if you logged in and found out that your friend had just joined Barack Obama '08, you were encouraged to check it out as well."

Obama was still a major underdog then, forty points down in the polls. But the volunteer energy and enthusiasm helped keep Meredith and Tobin going. "Lots of my friends," Meredith said, "would ask me 'Why are you dedicating your life to someone who's obviously going to lose?' Others would say, 'How many black presidents has America had?'" Some of those same people later became involved.

As Meredith remembered, "We had a sense that if we could get volunteers knocking on enough doors, making enough calls, and turning out enough people for the Iowa caucuses in particular, we had a real chance for it to end in victory. People were always saying that young people may join Facebook but they won't vote. But they weren't just signing up in our group. They were hanging signs in the dorms, registering their friends, coming to meetings, and knocking on doors. So why wouldn't they vote?"

The more people signed up, the more they enlisted their friends, calling and e-mailing them and using their personal Facebook pages to remind them of registration deadlines and ways to volunteer. By Fall 2007, the group included 600 chapters, with coordinators in virtually every state. They held contests to see which statewide leaders could establish more chapters and enlist the largest number of volunteers. "I'd fly in," Tobin said, "not even knowing where I was staying, and someone would find me a sofa bed. It's very much not in my personality to do something like that, but after a while it became routine."

Because Obama had to do well in the early contests, Meredith and Tobin asked students in states with late-breaking primaries or caucuses to focus on calling peers in the earlier ones, using extra cell minutes and campus directories that student volunteers scanned in to an Excel sheet. The group also targeted high school students who'd turn eighteen by November, so were eligible for the caucuses and primaries. With a national structure in place, it was easy for Meredith and Tobin to shift their focus to each successive primary state, "reminding California or Wisconsin students that their work wasn't done, and that they could still make a huge difference calling peers in Ohio, Texas, or North Carolina." Young voters and volunteers provided the critical margins in state after state, as they would in November.

"At the beginning it was important to demonstrate as much activity as we could," Meredith said, "so that people took the Obama campaign and the role of students seriously. After we'd proved that, we focused more on effective action. We started working on what each chapter could do to make the maximum impact, instead of just adding new ones."

Things shifted again once Obama clinched the nomination. In key battleground states, the campaign folded the student networks into their larger coordinated efforts, while Students for Barack Obama primarily focused on the remaining states, where they enlisted students in virtual phone banks and encouraged them to travel to key neighboring battlegrounds. Their official Facebook network now had 150,000 members, complemented by parallel state networks.

"Most of our leaders hadn't been active before," Meredith said. "But they got the training and experience of getting out the vote during the primaries. We made sure that school chapters led by seniors had strong younger members who'd be around in fall. When the home stretch hit after Labor Day, they were ready to funnel all of their energy into knocking on doors, making phone calls, and volunteering wherever it would make the most difference. We'd spent two years building our network. Now we had a chance to mobilize it."

Amid all her political efforts, Meredith somehow managed to graduate the June before the election. Since the group was designed to be run by students, she turned the prime leadership over to Tobin and the others, and switched to helping run the national campaign's Philadelphia offices. "We started off being part of a movement that hardly anyone believed had a chance. In the primaries, we knew the odds were against us, but we kept on anyway and changed them. Now everywhere you went you saw Obama signs, Obama gear, street musicians playing Obama songs. We just had to keep doing all the necessary tasks, with the same intensity and drive." After spending Election Day on the final push, Meredith boarded a plane to Chicago and arrived at the Grant Park celebration just in time to hear Obama speak.

Meredith and Tobin were certainly exceptional organizers. But like anyone who acts, they grew into their skills. They had plenty of reasons to stay on the sidelines, from their regular student obligations to the sheer improbability of Obama's initial candidacy. But like many others, they took one step, then another, getting more deeply involved, each new effort preparing them for the next. Refusing to be daunted by the perfect standard, they were unwilling to wait to take up such huge responsibilities, or wait until Obama's chances improved. Instead, they took a leap of faith, trusting that their efforts and those of others could matter. Recognizing from the start that the campaign could succeed only through a nearly unprecedented level of community engagement, they set out to build that community in every way they could. "There were millions who did something," Meredith said, "even just making one phone call."

For all the elation Meredith felt at Obama's victory, she also emphasized that it was just one moment in what she hoped would be a larger process of change. "Your candidate gets elected," she said, "Obama or anyone else. People think, 'Here's their platform, here are their policies. They'll magically become law.' But that's never the way things change. You have to keep pushing. You have to keep working. You have to keep building that engaged community. You can never expect any elected official to do it all on their own, no matter how much you admire them or how hard you worked to help them win. Your election night victory is just the beginning of the process."

CHAPTER FOUR

The Cynical Smirk

Irony has only emergency use. Carried over time, it's the voice of the trapped who have come to enjoy their cage.

—*LEWIS HYDE*

I remember seeing an ad for *Slate,* the online magazine founded by Microsoft and now owned by *The Washington Post.* "It's what everyone is talking about," the ad proclaimed: "media, politics, technology, high and low culture . . . all with a certain insouciant smirk that thinking people find compelling."

Which insouciant smirk, and which thinking people? My dictionary describes insouciant as "carefree" or "blithely indifferent." "Carefree" seems innocuous enough, but is indifference a virtue? Did the ad mean to suggest that *Slate*'s editors and writers stand above it all, and nothing they say really matters?

People smirk when they're full of themselves, smiling arrogantly, "in a self-conscious, knowing, or simpering manner." They know the score, you don't, and they're about to put you in your place. Exxon and AIG executives smirk. So do grade-school bullies and hedge-fund speculators. Donald Trump and Bernie Madoff smirk. Marie Antoinette's famed "Let them eat cake" was an ill-timed smirk that cost her her head.

Yet *Slate,* or their ad agency, decided that an ethic of contempt boosts sales. They presented it as something to be proud of. All of us, the ad suggested, should approach life with such hip detachment.

Merely knowing the right people and being able to drop the right insouciantly clever phrases exempts us from any broader responsibility to our fellow human beings. The ad implies that we simply need to acknowledge that the world is inherently corrupt, bought and paid for, and that all talk of changing it is naïve.

In her poem for Bill Clinton's inauguration, Maya Angelou called this kind of cynicism "a bloody sear" across the brow of our nation. "Everybody lies," says a veteran newspaperman quoted in the *Utne Reader,* "but it doesn't matter, because nobody listens." In a more extreme example, imagine a man who tells his young son to jump from the stairs into his arms. The father catches the boy twice, but the third time steps back and lets him fall. "That's to teach you never to trust anyone," he explains, "even your own father."

We're particularly taught to expect such betrayals when we think about trying to change things, whether in our community or on a larger scale. "You can't really do anything about it," people say, and when they repeat it enough we start to believe them. "That's just how things are," we agree, then shrug and move on. We give up hope before we even start.

When I first wrote *Soul of a Citizen,* it was the end of the Clinton era, and cynicism reigned. Those at the top smirked down from on high, making choices that hollowed out the American economy, including ending Depression-era banking and finance regulations that would likely have prevented economic meltdown. Most of the rest of us focused on our private lives. Whether riding an apparent boom economy or struggling to get by, we pretty much gave up on the possibility that our public actions could matter. While the Bush years saw even more cynicism at the national level, there was also a surge of renewed citizen involvement, although many felt frustrated at their inability to change the administration's policies.

I've now rewritten this book in the midst of massive economic and environmental crises, and with a president who ran explicitly on hope, while blasting cynicism as "a sorry kind of wisdom." Inspiring millions of ordinary people to join his campaign, Obama asked participants to view themselves in the tradition of engaged movements from the past—like those I explore in this book. This link between past history and present possibility was one reason supporters literally danced in the streets when he was elected.

As I write, it's unclear whether Obama's presidency will be able to restore a broader sense of our fates being tied together, and of government and ordinary citizens being able to make a difference. For far too many people, the very expectations he raised have fed dashed hopes and disillusionment, not only with his administration, but with public engagement in general. Those who've withdrawn cite frustration with Obama's compromises and policies, and his failure to passionately speak out on key issues. They talk of how powerful interests have blocked progress in so many critical areas that challenging them seems almost impossible. Those who withdraw also voice a sense of being overwhelmed at the sheer magnitude of the crises we face, and the sheer difficulty of addressing them.

If America is to turn away from cynical resignation, our own participation is crucial. So is remembering that, as I explore throughout this book, social change requires people staying involved despite inevitable setbacks and disappointments. Even the best political leaders need citizen involvement to help them pass critical programs, challenge them when their approaches fail or fall short of what's necessary, and model wise and creative solutions in their local communities. Otherwise we leave the field to the same powers and principalities that helped create and perpetuate our current problems. So if we'd like to see a renewed culture of hope, our best chance is to help develop it ourselves.

To do this, it helps to understand the interconnected barriers that stand in the way of involvement: the cynical smirk that mocks those who work for change; the corollary shrug of resignation when we decide the deck is so stacked that there's nothing we can do; the false alternative of blind trust, by which we defer judgment on critical choices to distant leaders; and the distancing mechanisms that render certain lives invisible, beyond the reach of moral concern. Add the more general challenge of people not having enough time, which I'll explore in a later chapter, and these obstacles create a powerful force for withdrawal.

Let's start with cynicism. In its most extreme form, cynicism enshrines as eternal truth the notion that every institution and every person is for sale. It assumes that human motives are debased and always will be. Implying that no traditions, truths, or community bonds are worth fighting for, it occupies the mental and psychological space we could reserve for hope—at least for the kind of hope that might inspire us to take public stands. Painting a categorically bleak portrait of human existence, with no redemption, cynicism convinces us that all businessmen and politicians are dishonest, all religious leaders charlatans, all journalists cheap-shot hacks, all social activists fools. Better to expect nothing, in this view, than to set ourselves up for certain disappointment. Taken far enough, it can become as great a barrier to meaningful public action as all the other barriers combined.

Cynicism wasn't always so disempowering. The first Cynics were a group of ancient Greek philosophers, most notably Diogenes, who caustically denounced the established culture of their time. Monklike ascetics who preached simplicity, self-discipline, and self-sufficiency, they offered a moral alternative to the empty materialism, legalism, and religious hypocrisy that had come to dominate Greek society. Back then, to be a Cynic meant to stand up for one's convictions.

To fully appreciate the corrosive effect of contemporary cynicism, imagine adopting the same approach toward our children, spouses, lovers, and friends that we often do toward public life. Pretend for a moment that instead of placing our trust in them, and forgiving their lapses and flaws, we greeted them with derision, suspicion, and indifference. How long would hope, love, or joy survive under those conditions? That's precisely the reason we resist cynicism in our personal relationships. We take chances on people, risking disappointment and heartbreak, to encourage their best qualities. Otherwise, decent relationships become impossible.

THE MEN WHO KNOW BEST

Cynicism in the public sphere is equally destructive, leaving us with a sense that working for a larger common good is a fool's errand, leaving no likely outcome except heartbreak. So what's the alternative? It certainly isn't blind trust, which is dangerous in its own right.

I saw both blind trust and cynicism during my three-year study of Washington State's Hanford nuclear complex, the largest in the world. Hanford's founding generation came in during World War II, producing the plutonium for the first atomic bomb (exploded in the New Mexico desert), the bomb that fell on Nagasaki, and the raw materials for a quarter of all the atomic warheads in the world. They were so proud of their work that the high school football team, the Richland Bombers, displayed a miniature mushroom cloud on its helmets, pep club banners, and school commencement programs.

To me, their work raised troubling moral questions. Hanford's repeated releases of radioactive gases, some deliberate, left a trail of cancers in communities 200 miles downwind. Hanford waste tanks, intended to be temporary, leached hundreds of thousands of gallons of radioactive liquids into the water table. With U.S. and Soviet missiles on hair-trigger alert, six minutes away from each other, bombs made with Hanford plutonium literally risked the annihilation of our species.

First-generation workers avoided these questions, choosing instead to immerse themselves in their jobs and in an ethic of invention. "I could just as easily have been making lightbulbs," said one. "My job," explained another, "was to make the machines work." Ultimately, Hanford's founding generation passed moral responsibility to those they referred to as "the men who know best." Hanford engineers believed that Congressional leaders and Pentagon officials had studied whether the building of nuclear weapons was right or wrong, and they trusted them to make that decision.

The notion that only a small group of specialists can understand critical national choices exemplifies the moral distancing mechanisms common among the generations of the 1940s and 1950s, a period some still idealize. When men and women who came of age during that period later stayed silent in the face of obvious social ills, they often did so because of their faith in our government leaders and their belief in technical progress. Both of these impulses were strengthened by the Second World War, when the United States pulled together as a nation to defeat a common enemy. Could the Allied forces have taken Omaha Beach on D-Day without a large number of young men willing to place their fate in the hands of the generals, their representatives in Washington, and ultimately their president? I'm not sure.

But blind trust has also made it easier to excuse and get away with questionable policies. When top Bush administration officials branded dissenters as allies of terrorism, it encouraged self-censorship and silence. As a University of Missouri student told me, "I'm trying to get people involved in debating our policies, and other students are saying, 'I'd like to, but I don't want to be told I'm helping Osama bin Laden.'" Many of us who spoke out at the time faced a similar response—supporters of the president said it was simply not acceptable to question him in a time of national crisis. This intimidation, fostered by a compliant media, helped the Bush administration promote false claims that Saddam Hussein possessed weapons of mass destruction, had ties to Al-Qaeda, and was importing weapons-grade uranium from Niger. The instinct to defer to those who presumably knew more convinced most Americans to accept these falsehoods, despite the many credible voices that challenged them. A different kind of blind trust fed the economic meltdown, as financial companies insisted that they could and should regulate themselves, and government officials went along with them. When we fail to ask the hard questions, there's almost always a cost.

A COMPANY DUE FOR EXTINCTION

If most of us no longer automatically believe the men who say they know best, that's because of repeated betrayals by individuals and institutions we once trusted. Yet we may also doubt that we can challenge their judgments. Too many Americans, convinced that the country is doomed to be run by greedy hustlers, have responded by retreating into private life, and trying to put out of mind whatever qualms they may have about our national direction.

Beginning in the late 1970s, a new generation of Hanford workers exemplified this cynicism. Unlike their older counterparts, most
of these young men and women mistrusted the nuclear enterprise,
but they still showed up every day to build three new commercial
reactors (only one of which limped to completion, saddling Pacific
Northwest ratepayers with a multibillion-dollar debt). They cultivated an attitude of detachment, treating their work as an elaborate
con game with an excellent paycheck.

"When these reactors go on line," several told me, "I'll be long
gone—as far away as possible." One computer scientist joked, "Maybe
the human species is like a company past its time—simply due for
extinction." The young Hanford workers often voiced misgivings
about the results of their labor and the process of their work. But
they quickly brushed aside higher ideals like so much smoke from
the high-priced dope they smoked. They joked about underground
pipes that led nowhere, improper welds, and other shoddy practices
with potentially catastrophic consequences. Then they laughed,
shrugged, and said they might as well get the money, since someone
was going to.

I'm not trashing dark humor. In a difficult era, an acerbic point
of view may be exactly what we need to keep on going. Sometimes
such fearless humor serves as one of the few sources of truth, a
good example being the scathing parodies of Jon Stewart and Stephen Colbert during the Bush administration. But as Colbert himself has said, "Cynicism is a self-imposed blindness, a rejection of
the world because we are afraid it will hurt us or disappoint us."

Cultivated or crude, cynicism is treacherous. It converts the understandable desire to not be lied to, into bitter protection against
dashed hopes: If we never fight for what we believe in and aspire to,
this removes the risk of failing and being disappointed. We can challenge "the men who know best" with contrary information and
counter-examples, particularly stories about how the powers that be
have misled us. But what can possibly challenge an all-encompassing
worldview that, in the guise of sophistication, promotes the bleakest
possible perspective on the human condition—the notion that

everyone lies? The answer requires giving citizens something to believe in, a vision of connection and effectiveness powerful enough to help us begin again to trust our fellow human beings.

WE DON'T CARE WHETHER THEY'LL EVER WORK

Of course, part of the reason we doubt our ability to make change is the runaway cynicism of powerful institutions and individuals. When I spoke to a group of employees at Lockheed Martin's Missiles & Space Division a couple of years before the 9/11 attacks, I mentioned the huge sums that America's top defense contractors were spending on political lobbying and contributions. I specifically challenged Lockheed Martin's role in promoting and building missile defense systems like the "Star Wars" project, which critics called politically destabilizing and technologically problematic (and which at that point had already cost $45 billion). An audience member quickly defended the system's necessity.

Then one of his colleagues spoke up. "Let's get real," he said. "We all know that if anyone ever attacks America, the bomb is going to be delivered by a suitcase, a car or a truck, or in a boat. It's not going to come from a missile, because you can track where a missile comes from and retaliate. We all know that we're lobbying for these programs because they make us money. We don't care whether they'll ever work, or even be useful. We just care that the dollars come our way."

The room was silent. The original questioner answered briefly, but no one else jumped in. After an awkward pause during which people looked down at their shoes, the conversation moved on. People seemed ashamed to respond.

In a parallel experience, I once flew from Dallas to Washington, D.C., while seated in the row ahead of two drunk arms traders, whose alcohol-fueled conversation was impossible to ignore. It soon became clear that they'd sold helicopters to both sides during the Iran–Iraq war. When the helicopters got shot down, the countries bought more, then more again, so the arms traders made more money each round. They laughed wildly about the story, considering it a perfect deal.

I thought of both of these examples in the wake of America's financial meltdown in late 2008. I also remembered the energy company Enron, George Bush's largest campaign donor. Before it collapsed in a massive corporate pyramid scheme, Enron had persuaded the government to remove barrier after barrier to energy price deregulation; when Bush became president, the head of the Federal Energy Regulatory Commission (hand-picked by Enron) accelerated the process still further. Meanwhile, as the company's energy traders manipulated West Coast utilities, they bragged (in a tape aired by CBS news) about stealing from "Grandma Millie" and jamming their inflated power prices "right up her ass." Enron was also breaking the law, but its actions weren't much different from those of the banking and finance executives who later accepted multibillion-dollar government bailouts as they continued buying corporate jets, handing out huge bonuses, and fighting new regulations. Their approach was the same as that of all the key players who helped destroy much of America's economy, yet continued to act as if the notion of a greater common good was only a fairy tale.

The more that powerful economic interests use questionable means to shape critical common choices, the more we feel that there's nothing we can do. That's the case when major banking interests and contractors manipulate the system. It's the case when greed-driven health interests do their best to prevent serious reform—as when the former CEO of HCA/Columbia, Rick Scott, whose company paid a $1.7 billion fine for defrauding Medicare and Medicaid, later attacked a public health care option with the help of the same public relations firm that had coordinated the notorious "Swift Boat" ads to undermine John Kerry in the 2004 election. It's also the case when Exxon and major coal companies like Peabody and Massey fund those who deny the human role in climate change.

From my perspective, the Bush years took institutional cynicism to depths not seen since the late-nineteenth-century "Gilded Age," whose politics Karl Rove consciously sought to emulate. Oil, coal, and nuclear industry representatives created energy policy in secret meetings with top administration officials. Pharmaceutical companies quashed every attempt to legalize importing cheaper Canadian drugs. Timber companies promoted a "Healthy Forests Initiative" that let them cut at will, and power plant owners did the same by gutting existing regulations on mercury and other noxious emissions under the so-called "Clear Skies Act," which the administration implemented through the Environmental Protection Administration when they couldn't get it through Congress. Credit card companies rewrote bankruptcy laws to protect themselves, while making it far harder for individuals to start over if their luck ran out. That doesn't even count the moral and political damage caused by actions like reclassifying torture as "enhanced interrogation."

To be fair, key Democrats facilitated many of the administration's most problematic actions. Roughly half of the Democratic Senators in the 2002 Congress supported giving Bush the authority to go to war in Iraq. Afraid of being branded unpatriotic, they never took the time to read a National Intelligence Report that challenged key administration claims or to heed any of the other contrary evidence. Instead they ran for cover like whipped dogs. The draconian bankruptcy bill would never have passed without just enough Democratic votes to get it through, including prime sponsor Joe Biden. And earlier, the Clinton administration played its own significant role in promoting cynicism: Before anyone had heard of Monica Lewinsky, Clinton left the Democratic Party demoralized and divided over his support for Republican proposals like the North American Free Trade Agreement (NAFTA) and Newt Gingrich's welfare reform, as well as his dismantling of key financial regulations (with a key role played by Lawrence Summers, who was then the Treasury Secretary and later the director of Obama's National Economic Council). Both parties have fostered the corrosive viewpoint that political participation is possible only when you surrender your ethical compass at the door.

HUDDLED IN THE BURROW

Ways exist to curb such abuses of power. Adopting Maine's Clean Election model nationwide would help immensely. So would restoring and reinforcing many of the very laws that HCA/Columbia, Enron, and similar companies have fought to dismantle or prevent. But make no mistake, the clout of these interests is real, and it is persistent, regardless of the party in control. In the face of massive financial bailouts and the political power of huge economic interests, it's tempting to resign ourselves and decide that this is simply how things work, that it's just human nature. Or to hope that Obama or some other charismatic leader can change things, without our having to do much but cheer from the sidelines.

Once we accept that we're powerless, our passivity turns into a self-fulfilling prophecy, a habit of mind that becomes harder and harder to shake. We decide that there's nothing we can do about key common issues, large or small, so we withdraw from public life before we give it a serious shot. We stop paying attention. After a while, we stop caring. Why break our hearts over things that are beyond our control?

In the judgment of the Princeton philosopher Robert Wuthnow, such cynical resignation has deep cultural roots. "In an individualistic society," he writes, "caring is sometimes seen as an abnormality. . . . We do not even believe in sharing too deeply in the suffering of others. Our individual autonomy is too important. If caring for others becomes too demanding . . . we call it an obsession."

Even if we believe in core notions of right and wrong, we often portray the unjust structures of our time as immutable, which leads to the conclusion that they can never be changed. A "radical" political scientist once explained to me loftily, "We're fooling ourselves if we think government doesn't serve powerful economic interests." True enough, for the moment. But he framed this as inevitable, with history being something that always happens to us, not something we can have a hand in making. He gave his students no vision to fight for, no foundation for action, only the prospect of joining him in the ranks of the all-knowing witnesses to human folly.

The political scientist also gave his students an all-purpose excuse for inaction and resignation. If nothing worthwhile can be done about the economy, climate change, global violence, or those suffering in our communities, then we bear no responsibility. Like the Kafka creature tunneling ever-deeper in his story, "The Burrow," we retreat into smaller and smaller spheres of private life, hoping the rest of the world will somehow muddle through.

Whatever issues we care about, and whatever our views on them, we're told that our actions can't matter. In a classroom at Central Michigan University, a young woman active in the pro-choice movement spoke up. "I work hard on this issue," she said. "It's so important to me. Most of the students I know agree with me. They're pretty much all sexually active, so this could affect them personally if they get careless or something goes wrong. But they don't get involved politically because they say it's not going to make any difference. They say I'm just wasting my time."

Then another young woman raised her hand. She was active on the pro-life side, she said, and even though it was a harder sell on their campus, some students definitely agreed with her. But she heard the same response. People told her that her efforts wouldn't matter. They didn't understand why she made the effort. On both sides, citizen efforts had in fact shifted both public opinion and policy, but most of the two students' peers said they were foolish to try.

Ironically, such resignation can exist without our being personally cynical. We still try to be caring toward family and friends. We may even volunteer at a Big Brother/Big Sister program or help at a soup kitchen, which are good things to do. But when we look at the larger issues, like why so many people in America are hungry or fail to receive an adequate education, we throw up our hands in frustration. Taking them on just seems too daunting, and our chances of success too elusive. It seems wiser and more practical to narrow our horizons.

Cynical resignation salves the pain of unrealized hope. If we convince ourselves that nothing can change, we don't have to risk acting on our dreams. But the more we accept this, the more we deny essential parts of ourselves. We deny even the possibility that our choices can matter.

RADICAL FUTURELESSNESS

Any problem whose magnitude is overwhelming can foster fatalism, and fatalism is just as much an obstacle to effective action as cynicism. Consider the global climate crisis. I've spoken of the judgment of the world's most respected scientists and scientific bodies that we need to dramatically change our course. Otherwise, they say, we'll be forced to endure temperatures and weather patterns qualitatively different from those we've experienced since before the dawn of human civilization. That's a terrifying thought, but it's not only climate change that makes us want to throw up our hands and retreat to purely private life.

As the Catholic monk Thomas Berry writes in *The Dream of the Earth,* "We can break the mountains apart. We can drain the rivers and flood the valleys. We can turn the most luxuriant forests into throwaway paper products. We can tear apart the great grass cover of the western plains and pour toxic chemicals into the soil and pesticides onto the fields until this soil is dead and blows away in the wind. We can pollute the air with acids, the rivers with sewage, the seas with oil—all this in a kind of intoxication with our power for devastation at an order of magnitude beyond all reckoning."

Merely reading this description can make you feel defeated. Though ways exist to address these problems and countless people are working to further hopeful alternatives, it's easier to adopt a kind of technological fundamentalism, like that of the initial Hanford workers, and assume that we can follow our current course indefinitely. Even if we don't think that's the case, it's tempting to succumb to what Robert Jay Lifton has called a "radical sense of futurelessness," and cease trying to imagine a better world, much less working to bring it about.

The prevalence of radical futurelessness is easier to understand when we realize that the problems we face today, environmental or otherwise, didn't reach their present scale overnight. They developed incrementally, which, in the case of a distracted and self-focused citizenry, means almost invisibly. We've heard how when frogs are thrown into boiling water, they jump out, but when they're placed in a pot in which the water is slowly brought to a boil, they let themselves be cooked to death. Similarly, we tolerate slow-burn crises so long as they don't touch us directly and we have time to adjust to their effects. Low-key yet devastating wars of survival occur daily on the streets of U.S. cities. Jobs disappear. Neighborhoods crumble. Lives are blighted. Young men and women die. Yet, apart from brief flickering moments, the toll is invisible, unless, of course, you're unlucky enough to live close at hand. The impact of our steady assault on the environment also doesn't register, except for those paying close attention, or during sudden, large-scale disasters like Hurricane Katrina. Similarly, until the economy crashed, the toll of building it on speculative greed was equally hidden from sight. We rarely get a clear, unequivocal signal to tell us when things have gotten so bad that we must do something to remedy them. By the time we do notice, the crises often have grown so large that their sheer size can intimidate us, even if we're inclined to help.

The vast number of problems America faces reinforces this impression. Commentators use the phrase "compassion fatigue" to describe the resulting sense of saturation and hopelessness. Change often takes time. We already feel overburdened. Few of us are familiar with the stories of how others persisted and eventually prevailed in circumstances at least as daunting as our own. So why not restrict our efforts to domains in which we can reasonably hope to exercise some influence? Why not retreat into private life?

DISTANT LIVES

Here's why not: Our personal lives are to a great extent shaped by decidedly impersonal forces. And we have far more power to influence those forces than we know. By retreating, we don't escape from the world so much as submit to it. We conspire in our own defeat.

I'll return often to these themes, as well as to their corollary—that the surest way to improve our private lives is to act together with others in the public arena.

But for now, I'd like to explore another element that makes it more difficult to engage with the world: our propensity to render certain kinds of people or certain communities invisible, even expendable, so we don't have to deal with their lives. Those of us who are relatively comfortable often do this with the homeless, immigrant farm workers, low-wage workers in general, and people starving halfway across the globe. The distancing impulse can become stronger as our country's economy gets meaner, and we fear for our own economic survival. We decide that the world will inevitably divide into the drowned and the saved, and we look away as the less fortunate slip beneath the surface.

Even when the American economy was supposedly booming, far too many of us faced what sociologist Todd Gitlin called the "soft apocalypse." As incomes at the top soared to unimaginable levels, the average earnings of those in the bottom 90 percent were lower in real dollars in 2006 than in 1973, and the wealthiest 1 percent controlled more wealth than the bottom 95 percent. These extreme discrepancies and the policies that produced them have left us with higher rates of infant mortality, homelessness, and child poverty than any other industrialized nation, and with the highest imprisonment rate on the planet. Poet Michael Meade once gave a workshop in the Southeast Ohio Correctional Institution, a facility that started out as a school, was converted into a minimum security prison, and later was upgraded to medium security. Meade called it "a metaphor for our times."

Yet many of us live unaware of these troubling realities. We're unaware in part because our society is so profoundly divided, and the lives of the poor are largely obscured. Jim Wallis recalls how a friend, civil rights historian Vincent Harding, began to weep after yet another young African American man whom they knew was lost to senseless street violence. "A whole generation of us is being destroyed," said Harding.

"At that moment," recalls Wallis, "I understood more clearly than ever before why our society was allowing the deadly carnage to continue. I realized that for most Americans who are white and middle class, it isn't a whole generation of 'us' that is being lost. Rather, it is 'them.' And we tell them what we think of them in clear messages every day: They aren't important, they don't count, they don't exist."

True words. Also discomforting ones, all the more so as desperation and dislocation reach many who were once economically comfortable. So what allows us to dismiss the pain of our fellow human beings as somehow unreal?

I once shared a train seat with a young man, just out of the army, who was heading back to the small northern Washington town where he grew up. Friendly, wholesome, and innocent, he described the tedious routine of being a soldier, and how much he looked forward to living in his hometown and seeing his family again. Then he stopped speaking for a moment, as if trying to puzzle something out, and told me about the sex bars he used to visit in Korea. The dancers there, he said shyly, squatted on the tables and picked up coins with their genitals. Once, a young woman about his own age was working, and he grew curious about what would happen if he heated the coins with his cigarette lighter. "I didn't mean any harm," he said. "I never thought it would hurt her." But she howled in pain, then ran out of the bar hunched over and screaming.

I believed the soldier harbored no conscious ill will toward that woman—or anyone else. But this only made his story more disturbing. It reminded me of our more general capacity for what theologians and ethicists call evil—the "militant ignorance," in the phrase of M. Scott Peck, that helps us deny the most destructive results of what we say and do. Did the military environment teach the young soldier to view the barroom dancer as something less than a full human being? Did he learn this lesson instead from his school, family, or friends? From his religion, or the TV news? He had to acquire it somewhere. He wasn't anymore intrinsically malicious than the rest of us.

Human destructiveness rarely comes in the shape of bloodthirsty madmen or sadistic monsters. In fact, those who cause the greatest harm are often so far removed from the consequences of their actions that they don't even perceive the connection. During my early high school years I had a friend named Tim. About the only thing we shared was a desire to go to Harvard. But we shot baskets in his backyard and speculated about sex. He taught me to play bridge, which he said would help me "get ahead in the world." When he termed our group of awkward nerdy friends "the minds," as if others had none, I felt uncomfortable at the smirking condescension but said nothing. Eventually I'd realize that we had too little in common to sustain a friendship.

Tim's father, whom I'll call Robert, worked for the Rand Corporation think tank in Santa Monica. As Tim told me proudly, his father had previously been offered the job as Nixon's national security advisor (the same job Henry Kissinger ended up taking). Although Robert had turned down the offer, he made regular trips to Washington, D.C., to meet with important people. What he actually did back there remained unclear until years later, when I came across some of Robert's essays. In his influential counterinsurgency studies, he wrote that any effort to win popular support in South Vietnam had little chance of success. Instead, he argued—in justifications anticipating those of men like Dick Cheney and other defenders of torture's necessity—that government forces should act as harshly as possible to prevent peasants from supporting our enemy, the Vietcong. We shouldn't be hamstrung by sentimental moralizing.

The ordinary soldiers summarized this strategy crudely: "If you've got them by the balls, their hearts and minds will follow." The language Robert used was more erudite and technocratic, far removed from the stench of death in the Southeast Asian jungles. But U.S. forces seemed to follow his maxims—from the designation of so-called free-fire zones where saturation bombing raids were conducted, to an assassination campaign that may have killed as many as 40,000 civilians. Given Robert's role as a top-level advisor, it seemed likely that he had contributed to these strategies. If so, he was responsible for vastly more suffering than the young soldier with his cigarette lighter could ever have imagined.

I still have a photo of a party Robert and his wife gave for the young men in Tim's circle and for our parents. We sit in their high-ceilinged living room, with a tiled fireplace, trees filling a picture window, a piano in one corner, and elegant drawings and paintings on the walls. Robert wears a suit and holds a drink. His wife sits next to him, listening attentively. The scene looks civilized, peaceful. Nothing links it to the massive death Robert helped bring about through his work.

Cynicism thrives in large, complex societies in which cause is easily divorced from effect. Under these circumstances, people such as Robert, the Hanford workers, or the investment bankers who did their best to turn the entire global economy into a pyramid scheme can participate in immensely destructive enterprises, yet feel no guilt, no ambivalence, no direct responsibility. By contrast, the young soldier I met on the train was forced to witness the pain he caused. It disturbed him, profoundly enough for him to confess it with shame to a stranger. This action didn't erase the consequences of his action, the scars on the young woman's body and soul, but I believed he would never do something like that again. Robert experienced no such connection. On the contrary, like Henry Kissinger, he viewed his readiness to help destroy ordinary lives as a badge of intellectual rigor and toughness. Remote and untouchable, he was too distant from the suffering he helped create to even begin to grasp its human impact.

To be sure, even the most callous and cynical people can change. But their doing so may depend on whether the rest of us find the courage to raise difficult and disconcerting issues. I think of a student at Connecticut's Fairfield University, a wealthy doctor's son I'll call Mark. "God helps those who help themselves," Mark said, when I interviewed him during his freshman year. "I feel sorry for those who get tough breaks, but we'll always have the poor. We gave the blacks a lot. Is it my fault if me or my parents make the bucks and they don't?"

"I want the things I have now," Mark continued, "a nice house, a nice car, a nice boat, if I get lucky, a plane. I want to make enough to be able to say 'Buddy, buzz off, this is mine. This is what I've paid for.' " His approach was as all-encompassing a distancing smirk as I had ever encountered.

Then, Mark went on to explain, a young professor had the audacity to bring environmental issues into the organic chemistry class that he was taking on his pre-med track. At first Mark resisted. "We were really pissed," he said looking back. "This was not going to be on the med school tests. Why was he wasting our time? But after a while, I realized that he wasn't wasting our time. He was passionate and taking a risk. We could have slammed him on our student evaluations. But the stuff he was talking about was important."

Mark was also challenged by a major medical waste spill that happened that same semester. He joined a campus environmental group and eventually went into environmental remediation as a career. When I last spoke with him, he cringed at his earlier attitude. "I can't believe I said those horrible things. If that professor and others hadn't pushed me, I just don't know where I'd be today."

THEY ALL SOLD OUT

I believe most of us want to live in a compassionate way, to move beyond cynicism, and to help shape a better world. But before we return to looking at how we can act, there's one more barrier to explore: our culture's tendency to demean any attempts to bring about change and, in particular, its distortion of the social movements of the 1960s as either fruitless, self-serving aberrations or as raising standards of involvement we never can meet.

In Chapter Two I mentioned how our cultural gatekeepers have buried or distorted the stories of the abolitionist and women's suffrage campaigns, union movements, and early civil rights efforts. By downplaying instances when seemingly powerless people persisted and changed history, they've denied us many of our most instructive and inspirational models. In the case of the 1960s antiwar movements, they've mostly caricatured them, twisting what could be powerful examples of citizens shifting their nation's course into images that cast a shadow over current efforts for change.

Far too often, activists from that era are portrayed as acid crazies wild in the streets, militants chanting mindless slogans, or protestors committing the ultimate callousness of spitting on soldiers. Yet when researchers tried to track down actual cases of the last stereotype, for example, they found next to none. Sociologists Richard Flacks of University of California Santa Barbara, Jerry Starr of University of West Virginia, and Jerry Lembcke of Holy Cross all concluded that to the degree such incidents happened at all, they were totally marginal. Yet a cynically smirking media has made them one of the centerpieces of the time.

The flip side of caricature is sentimentality, an unwarranted nostalgia that equally undermines our ability to act in the present by creating yet another impossible standard. The more we romanticize the period as a Shangri-La when everyone seemed to care, the easier it is to treat current efforts toward change as naïve and trivial by comparison. Forty years later, reporters still describe all manner of dissident efforts as "Sixties-style protests." It's as if present actions can amount to no more than pale imitations.

If we spend our time mourning the eclipse of a supposedly more compassionate time, we forget how hard and lonely it often was for activists then, and how challenging it was to sustain momentum. As late as 1966, no national antiwar demonstration drew more than 25,000 people, and more than 70 percent of students at the University of Wisconsin, a future radical hotbed, still approved of America's involvement in Vietnam. In the spring of 1968, not one of thirty-nine major newspapers in a *Boston Globe* survey favored pulling out our troops. Even Martin Luther King, as I've mentioned, got savaged when he finally mustered the courage to speak out.

The most cynical media myth regarding the 1960s is that of the great betrayal—the notion that those who campaigned most fervently for change back then abandoned their various causes as soon as they had the chance, compromised all their principles, and headed straight to lives of predatory greed. Some commentators even assumed, with zero evidence, that the right-wing screamers at the 2009 health care town halls were the former student radicals of 1969. This omnipresent yet overwhelmingly false story suggests that it's impossible to remain socially committed over the long haul. It makes social involvement in general look shallow, hypocritical, and opportunistic—hardly something to which we'd want to devote our lives. It's also made younger people feel isolated, abandoned by earlier generations. It has facilitated their dismissing peers who speak out for change, on the assumption that they, too, will eventually betray their beliefs. "How can they tell us to take a stand," young men and women have asked me repeatedly, "when they gave up all their values and left us the mess we're now facing?"

The notion of the great sellout stems largely from a conflation of the period's citizen movements with a far broader but often apolitical counterculture. Both antiwar activists and leaders like Nixon found it convenient to magnify the movement's strength by claiming that every longhair was a potential comrade, either a card-carrying member of "Woodstock Nation" or, in Nixon's view, a dangerous subversive. Those dressing and acting the hippie part often wanted a more compassionate world, and opposed the carnage in Vietnam. But smoking dope at a rock concert or growing out your hair wasn't the same as working for civil rights in Mississippi, handing out antiwar leaflets, or organizing a march at your school. You didn't have to figure out how to communicate your message, bring people together, or shift entrenched constellations of power. You merely had to pursue your "alternative" lifestyle. Yet repeated studies of those who spoke out have verified the conclusion that the more they were genuinely involved as students, the more likely they persisted. Compared to peers who never marched, or stood on the periphery, this group remains far more engaged.

I don't want to make the picture sound too rosy. Many who acted on their convictions back then certainly went through periods of dashed hopes and withdrawal, when people, institutions, ideas, and movements they once believed in turned out to be all too human and fallible. We face this possibility in our time as well, as we seesaw between cynicism and hope. I'll talk later about ways to stay involved without burning out from the inevitable obstacles, pressures, and disappointments. But even among those who shifted from large-scale social-change efforts to more modest endeavors aimed at, for example, filling in the gaps left by shrinking social programs, or even simply to leading ethical private lives, few fit the prevailing stereotype of selling out and embodying all that they once opposed.

Democratic societies progress by democratic means—that is, when citizens participate fully and fairly in public life, working for the common good. The myth of generational betrayal disrupts this process by instilling the belief that speaking out for justice and standing up for freedom are transient youthful pursuits, and misguided ones at that. It implies that they'll be inevitably replaced by grown-up, realistic priorities, like making sure we come out on top in a world that's getting perpetually meaner. It forecloses the prospect of leading lives of conviction.

RECLAIMING OUR HISTORY

As an alternative to this impotent "realism," I'd like to propose a clear-eyed idealism, which recognizes that these are bad times for many people, and maybe getting worse, but refuses to accept that the bad times are inevitable. This bears repeating, so as to avoid misunderstanding. I'm not promoting a culture of happy talk. It's important to dissect institutional arrogance and greed, to assess how it damages lives, neighborhoods, communities, and the most basic life systems of the earth. It's critical to hold powerful institutions accountable, including political leaders we may have worked for and voted for, and may in general still support. But too many social activists almost delight in rolling around in the bad news, like dogs in rancid fish. If that's all we do, we'll reinforce the belief that efforts to change things are doomed. We'll foster resignation and despair. So along with the bad news, we need to convey that which is capable of inspiring hope.

I'll explore how we can find this hope in the unexpected heroism of ordinary people, and in the movements for change that they've created. We can find it in our religious traditions—in the sense, as Virginia Ramirez and Rich Cizik said, that God provides strength for even the most difficult challenges. We can find it in the awe we feel at the complex majesty of the natural world, when watching an

eagle or feeling the power of a river. And we can find it by reclaiming the historical legacies that can most inspire us.

It may always feel more than a little absurd to think that we
might be able to change history. Recognizing that fact, and appreci-
ating the irony in our situation, can be useful, especially when our
efforts don't go as planned. But that same sense of irony becomes
dangerous when it's used to justify passivity. As the poet and essayist Lewis Hyde points out, it becomes "the voice of the trapped who
have come to enjoy their cage." Accordingly, we might think of a
modern cynic as someone who's given up all hope of finding a door,
much less a key. And we might remember that there are better ways
to live.

CHAPTER FIVE

Unforeseen Fruits

Most of the things worth doing in the world had been declared impossible before they were done.

—*JUSTICE LOUIS BRANDEIS*

I once went for a run in Fort Worth, Texas, in a grassy park along a riverbank. I came upon a man shaking a tree. I hesitated, then stopped and asked, "What are you doing?"

"It's a pecan tree," he said. "If I shake it enough, the nuts will come down. I can't know exactly when they'll fall or how many. But the more I shake it, the more I'll get."

This seems an apt metaphor for social involvement. Often our efforts may yield few clear or immediate results. Our victories will almost always be partial. But we need to draw enough strength from our initial steps to help us persevere. "You have to begin with small groups," Modjesca Simkins, a veteran South Carolina civil rights activist told me when she was eighty-four. "But you reach the people who matter. They reach others. Like the Bible says, leaven in the lump, like yeast in the dough. It rises somewhere else."

We liberate ourselves from cynicism by replacing the all-knowing but soul-destroying smirk and the hopeless shrug with compassionate curiosity about our fellow human beings. When we do so, we find that there is ample reason for hope. It's easy to highlight the discouraging aspects of any historical time. And we're inevitably

going to hit disappointments. Yet every effort for change has its
uncertainties, and every era its barriers and possibilities.

RIPPLES OF HOPE

We never know how acts of generosity and faith will resound in the
world. In 1978, Seattle therapist Ginny NiCarthy decided to write a
book for the participants in her groups for battered women. Ginny
ran the groups without pay, through the YWCA and a women's shelter called New Beginnings, while she scraped together a meager
living doing outside counseling on a sliding scale. Wanting to give
the women a glimpse of the road they'd have to travel to get out of
their abusive relationships, Ginny assembled some makeshift hand-
outs. The public was still largely unaware of the scope and seriousness of domestic violence, and the few existing books on the subject
were, as Ginny said, academic tomes "hardly appropriate for women
in the middle of the soup." So she began writing her own, drawing
on the stories she'd heard.

Twenty-four publishers rejected the book. Although they liked
the writing, the editors thought there weren't enough battered
women in America to make up an audience—and that even women
who were abused wouldn't walk up to a bookstore clerk to buy a
copy.

The rejections left Ginny frustrated. "I knew the women needed
the book. Every week more came into the group with black eyes
and broken spirits. But I didn't know just how it would get out. I
was already so stretched working umpteen hours a day on different
projects, with things so scraggly in terms of money. The whole situation felt overwhelming."

Ginny mentioned her circumstances to a group of friends who
met weekly to decompress and reflect on their work. Jane Klassen,
a therapist who co-led the New Beginnings group, knew how much
the book would mean to battered women. Though she had few extra resources of her own, Jane decided to give Ginny $500 to help
her finish the book. "I was trying to live simply," Jane told me later.

"I got a particular satisfaction in helping a friend do something that mattered."

Ginny was astonished. As she put it, "It was such a testament of faith. It doesn't sound like much money now, but back then it was a month's living expenses. With Jane's trust in the project, I had to complete it."

Buoyed by Jane's faith and generosity, Ginny finished the book and showed it to a friend at a small publisher called Seal Press. Despite not having published anything similar, Seal decided to go ahead with the book. *Getting Free* sold modestly at first, primarily through battered women's shelters and support groups, but it has now sold 175,000 copies, and has become the bible for women concerned about domestic violence. It paved the way for a slew of related books and helped move the battered women's movement from the margins to the mainstream. "Back then," Ginny said, "no one wanted to touch the subject. The problem hasn't gone away, but at least people recognize the right of women not to be beaten. Now concern about domestic violence is respectable. It's social work."

Social change always looks a lot more inevitable in hindsight than when you're trying to make it happen. Ginny could never have predicted the results of her efforts, nor Jane the results of a gift that helped Ginny complete the book despite all the obstacles and frustrations. Together, they helped it get out and make its impact.

The risks we take make a difference. As Robert Kennedy said, "Each time a person stands for an ideal, or acts to improve the lot of others, or strikes out against injustice, he or she sends forth a tiny ripple of hope. And crossing each other from a million different centers of energy and daring, those ripples build a current that can sweep down the mightiest walls of oppression and resistance."

CHAINS OF INSPIRATON

Our actions don't always transform institutions directly. Change comes, to be sure, when we shift corporate or governmental policies, elect more accountable leaders, or create effective institutional alternatives. But it also comes when we stir the hearts of previously disengaged citizens and help them take their own moral stands. We never know whom we'll draw in, or how their newfound involvement will influence the rest of their lives, but if we inspire enough people to become socially and politically engaged we can sometimes transform history.

Under Czechoslovakia's Communist dictatorship, playwright (and, eventually, president) Vaclav Havel helped build the country's nascent democracy movement through such apparently futile actions as defending a Czech rock band, Plastic People of the Universe, when the authorities broke up their concerts with police raids and sentenced key members to prison. As explored in my book, *The Impossible Will Take a Little While,* the defense committee Havel created to defend the band evolved into the country's key human rights and democracy group, Charter 77. Later Havel launched a petition, together with other writers and civic activists, to free a group of different political prisoners. Even though they were only asking the president to include the group in a Christmas amnesty, critics said that those who circulated the petition were being "exhibitionistic," dismissing their motives as nothing more than an attempt "to draw attention to themselves."

When Havel reflected on the incident seven years later, he acknowledged that they hadn't succeeded in freeing the prisoners at the time. But he still didn't think the critics were right. When the prisoners finally got out of jail, they said it had helped them to know that they weren't alone. This mattered because the movement needed their courageous voices. More important, for many of the people who signed the petition, it was their first step in standing up for their beliefs. And it wasn't their last. They went on to play dissident music, put on dissident plays, speak out in classrooms, preach from pulpits, and challenge the regime in a hundred different ways—until there were so many speaking out that the government couldn't put them all in jail. Eventually, they brought down the dictatorship without a shot being fired. Had Havel and the others not persevered with efforts that seemed fruitless at the time, they'd never have built the movement that ultimately prevailed.

Havel's story reminds us that even in an apparently losing cause, one person may unknowingly inspire another, and that person yet a third, who may then go on to change the world, or at least a small corner of it. Rosa Parks was part of a similar chain of inspiration. Her husband, a barber named Raymond Parks, co-founded the Montgomery NAACP. After Raymond and Rosa met and married, he convinced her to attend her first NAACP meeting, a key step on the path to her stand on the bus. But who first convinced Raymond Parks to speak out, at a time when progress was elusive? Although we'll probably never know, it almost certainly took a succession of people and conversations. The links in any chain of influence and inspiration are too numerous, too complex to trace them all. But they remind us that, by encouraging others to get involved, we can have a continuing impact through all of their future actions.

Vincent Harding, the civil rights historian who reminded Jim Wallis that the young men dying in America's streets were "us" and not "them," describes what he calls a river of social justice. It includes all those who ever worked for change and all who ever will. If we draw in enough new people and broaden that river sufficiently, it can become, in the words that Martin Luther King borrowed from the prophet Amos, "a mighty stream," large enough to be potentially world-changing. That's true even if we fail to reach our initial goals.

These chains of influence almost always have humble beginnings. A few years ago I heard a talk by Wangari Maathai, the Kenyan Nobel Peace Prize winner. She described attending a small Catholic college in Atchison, Kansas, where she engaged in conversations about social justice that were critical to her transformation into a social activist. Both fellow students and faculty opened up new worlds to her. They got Maathai thinking about what needed to be done and what she could do. After returning to Kenya to become the first East African woman to get her PhD at the University of Nairobi, she founded the Green Belt Movement, which has planted 40 million trees in an effort to reduce soil erosion. She also challenged the dictatorship of Daniel Arap Moi, demanding multiparty elections and an end to political corruption. The government imprisoned and violently attacked her, but a year after Maathai won the Peace Prize she was elected the first president of the African Union's Economic, Social, and Cultural Council. None of this would have happened, she said, were it not for the conversations with those who'd inspired her when she was in college. As I listened, I wondered what it would be like to have a young Wangari Maathai sitting next to you in a classroom or dorm, and discovering years later that you'd helped set her on her path.

I KNEW I'D CATCH SOME HEAT

A similar example of what Nelson Mandela calls "the multiplication of courage" furthered my own political development. When I was fifteen, the rabbi of my West Los Angeles temple, Leonard Beerman, gave a talk in the wake of Israel's recent victory in the 1967 Six–Day War, when the country first occupied the West Bank territories. We should be glad for Israel's survival, Beerman said, but wary of blindly celebrating military force. He believed the newfound occupation would cause problems enormously difficult to solve.

The message disconcerted even this liberal congregation. Many bristled, sitting with folded arms and clenched jaws. But it struck a chord inside me. It taught me the importance of raising hard questions, even if people won't always like what you say. That lesson has stayed with me to this day.

As a rabbi, Beerman was entrusted with offering a larger moral vision. He had a ready-made podium. But too many rabbis, ministers, and priests are silent on difficult issues, or gloss over them, offering platitudes instead of guidance. Beerman grappled with his own fears while writing this talk and others. Years later, he told me that he still remembered the occasion, "because I knew I'd catch some heat for it." He kept his job, despite the hostile responses, but others in similar situations did not—as when Pete Knutson's father, a Lutheran minister, was forced out of his congregation in a mill town north of Seattle for challenging the Vietnam War and demanding that the local Elks Club admit African Americans. Both spoke out despite the potential costs, and Beerman helped inspire me to do the same.

Some issues touch us directly, impelling us to immediate action. More often, though, our responses are delayed. We hear about common concerns on the TV news or read about them in the newspaper, our favorite blog, or maybe a friend's Facebook page. We may even learn that local citizens have made this or that issue their cause. But we still may pay little heed until a friend or two get involved. When we do finally join them, we realize that all the other voices we've heard have led the way.

Historian Howard Zinn witnessed this phenomenon in the late 1950s and early 1960s as a young teacher at Spelman, Atlanta's esteemed black women's college. In the classroom, he spoke out for justice and encouraged his students to get involved in the nascent civil rights movement. At first, they held back. But as the movement grew, a few decided to take part, initially in modest ways. As that early group became more confident, taking increasingly greater risks, others joined. In time, Zinn's students helped play key roles. And some, like Alice Walker and Marian Wright Edelman, went on to inspire thousands of others.

"Even the smallest, most unheroic of acts," Zinn wrote, "adds to the store of kindling that may be ignited by some surprising circumstance into tumultuous change. . . . What the [civil rights] movement proved is that even if people lack the customary attributes of power—money, political authority, physical force—as did the black people of the Deep South, there is a power that can be created out of pent-up indignation, courage, and the inspiration of a common cause, and that if enough people put their minds and bodies into that cause, they can win. It is a phenomenon recorded again and again in the history of popular movements against injustice all over the world."

Courage can be contagious, spreading from those who first raise their voices to others on the sidelines, helping them overcome their isolation and fear. It also nurtures the souls of those who are already involved, reminding them that they aren't alone.

A YOUNG BARACK OBAMA

Virtually all of America's most effective historical movements met with repeated frustration and failure before making significant progress toward their goals. At few points prior to victory could participants prove that their individual efforts mattered. As Justice Louis Brandeis once wrote: "Most of the things worth doing in the world had been declared impossible before they were done." Only in retrospect does the link between small beginnings and profound social change become fully evident. Only then is the true value of persistence in the face of difficulty revealed.

Think of the apartheid-era campaign for South African divestment, now largely forgotten. American economic interests had supported the South African apartheid government almost from its inception. An early example occurred after the 1960 Sharpeville massacre, when a consortium of U.S. banks led by Chase Manhattan invested heavily to shore up a Pretoria regime that seemed on the verge of collapse. In response, one of the first Students for a Democratic Society (SDS) protests was held on Wall Street. Challenges to American involvement surged and receded for the next fifteen years, then escalated after the 1976 Soweto massacre and the death a year later of South African student activist Stephen Biko.

These events helped trigger a global protest movement that included large-scale campus activism. Even as their generation was being maligned as apathetic and uncaring, American students organized rallies, petition drives, and marches, built protest shanty towns, and staged sit-ins and blockades—all aimed at persuading colleges and universities to heed the request of South African activists to divest themselves of companies that did business in the country. Community activists embarked on parallel efforts to get state pension funds to divest. The movement caught fire as global television showed the South African government beating, gassing, and shooting peaceful demonstrators who challenged worsening economic conditions, substandard education, and a new constitution that would permanently disenfranchise African citizens.

When Nelson Mandela was finally freed, Winston Willis, who

had been active in the anti-apartheid movement at Columbia University, heard him speak in Harlem. As Winston recalls, he went "with a sense that I'd played a part, no matter how infinitesimal, in helping to get him out." Winston told me that when another friend from those days went to South Africa, "Archbishop Desmond Tutu shook his hand and said, 'You don't know how important it was what you American students did.' We had no idea our actions would have such an impact."

One of the many students who got involved as a result of these efforts was a young man named Barack Obama. He'd certainly thought about larger political issues in high school, but it wasn't until he went off to Los Angeles's Occidental College that he first took a public stand. Occidental's anti-apartheid movement began in 1978, when a former Green Beret named Gary Chapman returned from Vietnam opposing the war and transferred from a local community college. After researching the impact of companies operating in South Africa, Chapman created Occidental's Student Coalition Against Apartheid. The group held rallies and debates, showed documentaries, brought in speakers, circulated petitions, and marched on their local Bank of America branch. With the help of some professors, they secured a unanimous faculty resolution to divest. But the college trustees—highly conservative Southern California business leaders—refused to go along, and the college president deferred to their judgment.

Chapman had just graduated when Obama arrived in the fall of 1979, and began working with the student coalition. Although Obama's role in the campaign was modest—he helped bring in touring speakers from the African National Congress, attended some organizing meetings, and spoke at a key rally—his involvement opened up a world in which he could connect his actions to his beliefs. With a diverse group of equally passionate friends, he spent long hours hanging out and talking about issues from human rights and poverty to apartheid, U.S. intervention in Central America, the lyrics of the latest Bob Marley album, and Jefferson's notions of participatory democracy. They talked in the dorms, at the Black Student Alliance, and at the Cooler, a campus coffee house where a friend recalled Obama as working part time. Obama was drawn to the movement, said one of his mentors, Professor Roger Boesche, "because of his concern for justice and fairness, at a time when his identity and values were just taking shape. And because he felt this issue was important enough to be worth taking on." In the process, he shifted from a political observer to a participant.

Obama regarded one particular moment as a turning point in his life. As he explains in *Dreams from My Father,* he was still wavering between cynicism and engagement when he agreed to speak at a rally held adjacent to an Occidental trustees meeting (and was mock-arrested by fellow students to drive home the South African reality). After the rally, he told a friend, "I don't believe we made any difference by what we did today." He said that he only spoke out "because it makes *me* feel important."

"Seemed to me like I heard a man speak who believed in something," his friend responded. In words that Obama would later incorporate into one of his core political messages, she continued, "It's not just about you. It's never just about you. It's about people who need your help." Obama said he took her rebuke to heart.

Others at the rally also felt Obama found his voice that day. "He was thoughtful and passionate," said another participant, "not strident, but reasonable. He made you want to listen to him." Another friend remembers Obama as being "eloquent and poised, disproportionate to his years," but she stressed that his participation was "almost accidental," a step that came out of "the influences around him, the opportunities that arose, and his core passion for justice."

While Obama's subsequent journey was neither automatic nor foreordained, his involvement in the anti-apartheid movement at Occidental, and later at Columbia, was the first time when he took a political stand. As such, he credited his student experience for laying the foundation for everything that followed, including his considering the vocation of community organizer. Had other students and faculty not taken the risk of standing up for what they believed— thus encouraging Obama's participation—he might never have started down the path that ultimately led to the White House.

BEFORE WATER TURNS TO ICE

None of us can predict when the causes we support will capture the public imagination, or our once-lonely quests become popular crusades. "Before water turns to ice," writes psychologist Joanna Macy, "it looks just the same as before. Then a few crystals form, and suddenly the whole system undergoes cataclysmic change." Paleontologist Stephen Jay Gould developed a theory he calls "punctuated equilibrium." Rather than occurring at a steady pace, evolution proceeds in fits and starts, Gould argued. Long stretches of relative stasis are followed by brief periods of intense transformation, when many new species appear and others die out. Although attempts to improve social and economic conditions usually proceed incrementally, it is impossible to foretell precisely when any of our endeavors will reach critical mass, suddenly creating change.

I once met a Wesleyan University student named Tess, who was inspired by an environmental conference. With a few friends, she registered nearly 300 fellow students concerned about environmental threats and cuts in government financial aid programs. Nearly all ended up supporting their strongly sympathetic Congressman, who won re-election by just twenty-one votes. Tess had hesitated before she began. She didn't think of herself as a "political person," and didn't want to come off like "a politician spouting a line." She wondered whether her efforts would even matter. Nonetheless, she decided to go ahead and do the best she could. Had she done nothing, her Congressman would have lost.

I had a similar experience in the 2004 election. As always, I spent as much time as possible making phone calls and knocking on doors in the weeks before the vote. It's the kind of action that, from a distance, can seem totally intimidating, but gets far easier once you begin to do it. On Election Day, I alternated between calls to Ohio and Florida, for the presidential contest, and getting out the vote for my local Washington State governor's race. Knocking on as many doors as I could, I turned out three supporters for my candidate who wouldn't have otherwise voted: One forgot it was Election

Day. Another didn't know if it was still okay to use an absentee ballot. The third needed a ride to the polls. My impact had nothing to do with any eloquence or skill, and everything to do with simply showing up. After three recounts, the candidate I supported won by 133 votes, and Washington's Republican Secretary of State resisted pressure from his own party and certified her election. If just a handful of our volunteers had stayed home, or if there had been a few more volunteers on the other side, the outcome would have been reversed. The same would have been true (leaving aside everything else that happened) in the 2000 Florida campaign that gave George Bush the presidency by an official margin of 537 votes.

My point isn't to argue for any particular candidate or party, though I'm glad my candidate won, but to remind us of the potential power of individuals taking action together. When enough people participate, even seemingly modest efforts, like making phone calls or knocking on doors, can combine with the efforts of others to change history.

GLOBAL RIPPLES

Sometimes we don't notice profound changes when they occur. Cultures shift, bit by bit. Ideas once branded as heresy become common currency. Under enough pressure, political and economic institutions follow suit. Think of the global shift toward sexual equality. It goes beyond the tremendous progress women like Ginny NiCarthy have made here in the United States on issues from domestic abuse to workplace opportunities to the admittedly contested right to abortion choice. Despite serious backlash, women throughout the world now expect vastly more from their men, work, and communities than they did as recently as the early 1970s.

Psychologist Jean Houston describes watching residents of a small village in India gather before their single TV set to watch a gorgeous dramatization of the Ramayana, an ancient epic central to Hindu culture. In the story, Princess Sita is abducted by a demon and carried away, then rescued by Prince Rama and an army of monkeys. Like the villagers, Jean was enjoying the production when an old woman turned to her and said, "Oh, I don't like Sita." The princess was too weak, the woman explained, too passive.

"We women in India are much stronger than that. She should have something to do with her own rescue, not just sit there moaning and hoping that Rama will come. We need to change the story." She said her husband was also named Rama and her name was Sita, and that he was "a lazy bum. If any demon got him, I would have to go and make the rescue." The woman's fellow villagers laughed in agreement.

Houston realized she was witnessing an ancient myth undergoing change, and with it fundamental relationships of power. No one can chart the precise route the global women's movement followed to reach this particular remote village, whether through Indian political leaders, outspoken local women, the international medium of television, or some combination of the three. But in Houston's estimation, the mere fact that the villagers were questioning traditional roles was an astounding benchmark of its progress and reach.

I JUST WANTED TO MAKE HIM LISTEN

As I've suggested, we never know how the impact of our actions may ripple outward, affecting others. We never know whom we may touch. In the spring of 2006, I read how a neatly dressed North Carolina commercial real estate broker had firmly but politely challenged President Bush at a town meeting in Charlotte, North Carolina. Sixty-one-year-old Harry Taylor raised his hand, waited for the mike, and then asked how Bush, with all of his talk of freedom, could "assert the right to tap my telephone, to arrest me, and hold me without charges, to try to preclude me from breathing clean air and drinking clean water and eating safe food."

People started booing, but to Harry's surprise, Bush said, "Let him continue." "In my lifetime," Harry went on, "I have never felt more ashamed of or frightened by my leadership in Washington. . . . I would hope, from time to time, that you have the humility and the grace to be ashamed of yourself." Harry then thanked Bush for letting him speak.

Harry was hardly the first to challenge Bush's policies, but the President's previous public interactions had been meticulously stage-managed. Dissenting voices were banned, people with critical T-shirts or buttons ejected, protestors kept far out of sight. No ordinary citizen had gotten the chance to challenge him in such an intimate yet public venue. Harry was covered in 500 newspapers, and on nearly every major network. A stranger's Web site, www.ThankYouHarryTaylor.net, received 18,000 supportive comments, including many from people in the military. *Congressional Quarterly,* the ultimate insiders' bible of Capitol Hill, said that his challenge "symbolized just how fully the president has lost his connection with many Americans," and concluded that it might be remembered as the "beginning of the end" for the Bush administration.

When I read the story, I assumed that Harry Taylor, like Rosa Parks in the mythologized version, had come out of nowhere. It turned out that he, too, had arrived at this moment on the national stage through an incremental process. Harry grew up in a strongly Republican family and served in the Air Force during Vietnam. Although he had reservations about the war, he kept silent. Later he volunteered for groups like Big Brothers and Outward Bound, because he liked mentoring young kids, "providing them," as he explained, "with consistent and trustworthy male role models, teaching them skills I had from the construction business." But beyond paying annual Sierra Club dues, he wasn't politically involved.

When Bush first ran, Harry was on the fence. He didn't like Al Gore, but he voted for him after reading about Bush's "appalling Texas environmental record." A year later, Bush flew to Charlotte for a $1,000-a-plate fundraiser, and the head of the local Sierra Club asked Harry to join a vigil highlighting the administration's actions that allowed more mercury in drinking water. Never having attended a protest, Harry hesitated. "Finally I said 'Okay, but I won't wear some stupid hat or a costume. I won't yell at people. I won't make protest chants.'"

Around the same time, Harry joined the progressive Internet-based organization MoveOn. "They're always labeled as these dangerous radicals, but the members I've met are just thoughtful citizens who care deeply about their country and want to get involved." Harry signed petitions opposing the Iraq war and the privatization of Social Security, and he joined a MoveOn vigil against health care cuts. Even when Bush was riding high in the polls, Harry felt sustained "just knowing there were others out there, that I wasn't alone."

The Town Hall opportunity came when the White House decided at the last minute to have Bush address the Charlotte World Affairs Council. The Sunday before, Harry had visited Charlotte's Museum of the New South, and stopped at a display commemorating the lunch counter sit-ins of the early 1960s, when students challenged segregation while patrons spat and poured mustard and ketchup on them. An accompanying video commemorated the Friendship Nine, a group of black students from nearby Friendship Junior College who, after a sit-in at one segregated lunch counter, followed a new strategy of staying in jail instead of bailing their way out. "I'd seen the exhibit many times, but for the first time I watched the video interviews—the men were now in their seventies. They talked about everything that led up to their action; their expectations and fears; and what it was like to look back fifty years later. I was really taken by how frightened they were that day, because they knew they could have been lynched, beaten, had their homes burned. I drove home thinking about their courage."

Harry woke up still thinking about them. Then he received an e-mail from the World Affairs Council. Bush was coming to town in three days, it said, and since Harry was a member, he could attend. "When I took my seat, I didn't know quite what I was going to say, but I wanted to be polite as I could be, and I wanted to be honest."

Bush finally called on Harry, who was "so nervous I was shaking. Our whole exchange took less than two minutes, but it seemed

like hours. I just wanted to make him listen." He didn't expect anything more to come of it, but he arrived home to find that his challenge was the major evening news story, and the phone didn't stop
ringing. "The next morning I did two national television interviews,
and then more TV, radio, and newspaper interviews. People seemed
to make me into a symbol. Just as the Friendship Nine helped give
me the courage to act, I became kind of a trigger for other people to
do the same kind of thing."

Harry also paid some costs. He'd been working for months on a
six-figure commercial real estate deal that was ready to be signed.
But a few days after the Town Hall event, his contact told him, "My
boss wants to fire you for talking that way to the Commander in
Chief." Harry kept working for several months more, trying to put
the deal together, but it never happened. The company had
quashed it because of Harry's polite but public disagreement with
his government's policies.

In 2008, Harry decided to run for Congress in an overwhelmingly Republican district that reached from wealthy Charlotte suburbs to rural counties that, in Harry's words, feel "like sixty years
ago." Incumbent Sue Myrick was among Bush's staunchest supporters, and when no other strong challengers emerged, Harry volunteered, thinking that "at least my notoriety might get some people
involved." He ended up losing, as he knew was likely. But the volunteers and voters he turned out helped Barack Obama to take North
Carolina by 15,000 votes, and Kay Hagen to unseat U.S. Senator
Elizabeth Dole. He also helped shift several close County Commis-
sioner races. Again, his efforts had an unexpected impact.

Whatever you think of Harry's criticisms of Bush, his story
serves as a familiar template for how many of us get involved. We
start in small and undramatic ways, often by connecting to larger
organizations. We then take further small steps, as with the rally
Harry hesitantly attended. We often draw courage from heroes of
the past, as he did with the Friendship Nine. And we sometimes exercise the greatest influence when we act despite self-doubt and apprehension. Harry simply hoped to raise a few questions. He could
never have predicted the response.

THE ONLY FAILURE IS QUITTING

Wholesale social change rarely happens all at once. Most successes are partial. "A final victory," Martin Luther King said, "is an accumulation of many short-term encounters. To lightly dismiss a success because it does not usher in a complete order of justice is to fail to comprehend the process of achieving full victory."

Sometimes we don't even recognize powerful victories when they occur, because their impact is hidden. In 1969, Nixon national security advisor Henry Kissinger told the North Vietnamese that Nixon was threatening a massive escalation of the war, including potential nuclear strikes, unless they capitulated and forced their allies in the South to do the same. Nixon was serious. He'd had military advisers prepare detailed plans, including mission folders with photographs of possible nuclear targets. But two weeks before the president's deadline for surrender, millions of people took part in a nationwide daylong "moratorium," with local demonstrations, vigils, church services, petition drives, and other forms of protest. A month later came a major march in Washington, D.C. Nixon's public response was to watch the Washington Redskins football game during the march, and to declare that the protestors weren't affecting his policies in the slightest. His contempt fed the frustration and demoralization of far too many in the peace movement. But privately, Nixon decided the movement had, as he put it, so "polarized" American opinion that he couldn't carry out his threat. Participants in the moratorium had no idea that their efforts may have helped stop a nuclear attack.

Nowhere is the need for a long view of social change more evident than in the case of campaigns that span generations. Think of the women's suffrage movement. When Susan B. Anthony began fighting for women's right to vote, her cause seemed like a long shot. She worked for it her entire adult life, then died fourteen years before suffrage was ratified. In retrospect, Anthony played as pivotal a role as any single individual. Yet during her lifetime, success seemed far from assured. Only by trusting that sooner or later their actions would matter could she and others keep on until they prevailed.

LETTING GO OF THE OUTCOME

Few of us, I hasten to add, can pursue a goal day in and day out, year in and year out, without experiencing success or satisfaction of some kind. So it's important to act as wisely as we can, in the hope of winning tangible victories. But no amount of thoughtful strategizing and prudent allocation of effort can guarantee a specific outcome. As a local leader in a successful United Parcel Service strike put it, "We couldn't promise anything at the beginning. We didn't know how it would turn out. We could only say that our cause was important and that the more we stuck together, the more solid we would be."

"If you get involved in trying to heal the world," says Marianne Williamson, "you're not guaranteed specific results as you define them. You're not promised that because you're doing this, a particular organization will work or a particular cause prevails. But you gain the satisfaction of living your life for a higher purpose." It's best to attend to the journey, in other words, and fret less about the destination.

While pregnant with her first child, my friend Stephanie Ericsson lost her husband to a sudden heart attack. In *Companion Through the Darkness,* her meditation on grieving, she explained, "Many books would prefer that we are neater about our pain. So they attempt to organize a process that is intentionally chaotic. . . . To acknowledge that there are mysteries we will never unravel is humbling and freeing at the same time. It is not a passive stance—resigning to darkness. It is an open stance, palms to the sky, as a receiving vessel. For vessels are meant to be emptied and filled, emptied and filled, emptied and filled."

Working for social change involves a similar process. The forces that impel us to act and take risks will always remain, at their core, a mystery, one that "the talkers talking their talk," to use a phrase of Walt Whitman's, will never be able to explain. We can only glimpse the reasons by means of what Whitman called "faint clues and indirections." Fighting for our deepest convictions requires relinquishing control and accepting messy uncertainties. It demands working as well as we can at efforts that feel morally right, and then having faith that our labors will bear fruit, perhaps in our time, or perhaps down the line, for somebody else. "If you expect to see the final results of your work," wrote journalist I. F. Stone, "you simply have not asked a big enough question."

The principle of keeping on regardless of apparent results recalls the religious view that true strength comes, paradoxically, from vulnerability, from knowing our limitations, and from a suffering that opens the door to compassion. As Jim Wallis of *Sojourners* writes, "Never achievement or success . . . but rather the giving of ourselves in faith leads to life." Our challenge, from this perspective, is not to predict what God has in store, or master some nebulous dialectic of history, but to live rightly, love our fellow human beings, and cherish God's creation. We can do this on a personal level, one to one. We can also do it politically, by working to create a society that nurtures human dignity.

America's dominant culture insists that our lives have no such broader significance, so we dare not vest them with purpose. Yet we can see how political silence feeds on itself, breeding isolation and despair. And how acts of faith and courage, conversely, can build on one another, opening up new possibilities. We owe much to those who acted with vision and conviction in previous times. The risks and commitments we undertake today may leave a better world for those yet to come. We can view our lives as a bridge between past and future.

"It helps to remember," says Atlanta's Sonya Vetra Tinsley, "how many changes there've been that were someone else's radical struggle for social justice. Whether the minimum wage, child labor laws, public schools, even jails instead of chopping people's heads off. When you first learn about injustice, you get all fired up. You want to fix it that day. You figure that if you only join this or that organization you'll solve it all in a couple years. After a while, you get humbled by the process. You realize that you're working for things you might not even see, and that you need to have faith that the effort is worthwhile.

"So much needs to be done to educate people," adds Sonya, "on how the freedoms and rights we take for granted didn't come about through chance, coincidence, or benevolence, but through struggle and intention. There's very little of worth in our society that someone didn't fight for."

We need to remember this even when our efforts appear utterly futile, when we seem to be rolling Sisyphus's rock up a hill only to watch it roll back again and again. In the early 1960s, my friend Lisa Peattie, now a retired MIT professor, was a young widow with four small kids. She took two of them to a vigil in front of the White House, to protest nuclear testing. The vigil was small, a hundred women at most. Rain poured down. Lisa's children were restless. Frustrated and soaked, the women joked about how President Kennedy was no doubt sitting inside drinking hot chocolate, warm, comfortable, and not even looking at their signs.

A few years later, the movement against nuclear testing had grown, and Lisa attended another march in Washington, considerably larger. One speaker was pediatrician Benjamin Spock, whose book, *Baby and Child Care,* had sold 50 million copies, making him probably the most influential medical authority in post–World War II America. Spock described how he'd come to take a stand on the nuclear issue. Because of his stature, his decision was immensely consequential, and would pave the way for his equally important opposition to the Vietnam War. Spock mentioned being in D.C. a few years earlier, and seeing a small group of women marching with their kids in the pouring rain. "I thought that if those women were out there," he said, "their cause must be really important." As he described the scene and setting, and how much he was moved, Lisa realized that Spock was referring to her group.

CHAPTER SIX

The Call of Stories

What is most important to me must be spoken, made verbal and shared, even at the risk of having it bruised or misunderstood.

—*AUDRE LORDE*

We work for justice, I've come to believe, when our hearts are stirred by specific lives and situations. Virginia Ramirez challenged the ills of her community only after watching her elderly neighbor die needlessly. She wasn't motivated by an abstract statistical analysis, however scandalous, of local poverty, deteriorating housing stock, or unequal investment in different neighborhoods. She learned those numbers later. Instead, she responded to a specific human story, which spurred her to rethink her own life. Virginia displayed a quality critical to social engagement: the capacity to feel empathy, to imagine ourselves as someone else. "Nearly all acts of altruism and self-sacrifice at any level are tied to this particular ability of the human imagination," says essayist Carol Bly.

Businessman Chris Kim was inspired to act by listening to the story of a fourteen-year-old African American boy. The boy stole a pair of pants from the clothing store Chris ran in his minimall in a poor south Seattle neighborhood. Chris and another Korean store owner grabbed him, called the police, and were ready to press charges. Then Chris thought about Christ's message of responding with forgiveness, not retribution. He decided to talk with the boy and his parents. "We always say we love our neighbors, but we never do it and risk something that belongs to us. He was a teenager, a young kid. It could have been anyone in a desperate situation, even one of my kids. I thought I should try and understand, not just turn him over to the police."

After Chris and the boy talked, the boy apologized, and said what he really wanted was a job. Chris hesitated briefly, then hired him as a clerk. The boy's mother sent Chris a note saying his compassion had changed her view of both Koreans and her son's life. Moved by the experience, Chris started working with local organizations that educate black youth. "Through my lifetime," Chris admitted, "I didn't have a good feeling about black people. It wasn't from direct experiences, but you hear so much in the media, about all the violence. So I tried to treat this kid as another human being, like myself, my family, my friends. I wanted to be part of solving the problems."

Chris's involvement was supported by an existing foundation of belief, in this case his Christian faith. But it took a direct connection with the boy and his world to induce Chris to put those beliefs into practice. It took a willingness to exercise his moral imagination and to expand his sphere of concern to include someone from a completely different background.

In the wake of this experience, Chris began questioning himself, especially his business practices. He consulted local neighborhood leaders, brought in new African American shops to his minimall, and sponsored an annual neighborhood festival. He tried to create a place where people of all races and ages would feel welcome. It still felt strange staking his money and time to try to help people who, as he says, "aren't even my own race of Koreans. But I wanted to set an example for my children. Once you start to share with others, it gets easier. What I did wasn't anything fancy. But I felt such a priceless taste of love coming back. I got closer to some other human beings who I'd never have gotten to know. Once I've done something like that, I can't go back to what I was before."

PARTICULAR LIVES

New information—the percentage of people out of work or children in poverty, the numbers behind America's record health care costs, the annual planetary increases in greenhouse gases—can help us comprehend the magnitude of our shared problems and develop appropriate responses. But information alone can't provide the organic connection that binds one person to another. By contrast, powerful individual stories create community, writes Scott Russell Sanders in *Utne Reader*. "They link teller to listeners, and listeners to one another." They let us glimpse the lives of those older or younger, richer or poorer, of different races, from places we'll never even see. Showing us the links between choices and consequences, they train our sight, "give us images for what is truly worth seeking, worth having, worth doing." Stories also teach us, Sanders suggests, how "every gesture, every act, every choice we make sends ripples of influence into the future."

This means that we are more likely to challenge homelessness if we hear the testimonies of individual people living on the street. We will work to overcome illiteracy after gaining a sense of what it's like to be unable to read. COPS derived its political agenda from stories like the one Virginia told about her neighbor who died. Psychological studies of those who rescued Jews during the Holocaust found they differed from their peers in their ability to be moved by pain, sadness, and helplessness. "If one woman ever told the whole honest truth about her life," writes poet Muriel Rukeyser, "the world would split open." I'd say the same would be true for any man.

As I've discussed, there are dangers inherent in trying to grasp too much at one time, in wallowing in the bad news. As psychologist Joanna Macy reminds us, "Information *by itself* can increase resistance [to engagement], deepening the sense of apathy and powerlessness." Stories about particular individuals and specific situations usually have the opposite effect. By giving unwieldy problems a human face, they also bring them down to a human—and thus manageable—scale.

Concrete stories help us feel moved by the world's troubles with out so overwhelming us that we despair of ever being able to change things. As philosopher Richard Rorty reminds us, the best way to promote compassion and solidarity is not by appealing to some general notion of goodness, but by encouraging people to respond to specific human lives. Responsibility in this view is not an abstract principle but a way of being. It exists only in the doing.

THE STORY OF THE EARTH

This same specificity can inspire us to act to preserve the natural world. Feeling the loss of a specific place that's been environmentally desecrated, or adopting and reclaiming it, can give us the strength to face the larger truth—that destroying our environment and what Catholic monk Thomas Berry calls its "modes of divine presence" has become our culture's routine way of doing business. Adam Werbach's concern was first aroused when he saw massive forest clearcuts. Key evangelical leaders began to shift on global climate change after Rich Cizik took them, together with Harvard scientists, to witness melting Arctic glaciers and permafrost. Michael Schut, of the faith-based environmental group Earth Ministry, describes the profound sorrow he felt hearing about Alaskan wolves being hunted from helicopters. "How am I possibly diminished by a wolf's death? What difference could the shooting of a few Alaskan wolves possibly make in my life? . . . Yet I tell the story anyway. . . . It speaks to me of the potential extent of the circle of human compassion, a sign of connection with all of creation. I felt and shared in another's loss, even when the 'other' is one with whom I didn't realize I shared an intimate connection. For the moment, the perceived walls of my separation came down."

We need not sentimentalize nature to recognize, as Scott Russell Sanders says, that "we belong to the earth, blood and brain and bone, and that we are kin to other creatures." Five hundred years ago, Martin Luther spoke to this kinship when he likened the world to a divine text: "God writes the Gospel, not in the Bible alone, but also on trees, and in the flowers and clouds and stars." Today, eco-theologians like Thomas Berry and ecopsychologists like Theodore Roszak offer a complementary image, connecting us with the largest possible story, what Berry calls "the grand liturgy of the universe."

This master narrative of existence doesn't provide specific prescriptions for our lives. But to recognize that we are joined to the forces that power the stars can remind us that when we work to heal the world, we do so in resonance with an immensely complex natural order that's been evolving for billions of years, and that has shaped who we are along with our layered experiences. As Roszak puts it, "The same atomic rudiments, the same chemical constituents, the same laws and principles extend from the cellular substance of our blood and bone to the farthest galaxies."

THE BROWN-EYED GIRL

Feeling part of a larger world and responsible to it can inspire us to act for human dignity, too. A Long Island teacher named Carol McNulty felt inspired to take a stand after watching a video of a brown-eyed girl, in a documentary called *Zoned for Slavery*. Though only fifteen, the girl had worked for two years making fifty-six cents an hour sewing clothes for the Gap and Eddie Bauer in a *maquiladora,* a factory inside a free-trade zone in El Salvador. Her eighteen-hour days left little time for eating, sleeping, or even going to the bathroom. She had to buy her food from the company store. Attending high school was out of the question, though she said shyly that she'd like to someday. The factory bosses prohibited workers from talking with each other, and when some of the bolder ones tried to organize, they were fired.

"I'm very intuitive about people's eyes," Carol explains. "I saw such a look of helplessness. My own children's eyes are so bright and cheerful. Hers were equally beautiful, but so beaten down and clouded by despair. It's wrong for children to live like that—undernourished, without hope, literally chained to machines. She was just one young woman whose life was so blocked. If you multiply that by all the others, it's horrendous." It angered Carol that this child—in Carol's words, "made in the image and likeness of God"— could be so abused for greed.

The group that started the Gap campaign, the National Labor Committee, was originally founded to support trade unionists and human rights activists who were threatened during the Reagan–Bush Central American wars. They then shifted to challenging companies like Walmart, Guess, Disney, Victoria's Secret, and the Gap for transferring production from U.S. factories to the cheapest possible overseas sites, then washing their hands of their contractors' abusive behavior. Shirts that cost thirty cents to make at the young woman's Salvadoran *maquiladora* sold in the United States for $20 or $30. The workers who sewed them could barely afford to eat. The situation outraged Carol to her core.

For years she had thought little about such matters. She considered Vietnam "a horror," as did her husband, Bill. But they were too busy raising their six kids and paying their bills to do anything about it. Then the first Gulf War erupted, and Carol and Bill joined a nascent peace and justice group in their local Catholic church. Shortly afterward, the group screened *Zoned for Slavery,* and Carol decided to take a stand.

Like Suzy Marks ducking behind her sign in West Los Angeles, Carol found it hard to be visible in her home community. Yet every Saturday for two months she and Bill stood in front of a nearby Gap store, braving biting winter rain and freezing snow. They were joined by a nun, some students, young mothers, a longshoreman, a union organizer, and a handful of others. Like citizens at other stores across the country, they handed out literature and talked with customers. They demanded that the corporation's contractors treat workers decently. Village trustees considered using anti-soliciting laws to force the group to leave. One claimed they had cursed people and harassed them in their cars. When Bill challenged this falsehood, the trustees refused to let him address their meeting. They said they didn't want to give him another platform for his protests.

This response frightened and disturbed Carol. "People lied so blatantly, it shook me up. It was so much easier to put a dollar in the collection plate each Sunday and think that this would buy eternal salvation. But I kept focusing on that young girl in the film and all the others she worked with. Their images kept me going."

Meanwhile, the National Labor Committee coordinated a nationwide effort whereby citizens picketed Gap stores, young *maquiladora* workers traveled to talk to TV stations, churches, civic groups, and schools, and the organization fed stories to the national media. "We felt these young women were incredibly courageous," said a National Labor Committee staffer. "If people just had a chance to hear them talk directly, we knew they'd be moved."

In the face of a growing public outcry, the Gap capitulated, pledging to ensure that contractors allow independent monitoring by churches and human rights groups and free access by unions, and treat their workers more equitably. Amazingly, the campaign had won.

"We celebrated with signs thanking the Gap for doing the right thing," said Carol. "Standing out there every week was hard. But it helped me to remember that the mothers in Central America love their children the same way I love mine. They bleed and feel pain like we do. We're not better than they are just because we're more comfortable."

Carol said that she and Bill had always been the "good Catholics who attended mass every Sunday, ate fish every Friday, and did all the rituals. But that's not enough. It's hard to worship God or find peace with your soul if people are starving in poverty, or when the air and water are filthy. It's wrong when companies fire people and their stock goes up. Or when they make money on the suffering of children—like that girl whose eyes grabbed my heart. We don't know that what we do will change this. But we've got to have the faith to try."

THEY DIDN'T KNOW THE LANGUAGE

Like the organizers who arranged the speaking tour for the young Salvadoran women, the most successful activists know the power of stories to move people's hearts, so they weave the richness of personal example into their arguments. If particular institutions are exploitive, racist, sexist, ecologically destructive, or otherwise oppressive, effective activists don't rely on mind-numbing rhetorical labels to arouse concern. Instead, they describe precisely how the institutions damage people's lives or degrade the environment. They frame policy proposals not in terms of arcane acronyms or bill numbers, but particular consequences. They continually link their arguments and visions to the narratives that can touch people's hearts.

I saw this when Oregon state employees, who were predominantly female and universally underpaid, began fighting for a living wage. Their unions started the campaign by hiring experts to draw up more equitable pay schedules. The resulting task force surveyed every category of job, then presented an elaborate report in the most neutral technical terms. At the request of top-level managers, they added more data. Eventually the study became so unwieldy and abstract that ordinary workers felt it had nothing to do with their lives, or their gut sense that their labor was undervalued. "Most of those affected couldn't even talk about the proposals," recalled the economist who chaired the task force, "because they didn't know the language, all the personnel-oriented, management-oriented terms. It left them completely out of the discussion." Lacking popular understanding or support, the effort collapsed of its own weight, dead on arrival at the legislature.

Then the unions shifted strategy, arranging for public-sector employees to speak for themselves to the media, community groups, and their elected officials. They posed simple but very telling questions: Why did women who took care of children at university day-care centers earn less than workers monitoring animals at local private research labs? Why did public-sector secretaries earn less than mail carriers? Why did nursing-home aides earn less than entry-level workers at insurance companies and banks? Testifying before the state legislature, they explained that their jobs mattered greatly to them, as well as to the community. Then they asked the senators how much they thought they earned. Holding up pay stubs as proof, they shamed the legislators with the reality of their economic plight:

Some made so little for full-time work, they needed food stamps to get by. The union won pay raises and other concessions that made working conditions more equitable. It triumphed by letting their members tell their own stories, in their own words.

STORIES AS TRAPS

But stories can mislead as well as reveal. How do we know which stories to heed? "Why, sometimes," the White Queen told Alice in *Through the Looking Glass,* "I've believed as many as six impossible things before breakfast." Stories betray the people and events they purport to depict when we're reckless with the truth or twist complex realities to make them fit what we happen to believe.

The problem includes outright falsehoods, like George W. Bush's claims that Saddam Hussein had weapons of mass destruction, active ties with Al-Qaeda, and was importing weapons-grade uranium from Niger. Or the assertion on Fox News that Barack Obama had attended a fundamentalist madrassa in Indonesia—refuted when CNN actually sent a reporter to check on what turned out to be a regular Indonesian public school, enrolling students of varied religious backgrounds. Or the arguments of some on the fringes of the political left that the 9/11 attacks were a government conspiracy.

Equally dubious is the practice of stripping stories of their actual contexts, highlighting the unrepresentative detail, the atypical incident, or the questionable source. A 2004 study published in the esteemed British science journal *Nature* found that out of nearly a thousand peer-reviewed articles on climate change from 1993 to 2003, not one took issue with either its urgent reality or the role of human actions in driving it. Yet much of the U.S. media continued to give equal weight to a handful of dissident "skeptics" whose work did not pass scientific muster. Not surprisingly, major fossil fuel interests either directly supported the skeptics or aided them in finding a platform for lodging their baseless criticisms.

One example: ABC's John Stossel announced, "You may have heard that sixteen hundred scientists signed a letter warning of 'devastating consequences.' But I bet you hadn't heard that seventeen thousand scientists signed a petition saying there's 'no convincing evidence' that greenhouse gases will disrupt the Earth's climate." As the media watch group FAIR pointed out, this seemingly impressive refutation didn't stand up to scrutiny. The first petition was signed by legitimate independent scientists, including 110 Nobel laureates, while the second was circulated by the energy industry, subject to no verification (which environmentalists exposed by adding blatantly inappropriate names like Ginger Spice and Michael J. Fox), and included a mix of random people who said they'd gotten a bachelor's degree in science but who lacked any relevant expertise.

Stories also mislead when ordinary citizens become poster children for the powerful. As journalist William Greider points out in *Who Will Tell the People,* corporations routinely push through self-serving congressional bills by hiring public relations firms to organize "Astroturf" lobbying efforts that give the orchestrated appearance of grassroots support. Responsible Industry for a Safe Environment? Actually a front group the National Agricultural Chemicals Association formed to thwart government pesticide regulation. The Foundation for Clean Air Progress? Created by the petroleum industry and PR firm Burson-Marsteller to fight federal clean air standards, building on Burson-Marsteller's creation of the National Smokers Alliance for Phillip Morris tobacco. And For the Sake of the Kids? A PAC through which the coal company Massey Energy spent $3 million helping defeat the incumbent Democratic West Virginia Chief Justice so his successor could reverse a $50 million jury verdict for fraud and breach of contract (a power-grab so blatant it inspired a John Grisham novel).

Talk show hosts and corporate PR flacks aren't alone in ignoring, obscuring, and misrepresenting context. When, for example, reporters describe pending legislation or policy decisions, they rarely mention, much less analyze, the behind-the-scenes role of money and power in shaping them. When George Bush signed major tax-cut legislation in 2001, he claimed that most of the gains would go to "low- and middle-income Americans." Those who supported the bill (including a dozen Democratic Senators) evoked images of Joe and Jane Taxpayer—overworked, overburdened, and much in need of relief.

You may be surprised to learn that by the time the bill's full impact hit, over half of the "relief" it supposedly provided would go to people whose income averaged $1.5 million a year, while the bottom fifth of taxpayers got under $100 apiece. Our political leaders didn't overtly say, "We're giving yet another tax break to the rich because they donate money to our campaigns." But with its deep cuts in taxes on capital gains, dividends, and inheritances, along with the lowering of top-bracket rates, the bill seemed to be the ultimate ratification of the belief that those who make money from speculative investments deserve to pay less for each dollar they make than teachers, factory workers, or anyone else who lives off what they earn from actual labor. It's helped create a situation in which, as billionaire Warren Buffett has pointed out, he now pays a lower tax rate than a receptionist in his office.

But you'd never know that from the way most of the media covered the story. Instead, they treated the cuts like populist manna from Heaven, referring again and again to the hardworking Americans who were about to get a long-awaited respite. Amid the debate, an article in my local paper's business section heralded how wonderful the tax cut on capital gains would be for investors. The same day, another section ran a piece on seniors at risk of losing their apartments because their federal Section Eight housing subsidies were about to be slashed. It was as if the two stories, and all that they implied about public policy, existed in two disconnected worlds. What was needed instead was a narrative that linked both cases, explaining how perpetually cutting the taxes of the wealthy makes it difficult for society to tend to the needs of its most vulnerable members.

CULTURE OF DISTRACTION

Seeing through the falsehoods and misleading frameworks is essential if we're going to tackle our most urgent issues. We'll also need to counter the media's tendency to bury the consequential beneath the trivial, helping foster a culture of distraction. Shortly after Iran's rigged 2009 election, CNN broadcast a clip of Obama talking about the massive street protests. "The President gave a really powerful Iran speech," said the anchor to his colleague. "Now what do you think about the death of Michael Jackson?" No wonder many of us know more about Jackson, Brad Pitt, Angelina Jolie, and others anointed by the celebrity gods than we do about our neighbors down the street. As psychologist William James wrote, "My experience is what I attend to." And to hear the stories that matter most, we need to reclaim our time and redirect our attention.

Here's another example of urgent issues getting lost in the clutter: In January 2007, the Intergovernmental Panel on Climate Change, the major international body of scientists working on this issue, released its Fourth Assessment Report, stating that global warming was unequivocally real and caused by human beings. The report warned of catastrophic consequences if we fail to address the building crisis. Even watered down to get unanimous agreement, it was a momentous and troubling report, one that led to the organization sharing the Nobel Peace Prize with Al Gore.

Yet when the story broke, as noted science writer Chris Mooney points out, it received much less attention than the U.S. Presidential election—which was almost two years away. And "by a week later," explains Mooney, "global warming had vanished from the roster of top stories entirely," supplanted by, among other things, the Super Bowl, the death of sex symbol Anna Nicole Smith, and coverage of the astronaut who drove 900 miles wearing diapers to attack the girlfriend of a fellow astronaut she had a crush on.

I admit the astronaut in diapers incident made for an alluring story. I wasted more than enough time on it myself. But I knew when to move on, unlike most of the mainstream media. Because global climate change proceeds largely invisibly, its most profound effects unlikely to be felt for years, it is particularly challenging to come to grips with. It is far easier to focus on the transient, the titillating, and the superficial.

SOLVING FOR PATTERN

So how do we separate true stories from false ones, the essential from the insignificant? How do we sort through contending claims without reverting to cynicism, or the perfect-standard argument that we can't act until we know every conceivable fact about the issues we'd like to address? How, in short, do we restore context? Appropriate solutions to social problems often represent compromises between legitimate competing interests, requiring us to listen to those who disagree with us, recognize and acknowledge what we find valid in their positions, and try our best to find common ground. People will always disagree over policy. But good policy can't be developed unless all relevant voices are taken into account, not only those of the well-connected.

One sign that a story properly takes context into account is that it acknowledges complex, sometimes seemingly contradictory implications. In her memoir, *Dead Man Walking*, Sister Helen Prejean describes feeling compelled to challenge capital punishment after she counseled convicted killer Pat Sonnier and learned the troubled history that led him to commit his unconscionable deed. Later, she came to know the parents of a girl whom another convict she was counseling had murdered. Through them, she also began to work with victims' rights groups. Acknowledging the pain that these parents suffered over the brutal killings of their children didn't negate Prejean's reasons for opposing capital punishment. But it challenged her vision, as she worked to take all viewpoints into account.

Another key to restoring context is asking who has lied or been honest in the past. That Exxon and the tobacco industry have consistently played fast and loose with the truth doesn't mean they always will, but it certainly is cause for closely examining any of their claims. The same is true of major news sources.

We can also ask who profits from certain institutional choices. Just because a policy benefits a particular interest or group doesn't automatically mean it's wrong. For instance, if we're going to solve global climate change, it makes sense to help support technologies

and industries that can lead the transition to alternative sources of
energy and more efficient use of the energy we have. If some companies or individuals get rich off this, more power to them.

But we still want to ask in any given situation whether the clout
of special interests is deforming policy choices and preventing us
from dealing with urgent common problems. And if it is, we need to
be honest about the destructive role that these interests are playing.
Pete Knutson took this approach when Washington State's giant
timber and aluminum interests tried to ban family fishing operations through Initiative 640. Together with his fellow fishermen and
their environmental supporters, Pete publicized Initiative 640's major backers, listed the amounts they donated, and provided numbers, maps, and charts to show how they'd degraded watersheds
and damaged salmon runs. Making clear that the initiative's claims
to environmental stewardship were false, they helped voters see
through the measure's self-serving misrepresentations, bringing about
its defeat.

Whatever the issues or interests may be in any given situation,
we can understand the relationship between particular stories and
their overall context by following an approach that Wendell Berry
calls "solving for pattern." "A bad solution is bad," writes Berry,
"because it acts destructively upon the larger patterns in which it is
contained . . . because it is formed in ignorance or disregard of them.
A bad solution solves for a single purpose or goal, such as increased
production. And it is typical of such solutions that they achieve stu-
pendous increases in production at exorbitant biological and social
costs."

Good solutions, Berry suggests, recognize that they are part of a
larger whole. They accept given limits and disciplines. They solve
more than one problem and don't create new problems. They answer the question "How much is enough?" A good solution, he says,
"should not enrich one person by the distress or impoverishment of
another."

To take one example, think about mountain-top removal, where
coal companies use millions of pounds of explosives to blow off the
tops of Appalachian mountains and extract coal from the rubble,

using a twenty-two-story $100 million machine called a dragline. The approach seems cost effective, because it requires few workers. But it also damages the mountains whose tops are destroyed and the valleys where the rubble is dumped. It has buried over 1,000 miles of rivers and streams, made floods more common, and created accident-prone tailing ponds holding hundreds of millions of gallons of contaminated water. The approach also produces little benefit for local economies, while the coal it produces emits mercury and contributes significantly to global climate change. Contrast mountain-top removal with wind farms that create no pollution. Tied to an updated national power grid to balance out local wind variances, they can provide a stable source of revenue for local family farmers, while creating high-wage jobs in the factories that produce their turbines. The first approach may seem to yield slightly cheaper energy. But even there the short-term costs are now almost equal. And the overall impact of the wind turbines is far more beneficial.

In fact, Wendell Berry considers mountain-top removal so much of "an abomination," that when environmental writer Bill McKibben asked him to join a nonviolent civil disobedience at the coal plant that provides heat and cooling for the U.S. Capitol, Berry agreed to risk arrest. At seventy-six years old, he joined 2,500 other people, blocking the entrances for four hours in subfreezing weather. Later Berry would get arrested at a West Virginia mountain-top-removal site owned by the coal company Massey Energy.

SELF-HELP FOR SOCIETY

I've talked of how other people's stories can expand our view of the world. Engagement in social change can also affect how we view our own personal narratives. When we reflect on where we've been and where we'd like to go, we can rely on larger explanatory stories to provide meaning and purpose, and to frame the choices we continue to make. We envision the kind of person we've been, who we are, and who we'd like to become. But most of us can't imagine developing an encompassing personal story where we might address the kinds of larger public solutions that Berry describes.

Two deep-rooted myths often prevent us from making this all-important connection. The first argues that we're masters of our fates, but only individually, since there's little we can do to act in common. The second contends that, because we create our own destiny, we deserve our fate—whether we end up at the top or the bottom. So all we can do is get our own lives in order and work to secure a spot among the elect. As a wealthy stockbroker's son insisted blithely when I interviewed him as a college freshman, "You make your own chances." He said this even though his father's money and connections paved every step of his path.

The stories that promote these myths are omnipresent, from rags-to-riches business chronicles to the latest self-help books that encourage us to take control of our lives, shed unhealthy relationships, pounds, or financial habits, and generally be all that we individually can be. To be sure, these stories teach some important lessons. We often can do more than we think possible. We have the capacity to transform our lives, and those of others, provided we stop viewing ourselves as passive victims of circumstances. We can grow, adapt, and escape old traps—and are stronger for doing so.

Self-respect and self-knowledge can also further common responsibility. "Love your neighbor as yourself," says the Bible, which means that we need to do both. If, as psychologist Jean Houston suggests, "another word for sin is unskilled behavior," then moral and personal development go hand in hand. "If we attempt to act and do things for others or for the world without deepening our own self-understanding," wrote Trappist monk Thomas Merton, "our own freedom, integrity, and capacity to love, we will not have anything to give to others. We will communicate nothing but our own obsessions, our aggressiveness, our ego-centered ambitions."

So there are reasons citizen activists should respect the universal need for psychological nurturance and individual growth. A scathing social critique is of little use in the absence of a hopeful vision of the future.

But a focus on personal growth and individual opportunity has its limits. It's easy for those of us who are blessed with comfortable circumstances to assume that everyone has options equal to our own. When we insist that we each have total power to shape the direction of our own lives, we ignore the social and economic context in which resources and opportunities are apportioned. It's a hard case to make for people who are starving, living in slavery, or just denied opportunities that many of us take for granted due to our own good fortune. Indeed, one reason for arguing that the poor choose poverty through their actions is that it avoids troubling questions about whether our own affluence might be due in part to privilege or chance rather than merit. If our only responsibility is to improve our own souls, we're off the moral hook for tragedies that may befall anyone else.

When educator and social critic Jonathan Kozol gave a talk to an affluent Dallas audience, he spoke of what he called the "savage inequalities" between rich and poor school districts across the country. At one point, he described how the desperately poor community of Camden, New Jersey, spent barely half as much per child as the affluent suburb of Cherry Hill, 5 miles away. Cherry Hill's children were growing up in homes filled with books and computers, while Camden's children faced every imaginable obstacle. But state education funding was based on local property taxes, and Camden's tax base was minimal. Pointing out that Texas had a similar system, Kozol suggested that statewide funding be equalized. The Dallas audience rebelled. Social problems can't be solved by throwing money at them, they said. Children can succeed if parents simply teach them persistence and promote character development.

Taking the audience at its word, Kozol then suggested that they send their own kids to Dallas's inner-city schools. Since their families possessed the necessary moral resources, they should have no problem flourishing, while the poor kids could commute to the suburbs. But the Dallas crowd didn't like that, either. Later, remembering all the sparkling diamond necklaces and bracelets he'd seen in the audience, Kozol said (referring to the famed phrase George Bush senior used to praise volunteerism), "I finally understood the meaning of 'a thousand points of light.'"

The most troublesome consequence of an overemphasis on individual responsibility is that it exempts even the most powerful economic, political, and social institutions from all responsibility for the state of society. It enshrines as gospel the pronouncement of former British Prime Minister Margaret Thatcher: "There is no such thing as society—there are only individual families." Yet such contemporary social problems as unemployment, inadequate health care, and global poverty require common public action, not only individual uplift. True, a few scattered individuals in difficult circumstances will, through uncommon effort, outside support, or enormous good luck, surmount the institutional hurdles that stand in their way. But until we begin to dismantle the hurdles themselves, the dreams of far too many in their communities will continue to be crushed. We might even say that the most stunted area of human potential is our capacity to think through our convictions and publicly act on them.

CHANGING THE THINGS WE CAN

Even the wiser perspectives in the tradition of personal uplift may inadvertently encourage passivity. They do so by downplaying the link between individual human pain and larger economic and political choices. I've found some valuable lessons in Stephen Covey's *The 7 Habits of Highly Effective People*. But it disturbs me when Covey writes that "it is our willing permission, our consent to what happens to us, that hurts us far more than what happens to us in the first place." He tells the story of a woman in one of his audiences who was a full-time nurse to "the most miserable, ungrateful man you can possibly imagine," a man who constantly harped at her and found fault with everything she did. Initially, the nurse was outraged at Covey's suggestion that "no one can hurt me without my consent, and that I have chosen my own emotional life of being miserable." Then she thought further and, according to Covey, realized that she did indeed possess the power to choose her response to her noxious patient.

I respect aspects of Covey's message: Sometimes we have to

make the best of difficult situations; it's better to come up with creative responses than to bemoan our circumstances endlessly, and although we can't always control the actions of others, we have control over our own responses, and needn't internalize the others' craziness. But such prescriptions, in isolation, fail to take into account the larger institutional contexts that so often constrain our choices. Maybe the nurse felt trapped, forced to keep her job, no matter how thankless or ill-paid, because no others were available. Rather than accept whatever tasks were handed to them, maybe she and her colleagues needed to organize a union to ensure that they could set limits to their commitments, receive a living wage, and get enough time off so they wouldn't burn out or take out their frustration on their families, themselves, or other patients. For all the importance of empathy, maybe this particular occupational setting wasn't the place for endless forbearance, or for automatically embracing the familiar women's role as long-suffering caretaker. Perhaps, instead, it was a place to challenge the unreasonable burdens that Covey's well-intentioned words ultimately rationalized.

Somewhere between the belief that all can be changed if we merely wish it so and the impotent resignation of the cynics, lies a far more practical yet hopeful outlook. It's expressed in the famous Alcoholics Anonymous prayer (adapted from an earlier version by social-justice theologian Reinhold Niebuhr) that has nourished millions of people: "God, grant me the serenity to accept the things I cannot change, the courage to change the things I can, and the wisdom to know the difference." We can view the prayer as a justification for timidity. It's been used at times for this. But we can also see it as a call for courage and wisdom—a challenge to choose our battles wisely as we continue to challenge injustice and to expand our definition of what we can change.

A SHELTER FOR MY GRANDCHILDREN

Even when we do engage and take responsibility for our society's problems, we're often taught to look for individual solutions, not common ones, and to favor purely personal approaches that don't require changing larger institutions. But in the process of scaling down our expectations and horizons, we risk allowing the problems we address to grow worse.

A Stanford student once explained how he'd learned more from his community volunteering than from all his courses in school. "I hope that one day," he concluded, "my grandchildren will get to have the same experience working in the same homeless shelter that I did." Friends gently reminded him that they were working for a future when people in a country this wealthy wouldn't need to sleep in shelters. The student meant no harm, but his words raised a question about the relationship between long-term change and the volunteer work that so many of us do in our communities.

Millions of us participate in voluntary activities, and our ranks are likely to increase with the passage, early in the Obama administration, of a $5.7 billion national service bill (co-sponsored by Democrat Ted Kennedy and Republican Orrin Hatch) that dramatically expanded AmeriCorps and related federal programs aimed at helping ordinary Americans volunteer to take on common challenges. We serve in soup kitchens and shelters, conduct literacy programs, read to otherwise isolated hospital patients or the elderly, work with Big Brothers, Big Sisters, Boy Scouts, and Girl Scouts. We teach Sunday school, coach Little League, work at our children's schools, and run churches, temples, mosques, volunteer fire departments, and historical sites. Usually, our motivation is the same as that of citizens involved in more political forms of advocacy: We want to alleviate human pain and affirm a sense of human connection. And we get back similar feelings of personal meaning and common purpose. Clearly, America would be a far meaner society without our efforts.

Yet many of us also find it easier to help our fellow citizens one on one than to exercise our democratic voice. We're far more likely to volunteer to meet a specific human need than to work to elect wiser leaders or pressure major economic, political, and cultural institutions to act more responsibly.

I'm troubled by the division between personal acts of compassion and the work that's necessary to bring about more structural change. As Jim Wallis points out, "In any good community center that deals with the problems of youth, the youth workers will spend most of their time talking about how the young people can get their lives together, find the spiritual and moral resources to make responsible choices, and take control of their own futures. Self-respect and mutual respect, cultural identity, community spirit, and social responsibility are all central. . . . But when describing the wider society, those same youth workers often will speak about the economic, racial, and social oppression that lies at the root of the problems their kids face."

Certainly, as Wallis suggests, the lines between service and institutional change often blur. I think of Chris Kim, who began, modestly enough, by extending a hand to the young man who'd tried to steal from his store, and ended up creating a center for his community. Meredith Segal began volunteering with Habitat for Humanity, then became involved trying to change policies and national leaders so that people wouldn't have to live in the streets. In the wake of Hurricane Katrina, MoveOn, which is primarily focused on political action, quickly set up a Web site to match evacuees with MoveOn members who had extra rooms in their houses to share; they ultimately provided temporary housing for more than 30,000 people.

Volunteer efforts can help us regain our sense of connection, offer lifelines to beleaguered communities, and change people's lives. Like Gandhi's "constructive program," where his supporters created local self-help projects, they can create new ways to address urgent problems, such as Habitat's pioneering work in building affordable houses. For certain kinds of crises, like the situation of young men and women trapped in bleak cycles of violence, the only solution may be to develop powerful relationships with people who can help them feel cared for in ways previously lacking, and show them a different way to live. Indeed, the best responses to many of our society's ills may be local and decentralized, drawing on such spiritual virtues as love, generosity, a willingness to listen, and the capacity to see a divine spark in even the most desperate and self-destructive of our fellow human beings.

Yet most of these one-on-one approaches require institutional
support. In his powerful memoir, *Always Running*, poet Luis Rodriguez describes his journey into East Los Angeles gang life in the
1960s—and how he finally left, thanks largely to the influence and
example of a former gang member turned community worker. Now
Rodriguez works with Chicago gang kids, running poetry workshops in which young people can express and exorcise their pain.
Without the resources that let the community worker turn social
intervention into a full-time job, enabling him to spend hours and
hours with Luis and his friends, Rodriguez might never have left the
gang culture in the first place.

We should work to heal the wounds of our culture whether or
not government programs support our efforts. But we should also
realize that gang members, for example, need more than mentors
and models. They also need jobs to teach them skills, drug treatment programs to help them overcome their addictions, and schools
where teachers and counselors can spend the time and energy it takes
to stop them from joining gangs or becoming homeless to begin
with. Our critical social problems demand both individual and
structural solutions. To rely on volunteer efforts is to duck the basic
issue of common responsibility, and to ignore the fact that individual crises often result from collective forces.

I've seen too many compassionate individuals trying to stem rivers of need, while national political and economic leaders have
opened the floodgates to widen them. We build five houses with
Habitat for Humanity, while escalating rents and government cut-
backs throw a hundred families into the street. We laboriously restore a single stream while a timber company clear-cuts a watershed
or global climate change turns once-fertile agricultural land into
desert. Environmental responsibility can begin with valuable personal steps, like driving our cars less or switching to high-efficiency
lightbulbs, but to solve global problems we're going to need common action. And when we do act in our communities, our volunteer
efforts may even produce, as Peter Cucchino, of Fordham University's community service center, worries, a "dissipation of energy
into all sorts of charitable activities, without a focus on any kind of

reform," averting "people's attention from the real victimization going on." As the Reverend William Sloane Coffin once said, "Charity
must not be allowed to go bail for justice."

Again and again, I've heard good-hearted volunteers who work
with low-income communities decry public decisions that they've
felt harmed these communities—such as Bush-era reductions in low-
income health care, housing, and energy assistance, or Clinton-era
reductions in child nutrition programs and food stamps. But when I
ask whether they've done anything to try to change those decisions,
they've said they stayed silent because they thought no one would
heed their voices. As a consequence, many of us who might otherwise be working for a more just social order spend our time instead
trying to fill the gaps in basic services created by several decades of
public cuts, and accentuated by the legacy of the 2008 economic
crash. Meanwhile, the victims of these cuts have even less time and
energy to make their voices heard, and their needs will be addressed—if at all—by already-stretched charities and caring individuals, rather than by social institutions and common resources. What
once was a shared responsibility has now been made private—and
voluntary.

THE POLITICS OF WITNESS

Greg Ricks, former director of Boston's powerful youth involvement
program, City Year, compared the situation of community service
volunteers to people trying to pull an endless sequence of drowning
children out of a river. Of course we must address the immediate
crisis, and try to rescue the children. But we also need to find out
why they're falling into the river—because no matter how hard we
try, we lack the resources, strength, and stamina to save them all.
So we must go upstream to fix the broken bridge, stop the people
who are pushing the children in, or do whatever else will address
the problem at its source.

How do we combine this with a more personal touch? How do
we proceed if we're inclined to act on a more personal level but also

want our individual actions to have an impact on a larger scale? The link, I believe, is the concept of witness, developed by people like Dorothy Day, who founded the Catholic Worker movement. We can use our service efforts to help cross daunting boundaries, like those of race and class. We can listen to those who come to the food banks, homeless shelters, and battered women's centers, and learn how they got there. We can talk to those on the street, and hear their stories. We can work to understand why our society produces so much needless human pain. Appropriate solutions will undoubtedly require supporting powerful local projects with common resources. And we may not always agree on the lessons. But whatever stories we encounter, whatever conclusions we draw, we can't keep them to ourselves.

The politics of witness involves taking these examples and lessons to the village square—or its contemporary equivalent—and then doing our best to convey them to as many others as possible. It means using them to refute myths that justify callousness and withdrawal. It also implies that we do all we can to help those who are habitually ignored or silenced to find their own voices and platforms.

An ethic of witness also affirms the bonds that link us. It helps us avoid being so ground down by our efforts to ease day-to-day miseries that we have no time to address their larger context. Given the deep roots of our culture's winner-take-all individualism, it's hard for those of us who work in beleaguered communities not to feel defensive, on the losing end of history. We may even mute our voices, lest we offend those whose financial and political resources our community institutions may depend on. Yet at least some of the energy we spend on volunteering should be directed toward the roots of the crises we address. If we don't look upstream, and try to act on what we see, we can hardly expect others to do so in our place.

LOVE YOUR HEART

In her novel *Beloved,* Toni Morrison describes the farm where her character Sethe grew up as a slave: "It never looked as terrible as it was and it made her wonder if Hell was a pretty place, too. Fire and brimstone all right, but hidden in lacy groves. Boys hanging from the most beautiful sycamores in the world." As in the farm of *Beloved*, our most urgent social crises are often hidden, and don't always signal their presence. They become apparent only when those who bear the scars of the crises speak out, insisting that their stories become part of the public dialogue.

This is especially true if we come from communities whose voices are habitually ignored, demeaned, or despised. It's our crises that the powers that be are likely to dismiss by explaining, in the words of the psychologist Edward Opton, "It didn't happen, and besides they deserved it." Our lives and those of our neighbors may refute such characterizations, but the only way others will know is if we tell them—which requires our actively speaking out to define who we are.

"No, they ain't in love with your mouth," says Sethe's mother, Baby Suggs, as she holds prayer meetings in the woods. "Yonder out there, they will see it broken and break it again. What you say out of it they will not heed. What you scream from it they do not hear. What you put into it to nourish your body they will snatch away and give you leavins instead. No, they don't love your mouth. *You* got to love it." And more even than your mouth, she says, "More than your life-holding womb and your life-giving private parts, hear me now, love your heart."

We need to embrace both our voice and our heart, even when the process is hard, and even in the face of people who will do their best to deny the very core of our being. "What is most important to me must be spoken," wrote poet Audre Lorde, "made verbal and shared, even at the risk of having it bruised or misunderstood." As our religious traditions point out, our very pain, vulnerability, and suffering can actually bring us closer to God by opening us up to compassion. For only when we begin to voice the difficult truths of our experience can we begin to change them and build better lives for ourselves and our communities.

Effective social movements often begin when once-silenced people resolve to tell their own stories. In different ways, under widely varying circumstances, they state, in effect, "This is who I am. This is how my community's hopes and dreams have systematically been spurned and destroyed. And this is how things have to change." Through the telling of these stories, people learn to view their lives as intertwined with history.

As we share our experiences with others, we often gain a broader perspective on who we are, on the forces that have shaped our circumstances, and on the evolution of what we believe. We develop a new sense of connection and responsibility, a new knowledge that our actions can count. "No matter who we are," writes Gloria Steinem, "the journey toward recovering the self-esteem that should have been our birthright follows similar steps: a first experience of seeing through our own eyes instead of through the eyes of others . . . telling what seemed to be shameful secrets, and discovering they are neither shameful nor secret . . . giving names to problems that have been treated as normal and thus have no names . . . bonding with others who share similar experiences . . . achieving empowerment."

I'm heartened, in this context, by the success of *Real Change,* a local Seattle street newspaper that has helped inspire a wave of others across the country in recent years. With the help of a small professional staff, those who live on the streets describe their experiences in the newspaper's pages for readers who think of homelessness as a faceless social problem. The paper also explores related social justice issues including how to create a city that works for all its inhabitants. The benefits to participants are both immediate and long-range. Money from selling the papers helps the homeless or near-homeless vendors survive. The very process of articulating their stories gives homeless men and women a new measure of control over their circumstances, and a sense of worth and purpose, while providing the rest of us a window onto their world.

BURIED LIVES

As the example of *Real Change* makes clear, problems tend to remain invisible, and thus unaddressed, until they're described in human terms. Just as stories can inspire action, those that gain public prominence significantly shape our political perception and choices. It's no exaggeration to say that the side of a particular debate that gets its stories before the public most widely and tells them most compellingly will likely win most political battles. As linguist George Lakoff stresses, it's critical to frame our issues in such ways that ordinary people will respond to them.

Think of the struggles of gays to be treated with equity and respect, and the resulting shifts in public attitudes over the past forty years. More than anything, progress has come from individuals risking their jobs, relationships, and sometimes physical safety to tell their stories, in private and public contexts. These difficult conversations and testaments have made it far harder for gay lives to be treated as abstractions, and have in turn inspired others to come forward. Changes addressing specific injustices have also been driven by storytelling, as when gay couples talk about being unable to visit their partners in a hospital, share medical insurance, or be considered legal guardians of each other's children.

In fact, the gay rights movement has made telling stories a deliberate political strategy, fundamental to its successes. As pioneering San Francisco supervisor Harvey Milk said, "You must come out. Come out . . . to your parents . . . I know that it is hard . . . Come out to your relatives . . . come out to your friends . . . if indeed they are your friends. Come out to your neighbors . . . to your fellow workers . . . to the people who work where you eat and shop . . . once and for all, break down the myths, destroy the lies and distortions."

Of course it's taken more than conversations to shift public perceptions and policies, and more than merely telling stories or even publicly coming out. It's taken organizing, registering voters, and pressuring elected officials to deal seriously with issues like AIDS, police harassment, and basic equity under the law. It's taken alliances, like the powerful moment (depicted in the movie *Milk*) when San Francisco gay activists persuaded their bars to stop serving beer produced by the union-busting company Coors, and then in return local unions supported the activists' efforts to get their community treated equitably. It's taken developing political power. But those who stepped forward and continue to step forward help make their lives real to people who once would have condemned them reflexively. They make the invisible visible—and in the process begin to win respect.

Not all critical stories get heard, though, and not all lives in the shadows get revealed. Like many Americans, I was shaken when the Space Shuttle Columbia disintegrated over Texas in 2003, killing the seven astronauts inside. Then I remembered seeing a tiny story just two days before, about an explosion at the West Pharmaceutical Plant in Kinston, North Carolina, that killed six workers and injured thirty-eight. The plant had been repeatedly cited for serious safety violations, which means the explosion might have been preventable. I wondered why it received barely a flicker of public attention.

The Kinston factory workers weren't the only Americans who risk life and limb at work. In a typical year, 6,000 people die from immediate occupational injuries, and 50,000 from longer-term occupational illnesses like asbestosis, brown lung, and workplace-linked cancers. But we don't talk about these people much. They're often immigrants and the poor, those most disposable in our culture. Their worlds are far removed from the media pundits. The lives of those who bravely rocket into the heavens just seem to matter more.

Those who die needlessly halfway across the globe are even less visible. As the respected Christian hunger advocacy group Bread for the World points out, every day, 16,000 children perish of hunger-related causes worldwide—the equivalent of five World Trade Center attacks. The toll is largely from infectious diseases that devastate undernourished bodies. The United Nations Development Programme (UNDP) estimates that for another $20 billion per year we could end this toll and meet the basic health and nutritional needs of the world's poorest people. That's less than what American and Europeans spend each year on pet food and less than a month of the cost of the Iraq War ($720 million a day at the peak of the occupation, as estimated by Nobel Prize–winning economist Joseph Stiglitz). But because the stories of these deaths are so rarely told, we don't feel their full human impact, making it easy for us to ignore the problem. Finding a solution requires telling some of these buried stories.

THE GIFT OF BEING HUMAN

If we've led relatively insulated and comfortable lives, hearing the stories of the less fortunate can open us up to a greater understanding. When we see the face or hear the voice of a person fighting for dignity, we enlarge our horizons, as happened with Carol McNulty after seeing the video of the Salvadoran *maquiladora* worker. Stories of the vulnerable or dispossessed can help us avoid becoming what Carol Bly calls "lucky predators," who by casually accepting the gifts bestowed by fortune, inadvertently circumscribe the lives and dampen the aspirations of countless others.

Conversely, too many of us purchase our comfort and security at the cost of building walls around our hearts, so the stories that might challenge us cannot penetrate. It doesn't help to wallow in guilt. But we need to look at how we've erected these internal gated cities, what it would take to dismantle them, and what we might gain by doing so.

Thus, it strengthens and deepens us to read Toni Morrison, listen to a laid-off autoworker, or hear the testament of a welfare mother. If we truly heed such stories, they can liberate us from insulation and nurture our sense of broader connection. By "connection" I mean much more than an increased willingness to give money to hungry children or recycle our trash. I mean the recognition that our fates are fundamentally linked to other people and to the earth, and that whether or not we're conscious about their impact, our choices do shape the world, making it more generous or more callous.

When we open ourselves up in this fashion, we gain powerful rewards. Psychologist Lane Gerber works with Cambodian refugees. Reflecting on the experience of listening to their accounts of the Khmer Rouge's violence and brutality—many had witnessed the killing of their families—Lane described an unexpected paradox. The refugees' stories were horrible. They gave him nightmares. Yet he also felt honored, even uplifted, to be able to listen in support. As a colleague of his recalled, "I felt such sadness and heaviness as I talked with a man about his suffering and loss. Yet I also felt more alive somehow. Those things shouldn't go together. But they did. I remember thinking that something sacred was happening, and thinking, 'This is why we were born. This is what it is to be human.' "

"There's something about what we hear from these survivors," said Lane, "that teaches us why we live. It's the opposite of a situation one woman described, where the Khmer Rouge prohibited her and the other concentration camp prisoners from even talking with each other—under threat of death. 'We all suffered,' the woman told me, 'but we suffered alone so the suffering was useless.' It shakes you to work with these stories. But you also feel privileged to hear another's cry and give recognition to their suffering. It touches your core vulnerability and lifts you beyond your individual self. It's a strangely hopeful experience."

DIGGING UP THE LAND MINES

We can gain this mix of strength and vulnerability from people who, with courage and generosity, work to create a more just world. Though vastly underrepresented in our national dialogue, their stories can help us envision a future of reciprocity and fairness, wisdom and compassion, in which the human spirit can flourish. Their examples can help us balance public goals and personal pressures, give us perspective on our journeys, and keep us going when times get tough. We need their stories to inspire us.

Many of the most effective and inspiring activists draw heavily on their own stories in charting their path. In 1992, East Palo Alto, California, had the highest murder rate in America and the highest rate west of Chicago of intravenous drug users infected with HIV. Five years later, serious crime in the community dropped nearly 90 percent and has remained there ever since—in large part thanks to a long-time San Quentin inmate named David Lewis, who'd spent seventeen years in the California prison system.

David still looks intimidating: He's a six-foot-two, 220-pound African American man with a shaved head, a handlebar mustache, and eighteen-inch biceps, one of which is adorned with a fading tattoo and a scar. But his eyes and voice are no longer edgy and desperate. Patient, reflective, and forgiving, David is a very different man today than he once was.

David started his downhill slide when he was ten. Though he was undiagnosed at the time, he had dyslexia. His school responded to his resulting slow progress by placing him in a class with mentally retarded kids, where the teachers did little but baby-sit. David's teachers told him he had no educational future, so he felt there was nothing to be gained by trying.

Bored, angry, and powerless, David began drinking and skipping school, making, as he now says, "a conscious decision to take whatever substances would change the way I felt." His grandmother used liquor as a medicine for sorrow. When President Kennedy was shot, she stared bleakly at the TV until David, age eight, brought her a bottle. The only time his dad could talk with his white neighbor was when they were drunk. David soon supplemented his own liquor consumption with marijuana and barbiturates. When David was fifteen, Nixon cracked down on the marijuana trade, and heroin flooded the streets. "It felt really good to take a shot of dope," he says. "It took all my pain away."

David soon found other kids who were also scorned, discarded, and wanting to get back a sense of worth however they could. "We'd come up to a random person, the biggest grown man we could find, and knock him unconscious with a single punch. I could do it with either hand. People on the street started treating me with respect."

David grew bolder, entering drug dealers' apartments with a sawed-off shotgun. "I'd fire it at the ceiling, then clean them out. I never killed anyone, but I was crazy enough to threaten people. I liked being the kid with no future, the kid people were afraid of." When David was eighteen, he and three friends were caught robbing a gas station of $156. The judge sent him to San Quentin.

David mastered the prison environment quickly. He felt at home with inmates who'd similarly learned to survive from score to score and crime to crime. Many shared David's dyslexia and had been excluded from school. The once-terrifying clanging gates soon became familiar, almost reassuring. Even when David joined a prison affiliate of the Black Panthers, he and the other key leaders spent most of their energy finding ways to get high.

Two-and-a-half years later, David was released, only to be turned in a month later by a onetime friend, to whom he'd sold $20 worth of heroin. This time the sentence was ten years to life. Prison became steadily more comfortable, despite its physical harshness. David found a pet mouse and "fed it, played with it, tried to teach it to play chess, did everything but make love to it."

He was released a few more times. But in each case, life outside prison seemed like a strange hiatus. An uncertain spectator in an alien world, he'd eat food from the kitchen pot and sit on the toilet with the door open. "I had no social skills," David says. "I felt like God had left a component out of me, and that I didn't fit."

He also kept returning to heroin. "I always thought I could regulate it, not let it master me. Then I'd do something crazy to get back inside, where I had a place and a reputation. If I was hungry, I'd get a gun to take what I needed. Someone else could work and stand in line, but I wasn't going to."

David's turning point came while he was getting ready to watch the World Series on a small TV set in his San Quentin cell. The ground started shaking. It was a major San Francisco earthquake. "I felt helpless and hopeless, locked in a cage. I heard the Bay Bridge had collapsed. I thought of my twenty-seven-year-old son, who I'd had when I was seventeen. I'd spent half my life behind bars. Now he seemed headed for jail, too. I wondered if both of us might die here."

This sudden sense of vulnerability, David now believes, was the key to his transformation. In prison, people admired his toughness. It didn't matter that it led nowhere. More respectable people practiced a similar denial, David felt, in their endless striving to consume. "Only when I began to doubt could I change."

But wanting to change wasn't enough. David was full of resolve the next time he got out, but still had no clear models for a different way to live. Aside from a few men who'd embraced more religion than he could handle, he knew of no long-term inmates who'd "broken free and gotten a regular life with the job, house, wife, dog, goldfish, and a car that you don't have to steal."

David's probation officer found him lying beneath a bridge with a needle in his arm, then got him into a rehab program. There he saw a video in which the veteran convict turned leadership trainer Gordon Graham described prison as a comfort zone, where people came to feel more at home than they did outside.

"I'd never seen anyone really change who was like me," David said. "Gordon spoke in a language I knew because he'd been there. He showed me how I was stuck, like a broken record going rup, rup, rup in the groove, and how the survival skills I'd learned didn't work. He helped me get past just endlessly repeating."

David stayed in the rehab program nine months, got a job as a painter, and began attending Alcoholics Anonymous and Narcotics Anonymous meetings. They were his medicine, says David, "just like someone sick with diabetes needs insulin, or someone whose kidneys don't work needs dialysis. If you don't remember what you've been through, you're doomed to keep doing it, which means something dreadful will bite your ass like you never want to think about." After David appeared in a Bill Moyers TV program on an African American men's support group, he got a call from East Palo Alto's mayor. "She wanted me to help stop the community violence. I was one of the people who'd helped sow the land mines of violence to begin with. When you have a war like the war in our streets, it's the people who sow the land mines who know best how to dig them up."

WE'D BEEN THERE

Drawing on his own story, and with support from San Mateo County, David started a drug and alcohol rehab center called Free at Last. Its approach stemmed from the lessons of the street culture he'd inhabited. Instead of hiding the program, the staff tied it to the community with a highly visible storefront center. They kept it open late, so people could drop in and get support at almost any time. By day, people enrolled in the center's education and health programs. At night, Free at Last outreach workers, led by David, visited bars, crack houses, and shooting galleries to test people for HIV and offer them treatment programs. "Most IV addicts are out at night. So it doesn't work to have a clinic that follows the standard medical model, open eight to five, and expect people to come to you. You have to go to where people are. We got trained in how to draw blood and give the tests, so we didn't need a nurse. We'd pass out bleach and condoms as a way to draw people into the rehab programs. They'd listen to us because we'd been in gangs with them and shot dope with them. We'd been there."

Monday night was a bad night for murders in East Palo Alto. "On the weekends you're getting high," David explains. "You've got your money, your drugs, maybe a girl. Then it's Monday, the money from your payday is gone. You have to start all over, broke and hurting. That's why all the blues songs talk about 'Stormy Monday' and 'Blue Monday.' You have to steal to get what you need. That's when you feel desperate and people kill each other.

"We developed one of the early Midnight Basketball programs for Monday and for Thursday, which is another bad night. To join you have to be a school dropout or on parole or probation. Our players attend a workshop at eight in the evening, where they talk about their lives and learn about alternatives. Then they play in the basketball games, with community coaches. We give them somewhere to go when they're likely to be the most vulnerable and reckless. They don't have to go blow someone away."

David built the clinic through state and private grants and community health program contracts. He drew no salary, keeping his other job as an HIV outreach worker. But under his guidance, the organization has grown over fifteen years. Like the community they serve, the fifty-four staff members are overwhelmingly African American and Latino, and two thirds are in recovery. Free at Last developed residential services for women going through rehab, so they wouldn't be separated from their children. They challenged liquor store licenses, advocated for access to treatment programs, worked with the local court system to offer alternatives to drug-related incarceration, and ran domestic violence groups for women and for the men who abused them. Together with Gordon Graham, David continued to lead prison workshops nationwide, developing prerelease programs to address the chasm between prison culture and the outside.

"Lots of things I do today use the same energy and drive as when I was crazy. You don't go into a person's house and rob them with a shotgun without emotional faith. It's just as scary as asking for a hundred thousand dollars from the president of the Robert Wood Johnson Foundation. I just discovered a way into being a powerful person instead of being a fool." Three-quarters of the people who graduated from the Free at Last programs remained clean, sober, and gainfully employed, and David has used their approach to develop similar innovative programs in Tanzania, Kenya, and Kazakhstan.

David wanted to see a new politics coming out of the stories of the recovery movement, where "we start in a dark room, lift the shades so we're able to see, and begin fighting for a fair chance for our communities. If they'd had 'three strikes' laws when I was in prison, I'd never have been released. But I'm not an exception, just an example of what can happen when people get the support they need, in a language they can understand."

SHARED VULNERABILITY

If we want to create a more just and humane common future, we can begin by acknowledging our shared vulnerability. David Lewis started to change not when he felt in command, but when the Bay Area earthquake made him feel like a helpless beast, confined and powerless. For Virginia Ramirez, change came when she witnessed but couldn't prevent her old neighbor's needless death. For evangelical leader Rich Cizik it was the unexpected fragility of God's creation. For Meredith Segal, of Students for Obama, it came when she recognized that, as much as she loved building Habitat houses, that alone would never end homelessness. We rarely change when

we're cruising along, insulated from the world—only when we drop
the barriers that separate us from other human beings, admit that
we don't know all the answers, and listen closely to others, to the
world around us. Our lives shift when our heart becomes so open,
in Alice Walker's words, that "the wind blows through it."

A parallel process occurs when we share our stories of engagement. Once we've been involved in social causes for a while, it's easy
to forget our initial hesitancy. Reflecting on common journeys can
remind us of the origins of our commitment and help us reach out
to people who are paralyzed by the fears and debilitating self-
definitions that once blocked our involvement, too. Theologian
James Cone describes how the black church uses religious testimony "not only to strengthen an individual's faith, but also to build
the faith of the community." The more we tell and retell stories about
our commitments, the more we can strengthen our hope.

At its best, reflecting on the larger contexts of our lives can help
us connect with the stories of others, and with a larger narrative of
being. If we focus solely on our own experiences, we will hear nothing but the echoes of our obsessions. But if we look for ties to a
broader common story, in which we all partake, we can develop the
vision we need.

CHAPTER SEVEN

Values, Work, and Family

Finding the right work is like discovering your own soul in the world.
—*THOMAS MOORE*

We often hesitate to get involved in our communities: We're too busy, we say. We've got all we can handle holding on to our jobs, paying the bills, and raising our children. Given our day-to-day responsibilities, we're lucky if we can find a few spare hours for pursuits that revive us. It's hard to imagine how we might make room for more public commitments.

The pressures are real, especially at our workplaces. Whatever we do, most of us work longer and harder than ever, while worrying more about our future in an uncertain economy. This is true whether we're low-wage workers holding two jobs to make ends meet, professionals working endless nights and weekends, or students beleaguered by outside jobs and debt. It's true for all of us squeezed between escalating workplace demands and a sense that we'll never catch up. The situation is even worse, of course, for those who are out of work and desperately struggling to get by. In *The Overworked American,* Harvard economist Juliet Schor examines the emergence of this Alice-in-Wonderland world, where we have to scramble faster and faster just to stay in the same place. Between 1967 and 2006, the average American worker's time on the job jumped by over 167 hours per year, or the equivalent of an entire extra month. And that number doesn't take into account the time spent in ever-lengthening commutes or all the work-related e-mails we send in what are supposedly our off-hours.

Meanwhile, guarantees that once allowed most of us to take our basic survival for granted have steadily eroded or, for many, collapsed altogether. Not only do we spend more time working, we take fewer vacations, receive fewer benefits, and face far more daily stress. As I write, more than 46 million Americans have no health insurance, and nothing to rely on but the prayer: "I hope no one in my family gets sick." Once, we could count on employer-funded pensions, confident that if we worked long and hard enough, our old age would be provided for. Now, retirement has become a crapshoot, as we've watched hard-earned savings evaporate in a crash provoked by speculation and greed, with few good options for trying to rebuild them in time to make a difference. Things would be even worse had engaged citizens not helped defeat repeated attempts by major financial interests to privatize Social Security.

If you're going to school, you face at least equal pressures. Even as higher education has become essential for most decent jobs, students face more and more economic barriers. If you grow up in the top economic quarter of the population, you have a 76 percent chance of getting through college by age twenty-four, after which point graduation grows substantially harder. But if you're in the bottom quarter, your chances are much worse: No matter how smart, ambitious, and hardworking you are, the odds are less than ten in a hundred that you'll get through by that same critical point and acquire the education you need without an immense and protracted struggle.

The gap is due to cuts in federal financial aid, the decline of the minimum wage, which is now lower in real purchasing power than in the mid 1950s, and the increasing deprivation of low-income communities. When Congress established federal Pell grants in 1965, they covered three-quarters of the cost of getting through the average public four-year college; now, even with increases under Obama, they cover just a third of the cost. Two-thirds of students now graduate in debt, owing an average of $23,000 each, despite most full-time students working at outside jobs, with a third working twenty-five or more hours a week.

The situation wasn't always this difficult. In the early seventies, I worked my way through my last two years of college as a bartender, making $5 an hour for twenty hours a week. I paid my living expenses and tuition at New York's New School for Social Research (a private university with costs as high as any in the nation), and still had enough money to go out on the weekends and graduate without a dollar of debt. Twenty-five years later, I met a student who lived on the same Brooklyn block where I had lived when going to college. He worked thirty hours a week for $6 an hour, a fraction in real dollars of what I'd been making. He commuted ninety minutes each way to the City College of New York, a public college with tuition far higher proportionate to his earnings than my tuition was. He kept dropping out and working full-time to avoid getting too deep in debt, even though he still expected to owe $15,000 by the time he finished. Though he was working harder than I had, the rules had changed to make his passage far tougher, and the costs have only continued to rise.

Even beyond financial survival, our lives in general seem more overloaded and uncertain, more at the mercy of distant powers and principalities. A key way to ease all these pressures is to make wiser public choices, and find common solutions to the pressures we face. Without the legislation that established rent control, for instance, an award-winning high school science teacher I know would not be able to live, work, and raise a family in New York City. Nor would tens of thousands of other teachers, subway conductors, garbage collectors, and janitors, without whose labors the city would grind to a halt. Income-contingent loan-repayment programs were piloted in the Clinton administration to allow young women and men to pursue occupations that are vital to the well-being of our communities, but that traditionally pay poorly. The Bush administration cut these programs, but they've been renewed and expanded under Obama, along with the previously mentioned increases in financial aid. Some of our country's pivotal advances came during periods

like the Great Depression, when those without work banded together
to demand innovative social programs whose fruits we still enjoy—as when I visit my Works Progress Administration–built local
library, or run in a WPA-created waterfront park. These and related
measures were brought about by elected representatives, advocacy
groups, and the collective action of ordinary citizens.

SLEEPING IN DUMPSTERS

For most of us, our time crunches are serious but not insurmountable. True, the amount of time we devote to work, school, and commuting has been steadily increasing. But these hours still aren't
comparable to those activists faced a century ago, like labor organizers who challenged the eighty-hour workweek even as they continued to put in their shifts. By and large, we have it far easier than the
black sharecroppers and domestic workers who made up the un-
glamorous core of the civil rights movement. They struggled to take
care of their families, faced pervasive racial discrimination, and still
made time to challenge their situation. The day after Rosa Parks was
arrested, she went in to work at her job as a department store seam-
stress. When he became head of the Montgomery chapter of the
NAACP, E. D. Nixon continued working as a railroad porter. Neither had a choice. Yet we forget that people like Parks and Nixon
had less latitude to act than most of us do.

Even individuals facing tremendous financial pressure can find
ways to take a stand. A student named Chaim Eliyah had lived on
and off the streets of Seattle's northern suburbs since the end of high
school, sleeping in his van, in dumpsters, and on the couches of
friends, while working a succession of minimum wage jobs at Mc-
Donald's, Starbucks, and a local hardware store. Chaim's parents
were barely surviving themselves, had major medical problems, and
lived in a trailer park where no one under fifty-five was allowed.
Things got worse after a street friend offered Chaim meth and he
spent the next year and a half alternately working and committing
petty crimes "trying to get back to that first wonderful high." Seeing

where he was headed, Chaim was finally able to kick his drug habit, but was still living on the edge when a sympathetic middle-aged woman let him stay in her house and save up for an apartment. He enrolled at a local community college, scraping together grants, loans, and a work-study job to make a go of it. A required multicultural studies class "felt like the story of my life," leading him to realize that "while I obviously made some very poor choices, part of what I was up against was coming from the bottom with absolutely no safety net."

Chaim did well enough at the community college to transfer to the University of Washington, but the dorms were too expensive and nearby apartments wouldn't rent to him because he had a criminal record. So he commuted ninety minutes each way by bus before finally finding an apartment close enough to bike. Securing another work-study job and more student loans, Chaim got involved first with Students for Darfur, then a campus affiliate of United Students Against Sweatshops. The anti-sweatshop group successfully pressured the university to allow the janitors in all the buildings it ran to unionize, and then to require any companies that furnished its sweatshirts, jerseys, hats, and other branded gear to join a consortium that independently monitored fair labor standards.

Chaim still lived on the financial edge. "When middle class students say 'I'm broke,' it means they've exhausted their monthly budget," he explained. "When I say that, it means I literally have nothing left. I'm also graduating with close to fifty thousand dollars in debt, between student loans, money I still owe the criminal justice system, and bills to doctors and hospitals for major foot problems and chronic allergy problems, neither of which my student health insurance would cover because they called them preexisting conditions." Despite these obstacles, Chaim's political involvement opened up new possibilities, like working with the labor movement, and new commitments that he eagerly embraced. Living on the streets, he felt, gave him more sympathy for people working in near slave-wage sweatshops. "It isn't the same, of course, but I have a sense of what it's like to be locked into bad situations because you feel you have no other options. It makes me more committed to act."

A LOW OVERHEAD

Although Chaim's situation was far more economically precarious, many of the most active students I've met have worked twenty, thirty, even forty hours a week along with going to school. They face constraints as great as their less active peers, but find creative ways to be engaged nonetheless. People will always have differing financial and time pressures, making it easier for some to spend more energy on community involvement than others. But it's important to realize that some of the stress we feel may be self-induced. "If you want to do anything creative," said writer and activist Grace Paley, "keep a low overhead." Public involvement can be an immensely creative, but a hard path to pursue if our lifestyle is so expensive that we need a six-figure income to get by. In *Your Money or Your Life*, Vicki Robin and Joe Dominguez explored this phenomenon, describing how the American addiction to consumption damages our souls. They then suggested systematic ways to examine how we spend our money, and to make sure we get enough satisfaction from each expenditure to justify the time and energy we invest in it. In the process, they encouraged us to ask a radical question: How much is enough?

Simple lives can still be rich—a lesson even more critical in difficult economic times. As a young street artist once told George Orwell, "The stars are a free show; it doesn't cost anything to use your eyes." In an experience that will be familiar to many parents, none of my stepson's toys gave him more pleasure than our daily rituals: We chased each other around and around the house, while I made monster noises and he responded with glee; then each night, before he went to sleep, we crowded onto his bed while my wife, Rebecca, read to him.

Robin and Dominguez aren't arguing for sackcloth austerity. They're fine with enjoying selected discretionary items and experiences that offer real and sustained satisfaction. But they insist, rightly I think, that many—if not most—consumer purchases do no such thing. If we spend less, we can work fewer hours, retire early, or pursue occupations more congruent with our values, not to mention lightening our load on the planet. True, this approach works best if we earn enough to allow for discretionary spending in the first place. But just about everyone in America is affected by our culture's pervasive materialism; poor teenagers, for example, crave the latest electronic toys or pricey brand-name clothing just as much as their affluent suburban peers. That means just about everyone can benefit from spending money more wisely.

The results of paring down our economic needs will vary from person to person, but often they're dramatic. For fourteen years, my friend Mary worked as a water treatment operator for Seattle's municipal utility, involving herself in peace and environmental issues on the side. Along the way, she bought a house, which she shared comfortably but modestly with three roommates. By the time she was forty-four, she was able to quit her full-time position. Since then, Mary has survived on the rent paid by her housemates and the income from working twelve hours a week. She devotes most of her life to her causes. "I get so much satisfaction out of my involvements," she says. "I don't feel a need for all that other consumption."

Similarly, a young woman who now works to reduce commercialism in public schools said, about her earlier employment with an accounting firm, "I didn't really fit that job. I made good money and bought a fur coat. But I don't need lots of money. Poetry readings are cheap. I'd rather go to a house party than a club. I don't feel I'm missing things."

I've experienced the benefits of a low overhead in my own life. I love picking up $350 suits at garage sales or used clothing stores, and second-hand electronics on eBay and craigslist. I've bought my last three cars when they were ten years old and kept them until they were over twenty. I really would rather go down to the beach and watch a sunset than eat at a fancy restaurant. These and other choices have saved me tens of thousands of dollars over the years, allowing me to keep writing when my income was totally marginal.

Being frugal has also enabled me to contribute more to causes I believe in and to afford major purchases that did seem worthwhile, like solar panels and a high-efficiency furnace (made in unionized plants in the United States). I love how my electric bicycle climbs

Seattle's major hills—and supports the new renewable energy economy. I enjoy watching my electrical meter spin backward—providing
tangible proof that, with the right government programs, entrepre-
neurial initiative, and citizen involvement, we really can meet our
energy needs without frying the planet.

My favorite song from the Jewish Passover ceremony is "Dayenu," which means "It Would Have Been Enough":

> *Had the Lord only brought us out of Egypt . . .*
> *   it would have been enough.*
> *Had the Lord only sustained us in the desert . . .*
> *   it would have been enough.*
> *Had the Lord only given us the Torah . . .*
> *   it would have been enough.*

We have too little of the "Dayenu" spirit in American culture.
We dream of making it big. We constantly pursue more wealth, status, and material goods, whether or not they bestow true satisfaction. When we joke that "he who dies with the most toys wins," we
underscore the extent to which we're possessed by our possessions.
As the historian William Appleman Williams wrote, "Once people
begin to acquire and enjoy and take for granted and waste surplus
resources and space as a routine part of their lives, and to view
them as a sign of God's favor, then it requires a genius to make a
career—let alone create a culture—on the basis of agreeing to limits."

TRUE REJUVENATION

Making the best use of our time and energy is more than a matter of
reducing expenses. Most of us spend time recuperating from stress—
time that we might use to get involved in our communities. We all
have our favorite ways to do this: hanging out with friends, running, dancing, gardening, or reading novels, posting on Facebook,
or even following every twist and turn of politics as if it were a
spectator sport. I'm not suggesting we necessarily give up these

activities. The tangible and intangible satisfactions we get from them can help us remain sane, relaxed, and healthy. All citizens possess souls, and all souls require rejuvenation. But in excess, even the most wonderful pastimes can swallow up our lives. And some are fundamentally distracting and numbing, like constant TV-watching, getting so drunk every weekend that we barely remember what we did, or texting so obsessively we're unable to focus on anything else. If we cut back on some of our diversions, we can use the time and attention we save for community involvement.

One of my own prime time-wasters is following the Seattle Mariners. The team gives me a sense of drama and excitement, makes me feel twelve years old and innocent, provides fresh hope each year. But baseball can also consume my life—if I let it. I can spend untold hours following each at-bat in every game, or following every twist and turn of the latest trade speculation. I can waste an even greater amount of time following political blogs and articles. They're vital to my work, but if I give them too much of my attention, the stories blur into each other, and, soon, my focus is so diffused I get nothing else done—and lose the chance to make my own modest impact on the world.

We need to strike a balance between the havens that nurture us and the work that needs doing in the world. That means learning to draw pleasure from our modest domestic comforts, our hobbies, our passions, and even some of our distractions—but refusing to let them dominate our lives.

WORKING TO GET BY

Even living simply, we need a means for surviving, for paying the bills. Often, we work at jobs that we hope are at least modestly useful, while acting for social change in our off hours. Alison Smith, of Maine's campaign reform initiative, had a low-level job at a university. Harry Taylor sold commercial real estate. Using skills she'd developed with COPS, Virginia Ramirez worked as a health outreach trainer, while continuing her community organizing. With enough ingenuity, we may carve out more time. A lawyer I know worked out a job-share arrangement whereby she and two others split two full-time positions at the Seattle Public Defender's office. This gave her four months on and two months off; she used the time off to join delegations investigating human rights crises in areas like Guatemala, El Salvador, and the Palestinian West Bank.

Some of us make a strong personal impact in demanding fields, such as teaching, medicine, or psychotherapy. But even here, as I've suggested, we're subject to larger social forces. Dedicated community doctors and nurses see their ability to do their jobs well continually undermined by excessive paperwork and bureaucratic tasks demanded by insurance companies. Teachers, counselors, and social workers face similar overloads, particularly if they're serving less affluent populations. Engineers, architects, skilled tradespeople, and green business entrepreneurs who would love to build a new renewable economy depend on common choices to level the economic playing field and make the necessary resources available. If we want to change social structures, much of our work will take place either outside the confines of our jobs, or by building on our workplace experience to serve as advocates.

RIGHT LIVELIHOOD

It's a gift to be able to work directly on issues we care about, and earn our living in the process. We don't have to divide our lives. We can fully invest our passions. "Finding the right work," says theologian and psychotherapist Thomas Moore, "is like discovering your own soul in the world." Usually the livings we make as community activists are modest. They require that we live frugally, sometimes skating near the financial edge in a context where life is already hard and getting harder for far too many. But when we do find such jobs, they let us focus our time and energy in ways consonant with our deepest personal urgencies. We may find such work by joining existing organizations, whether local community projects or affiliates of national groups. We can also start our own institutions, like

David Lewis with Free at Last, or Sonya Vetra Tinsley with her Serious Fun community music project.

Sometimes social engagement can lead to unexpected career opportunities. When a young woman named Barb Meister was a "fragile and self-conscious freshman" at the University of Nebraska, she rarely read a newspaper, didn't vote, and rarely spoke up in class. Her most daring accomplishment had been entering her prizewinning cows in local fairs.

Then America's family farms began going belly-up. Barb's parents were forced to file for bankruptcy, but they also joined some activist farmers' organizations. They inspired Barb to start a student group so she and others could educate their peers on the issues that affected Nebraska's farm communities. Later, she based a career, as she says, on "what I'd done, what I knew, the issues I was grounded in." By age twenty-five, she was second in command of the entire Nebraska Department of Agriculture.

We never know where we'll find what the Buddhist tradition calls "right livelihood." I was recently stunned to see my friend John Weeks interviewed in *Best's Review,* the bible of the insurance industry. John talked about the future of alternative medicine, arguing that it should be integrated into HMO and insurance plans. He'd entered the field in 1983, doing fund-raising and public outreach for Seattle's Bastyr University. Bastyr gave John "a chance to build something, and to fully engage myself for the first time in my professional life." He'd dropped out of Stanford, worked as a furniture mover and taxi driver, written for an alternative paper, assisted a maverick state legislator, and organized eastern Washington wheat farmers to fight a huge proposed coal plant. But he'd always felt rootless, drifting from cause to cause. Bastyr provided both a paycheck and a home.

John used his organizer's skills to reach out to initially wary media. He helped shepherd Bastyr through the lengthy process of becoming accredited, making it the first naturopathic university in the country to gain this legitimation. "We had to pass through that narrows," John says, "to have any significant influence on health practice in America." John then helped secure research grants that enabled alternative medicine advocates to begin proving to critics that their treatments were legitimate—including one where Bastyr beat out Harvard for a major National Institutes of Health (NIH) grant. And he helped pull together a multidisciplinary team of natural health professionals whose knowledge and credentials gave them a chance to be heard by Congress. They convinced political leaders as diverse as liberal Tom Harkin and conservative Orrin Hatch to support the federal government's first Office of Alternative Medicine within the NIH. John also helped the alternative health care movement reach people outside the middle class: He worked with local Washington State authorities to help develop the nation's first publicly funded community clinic where conventional physicians and naturopaths work side by side, learning from each other, while providing services to low-income patients. More recently, he's navigated the complex terrain of HMOs and giant insurance companies, showing them cost-effective ways to integrate alternative medicine into their plans, and has brought together licensed chiropractors, naturopaths, massage therapists, and acupuncturists and homebirth-oriented midwives to forge a common political voice. John's work has evolved over time, but he's been fortunate enough to earn a living helping huge institutions incorporate alternatives that promise both to save money and to improve their participants' wellness.

Whatever our jobs, we can use them to address larger questions. Physician Deborah Prothrow-Stith was a third-year medical student when a teenage boy was admitted to Boston's Brigham and Women's Hospital with a stab wound. As she stitched him up, he described the argument that prompted the attack, and said he'd take his own revenge as soon as he got out. "Don't go to sleep," he warned her, "because the guy who did this to me is going to be in here in about an hour, and you'll get all the practice stitching you need!"

His words stayed with Prothrow-Stith and raised questions about the scope of her responsibility. "Had he been a potential suicide who had taken an overdose of barbiturates," she says, "my job would have extended well beyond the lavage of his stomach." She wondered why physicians educated the public about cigarette smoking, excess weight, and safe sex but did nothing to address street violence. "We were just stitching them back up and sending them back out on the streets," back to the domestic equivalent of a war zone, where in some neighborhoods a quarter of all children had witnessed a murder. Prothrow-Stith realized that this violence had reached epidemic proportions; it was a public health problem that called for a public health solution.

Drawing on the experience that had moved her, Prothrow-Stith began working with city hospitals to develop follow-up strategies for patients admitted with gunshot or stab wounds, so that the factors that led to the incidents were addressed as well. She spent fifteen years developing violence-prevention curriculums for schools, and programs that taught conflict-resolution skills to teachers, students, police officers, health workers, businesspeople, church members, and public housing residents. At one point, more than two years had passed without a single person aged sixteen or under dying from a shooting in Boston.

Apart from the powerful results, what's most instructive about Prothrow-Stith's experience is that everything she did was an extension of her role as a physician, meshed with the broader sense of responsibility she learned from the African American church that helped anchor her soul. She merely expanded her mission as a healer beyond its traditional bounds.

We've seen a similar expansion of boundaries when Chris Kim transformed his minimall into a center that helped tie together the surrounding community. Or when fisherman Pete Knutson brought the lessons of an ancient way of life to bear on current environmental issues. What would happen if every teacher spoke out concerning the social inequities that drastically hinder learning for far too many children? If doctors and nurses fought to guarantee genuinely affordable and comprehensive health care for every American? If police, firefighters, and social workers talked openly and compassionately about the homeless families they see on the street? If more scientists became advocates for the environment? Wherever we work, we can encourage our employers to make their production, purchasing, and daily operations as ecologically sound as possible, to treat our fellow workers equitably, and to benefit whatever external communities we work with.

To do this, we'll need to join forces with others. Indeed, viewing our workplaces as mini-societies is the first step toward trying to make them responsible. Former Dominican priest Matthew Fox suggests we take an active role in forming workplace communities, so we can "gather to tell our stories" and as a group create new and more generous visions of our vocations, "whether it's education or health work, religion or parenting." Without such support, Fox suggests, our best instincts will be frustrated, no matter how committed we may be.

WE ENERGIZED EACH OTHER

No one is saying this is easy, or always successful, particularly in contexts we neither own nor control. But employees working in concert can produce astonishing transformations. At Chicago's Inland Steel, four African American employees became concerned about how minority employees were treated. "The paper policies were fine," says saleswoman Scharlene Hurston, "but they weren't carried out. When you were involved in meetings, you always felt like you weren't part of the group. You felt you were invisible. Although you'd speak up and have a reasonable opinion, your ideas would be ignored or discarded. Then someone who was white would bring up an almost identical proposal, and everyone would jump to embrace it. Forty percent of our plant workers are minorities. But it stopped when you got to the upper levels. Out of two hundred managers in sales and marketing, we had three African Americans. We felt totally isolated."

Fed up with the lack of progress, Scharlene began meeting informally with three other African American colleagues who had individually approached management to discuss advancement practices, only to find their complaints dismissed. They echoed Scharlene's judgment that "the situation violated principles I hold very dearly, about doing what's right and truthful and honest." Over a period of months, they brainstormed together, finally deciding to approach Steven Bowsher, a white general manager they respected. Inviting him to dinner, they told him about the racist jokes, derogatory comments, and overt and covert obstacles that they and others had faced at Inland. Although Bowsher was sympathetic, he found the examples abstract and remote from his experience. But he was interested enough to take a two-day race relations seminar led by a longtime civil rights activist, and unexpectedly saw his company with new eyes.

"Suddenly, we weren't talking at each other," Scharlene Hurston recalls, "we started to talk *with* each other." Bowsher had his entire team of managers attend the seminar, then established an aggressive affirmative action plan. His department began to systematically promote minorities on the basis of their total years of experience and the general strength of their skills, even if they'd been stuck for years at the lower levels of the corporate hierarchy. After some prodding from Bowsher, Inland's president attended the same seminar, convened a meeting of top officers to deal with racial issues, and seriously solicited the opinions of women and minority employees.

Scharlene's group met resistance, of course. "When you take on something controversial, you're going to get shot at," she says. "We all had colleagues who explained to us how our future looked so bright—if we just divorced ourselves from those other people who were causing trouble. Most of our opponents weren't bad people. They were simply ignorant, afraid of controversy and change."

But that didn't stop the reformers. "We energized each other," said Scharlene. "When one of us got tired, the others were there to pick them up." Besides, it was no longer just the four of them. Each major department and manufacturing plant now had a group to address racial and sexual inclusion. When Bowsher became head of Inland's now-independent Ryerson Coil division, he appointed the company's first African American general manager and first Latino and female plant managers, conducted a major campaign against sexual harassment, and revoked a longstanding policy that made the office areas off-limits to ordinary workers. When the division finally turned a profit, after years of losing money, he attributed its success to unleashing the energy and creativity of workers who finally felt they had the respect and support of management.

"A corporate culture takes forever to create and forever to

change," said Scharlene. "But the issues have been legitimized. We've learned the art of negotiation and the strength of solidarity. Before, there were little pockets of questioning, or people denying that these issues existed at all. Now people aren't nearly as afraid. They're much more ready to speak up."

PART OF A MOVEMENT

Scharlene and her coworkers were fortunate to find a sympathetic senior manager. But their approach—building a supportive community, telling their story as powerfully as they could, and then being strategic (and persistent) about how to make changes—applies to any situation in which you're trying to change your workplace, whether to make it more environmentally responsible or to secure more equitable treatment for fellow employees (or yourself). Particularly in a difficult economy, it's challenging to attempt to change the culture of our workplaces while navigating the accompanying personal politics and accomplishing our assigned tasks. But it's not impossible. And when companies shift toward serving a greater common good, they often do so in response to an impetus from below. In his book *Aiming Higher,* David Bollier describes an inspiring array of businesses that have combined ethical action with marketplace success—many in exactly this fashion.

But what if our employers are completely resistant to ethical claims and threaten us for just speaking our minds? I've talked much in this book about finding our moral voice, but many of us risk losing our jobs if we express this voice at work. Our task becomes a lot less daunting if we have some protection against being capriciously fired—if we can express our beliefs without fear of losing our jobs. And the only source of such protection I know of— unless we're at the absolute top of the hierarchy—is that much-maligned institution, the labor union.

Unions seem far from the domains of the soul. Hostile stereotypes associate them with corruption, ruthless power, and needless confrontation. They seem to belong to an earlier period in this

country's history, one whose brute industrial forces and harsh working conditions many of us would prefer to think we've left behind.
Yet since most of us work for others, no other institution can more
effectively help us bring our values into our workplaces.

In his compelling memoir, *Which Side Are You On?: Trying to Be
for Labor When It's Flat on Its Back,* labor lawyer Thomas Geoghegan describes a dispatcher who'd worked at a trucking company for
years, then was abruptly fired following a heart attack. When the
dispatcher wanted to challenge his firing, Geoghegan asked if anyone could testify about his work record. But everyone the man
could think of was either a fellow dispatcher or a foreman, and they
were afraid to risk their jobs. Finally, the man had an epiphany:
"Hey, why didn't I think of it? The guys in the *union*. They can testify for me, and they won't get whacked."

Like all other nonunion employees in America, Geoghegan writes,
everyone else in the company could be fired "at will . . . for any
reason, good or bad . . . or for no reason at all." But the union men,
who happened to be truck drivers, could be fired only for cause.
"They, unlike the supervisors, could stroll into court, testify, and
just walk past the Boss and wave."

Although they've sometimes betrayed their promise, unions give
those of us who are ordinary workers our best chance at a genuine
say in our workplaces, with security grounded in more than employer benevolence. They protect us against capricious management
decisions—for instance, being fired for voicing discomforting truths.
If we're in a union, employers find it harder to play us off against
each other, as expendable pawns in the global marketplace. Unions
also build that threatened but essential quality called solidarity, a
sense of common purpose. They promote the profoundly spiritual
recognition that "an injury to one is an injury to all" and that our
fates are inextricably joined, as Martin Luther King said, "in an in-
escapable network of mutuality, tied in a single garment of destiny."

Unions can also give us a say in shaping history. We forget, or
are never taught, their role in helping to bring about the eight-hour
workday, Social Security, unemployment insurance, and Medicare.
Nor is it widely known that unions like the United Auto Workers

provided key support for the civil rights movement, or that long-shore workers' locals worldwide helped end apartheid by refusing to load ships destined for South Africa.

In the United States, unions have been in decline since the late 1970s, even as union membership has grown in Canada, where economic conditions are comparable but workers face far less hostile labor laws. Yet a wave of new leaders offers fresh hope, primarily through building alliances with community and environmental groups.

Even in the anti-labor climate of the Bush years, United Steel Workers president Leo Gerard helped found the Blue Green Alliance with the Sierra Club, and brokered solutions like using state and federal incentives to help create a unionized wind turbine plant on the site of a closed Pennsylvania steel mill. During the same period, the Service Employees International Union (SEIU) grew from 1 to 2 million members, organizing traditionally low-wage workers like janitors, home health care workers, nurses' aides, and security guards, and drawing on students, religious leaders, and community members to support campaigns like Justice for Janitors. In 2003, 87,000 Communications Workers of America members successfully struck the telecommunications giant Verizon, challenging mandatory overtime and workplace speedups.

Nearly all these victories required major public involvement, and with enough support, unions were able to make headway against even the most resistant employers. For fifteen years, the United Food and Commercial Workers (UFCW) fought to represent 4,000 workers at a hog slaughterhouse owned by Smithfield Farms in Tar Heel, North Carolina. The mostly African American and Latino workers braved firings, physical violence, repeated immigration raids, and intimidation so blatant that even the Bush-era National Labor Relations Board threw out the elections in which the company prevailed. Meanwhile the UFCW established a nearby workers center where fired organizers could hold English classes and classes on labor rights, and the campaign could build a base outside the plant. Workers inside wrote "Union Time" on their helmets and slowed down the slaughterhouse line to gain a sense of control.

Outside supporters promoted a national boycott, which led to the city of Boston canceling orders for all Smithfield products. In February 2009, the union finally won.

The Coalition of Immokalee Workers used a similar national boycott to pressure Taco Bell—and then McDonald's, Burger King, and Subway—to require their contractors to improve wages and near-slavery working conditions for tomato pickers in the Florida fields. They focused on Taco Bell first, with students organizing "Boot the Bell" campaigns on their campuses, then pressured the chain's parent company to sign a landmark agreement in 2005, leading to similar concessions from the other major chains.

THEY LEARNED TO STAND UP

The starting point for many involved in such efforts is a basic wish to preserve their dignity—a desire they share with other community activists. When Jorge Rivera was hired at ASI, a small Boston mattress factory with forty production employees, he was paid only $7.50 an hour, but was promised quick raises to $11 an hour. Once on the job, Jorge learned how to coil inner springs, build frames, and sew padding and fabric. He assembled displays for trade shows and helped sell the company's high-end mattresses to customers. Some days he'd work sixteen hours straight. But his promised raises never came.

Jorge let it pass for six months. "Then after another six months I asked what happened to the original offer," he said. "I was giving the best of myself, but they said I had to wait a little while." He finally got a fifty-cent raise, but by that time well over a year had passed. "It was like they were using me, acting like I was stupid, so I said, 'I want the raise that you talked about when I got hired.' I was getting madder and madder, until one day I just stayed home and told them I was going to look for another job. They called and offered me nine-fifty because they didn't have anyone else to do the work I was doing."

At that point Jorge realized that "all these other people in the company hadn't had a raise in three years. People wouldn't even get their overtime unless they went to the office and complained. I told them, 'You have to do what I did. Go and speak up.'" But most were afraid to. While Jorge was born in New York City of Puerto Rican parents, most of his coworkers came from Central America and knew only Spanish. "So I started speaking out for other people, because I spoke English."

The factory had other problems. The workers' bathrooms were filthy, "like we were animals. Nobody cleaned them. The drinking water from our fountain came out green. They didn't give you safety belts for your back when you lifted heavy mattresses. We used hot metal glue from a pump gun, but they didn't give us gloves or masks."

When Jorge began talking openly about these and other issues, he says, "the manager told me to look out for myself and they'd take care of me. I felt bad because these were my partners. I was trying to make conditions better so people would be happy and increase production."

When Jorge heard about workers at another Boston firm who won the right to be represented by the textile union UNITE, he and a few coworkers quietly met with a union representative. "I also started talking with people inside the plant and asking them how they felt about getting paid just five or six dollars an hour, when in that same hour they made three or four top-quality mattresses that sold for eight hundred dollars each. 'You can't buy a house with that money,' I said. 'You can't raise a family.'"

Jorge knew his actions were risky. "But I had to do it for the people who were there, even if I lost my job." The managers called a series of company-wide meetings. "They said that if the union came in, the owners would have to close the plant. That's the first thing they always say."

But momentum kept building. Jorge addressed groups of people during his lunch breaks. "The management could see us, but they didn't know what we were saying, because we spoke Spanish and they didn't." When the mattress workers finally had a vote, the union won. But ASI offered to increase base wages by only sixteen cents an hour. Jorge and the other workers felt they had no choice but to strike.

"Only five workers crossed the picket line," Jorge recalls. "Even some people who'd voted against the union and had been with the company for years were with us. These were old men and women who'd worked hard all their lives and gotten nothing. I was so happy to see them I almost cried."

The workers built outside support with the help of UNITE, organizations like Jobs with Justice, and members of other unions. "We told our customers about the strike," Jorge says, "so they'd call and put pressure for delivery. The company ran out of inventory."

After five days, the company settled. Workers received an immediate dollar-an-hour raise and a guarantee of additional raises for each of the next two years, plus sick days, health insurance, and two weeks' paid vacation. The bathrooms were cleaned, and there was talk of a cafeteria. "Now people dare to talk with the boss and tell him what they feel," Jorge explains. "They go by themselves to the office, with the problems they have. They learned to stand up for themselves."

OVEREXTENDED PARENTS

Gaining more dignity and security at our jobs is one example of how common public efforts can give us more personal breathing room. Public commitments can also influence other aspects of our private lives, including our roles as parents. That connection can be harder to see, and we often tend to shy away from social action precisely because we fear we'll make our childrens' lives more difficult or financially insecure. "You want to protect the institutions instead of challenging them," explained a woman who cut back her community organizing when the stresses of single parenting grew too harsh. "Once I had a kid, I was no longer a single person. I had to balance everything against what it would mean for my son."

Our children do take time and attention, and they should. We race constantly to find babysitters, juggle money, keep track of their schoolwork, and make sure they are fed, bathed, and have clean clothes. Middle-class parents can spend practically every free hour shuttling children from lesson to sports team to play date. This frantic way of life can leave everyone exhausted. What's the alternative, we ask, in these perilous times? We think children must always be supervised, even if it means scheduling their every free minute.

Especially when our children are toddlers—and most in need of parental care—it may be all we can do just to go to work, come home, pay attention to their needs, and catch a few scarce hours of sleep. Pete Knutson recalls feeling totally overwhelmed while trying to keep his domestic world afloat early in his marriage, although the desire to preserve a decent future for his kids later fueled his public stands. Virginia Ramirez's children were largely grown when she first got involved in COPS, but her husband and mother still pressured her to keep her focus on her family. "My kids are three and nine now," explains a therapist who has long been involved in global peace issues. "They've brought a radical change in my life. I find myself doing things I can work into family life: tutoring at their inner-city public school; making phone calls; writing letters; staying involved through my Catholic church, which is a very engaged, multiracial congregation. But I'm not going to as many meetings. I'm not doing civil disobedience. I see time opening up as they get older, and look forward to all the things I'll be able to do, political and otherwise. I see myself as one of those women who will jump back in intensely when my kids are just a bit more grown."

Collaborative approaches can help us find time: When my wife, Rebecca, was pregnant with my stepson, she approached another pregnant woman in her apartment building and initiated a babysitting co-op that quickly spread to twenty families. The group soon became a close-knit extended support system, watching each other's children daily, holding a weekly play group, volunteering together at a local community help line, and sharing emotional support. Similarly, if we want to attract parents to political events, we'd do well to offer child care, or find ways for people to bring their children along. But many of us will have to back away, at least briefly.

However we handle the time constraints, raising children can make us more economically fearful. Because we're concerned about their future, we shy away from public controversies that might risk our jobs. We buy life insurance, save for college, move to pricier neighborhoods with better schools, and provide every material convenience we can. No matter how economically successful we are, we can always justify the struggle to earn more by saying that we're only trying to give our children the additional comfort and security they deserve.

We also want to shelter them from the ills of the world. The need is obvious in poor communities where children live closer to violence. Social injustices affect them more personally and at an earlier age. As parents, we may have to explain fear, bigotry, greed—and why they can buy guns, liquor, and drugs at any hour of the day but have to take a bus for miles to find school supplies, library books, or fresh, unprocessed groceries. As psychiatrist and social critic Robert Coles writes, "A black child of eight, in rural Mississippi or in a northern ghetto, an Indian or Chicano or Appalachian child, can sound like a disillusioned old radical."

Even for more affluent families, public commitments can bring difficult choices. In their study of community involvement, *Common Fire,* Larry Parks Daloz, Sharon Daloz Parks, and their colleagues profiled the director of a community credit union who raised her children in the same low-income neighborhood that the credit union served. She and her husband had alternatives, so wondered whether it was fair to raise a child in this setting, seeing poverty and despair "instead of waking up in the morning and seeing lots of lovely flowers and beautiful homes. Is it good for your child to see children with no decent shoes or sweaters in winter? Is it good for your child to see people whose only home is a grocery cart?" But the woman also remembered looking out the window and seeing her husband and daughter helping a homeless man gather and crush cans for refunds. "Then again, they benefit from this, too—maybe more than we know." She taught her daughter an ethic of connection, rather than one of retreat.

Each of us will resolve these intimate dilemmas in our own ways. But as Marian Wright Edelman puts it in *The Measure of Our*

Success, protecting our own children "does not end in our kitchen or at our front door or with narrow attention just to [their] personal needs." Writing to her own sons, she says, "You must walk the streets with other people's children and attend schools with other people's children. You breathe polluted air and eat polluted food like millions of other children and are threatened by pesticides and chemicals and toxic waste and a depleted ozone layer like everybody's children. Drunken drivers and crack addicts on the streets are a menace to every American child. So are violent television shows and movies and incessant advertising and cultural signals that hawk profligate consumption and excessive violence and tell you slick is real. It is too easy and unrealistic to say these forces can be tuned out just by individual parental vigilance." If we want our children to lead generous lives, we need to give them ideals to inspire them.

COMMON SOLUTIONS

In addition to giving our children ideals, if we want truly to protect them from the destructive forces of contemporary society, we have to meet those forces head-on, through common solutions. And that effort will work best if conducted in a spirit that affirms our human connections. Think of the possibilities: The stronger our public schools, the less we have to fear that our daughters and sons will be unsafe, neglected, or poorly taught. Those of us with the latitude to do so wouldn't have to spend hours navigating them through ultra-competitive magnet programs, or working extra to pay for private education. If we created a decent social safety net, we'd worry less about where to find the money to pay our kids' medical bills. If our society were less violent, we'd more readily let our children roam the neighborhood with friends, instead of watching their every move or keeping them in the house in front of the TV. If we could worry less about their economic futures, maybe we'd also be less obsessed with shuttling them to round after round of outside lessons and activities, all supposedly to prepare them to succeed. We may believe we can make our homes into castles, but whatever we do, the world will intrude.

Instead, we can affirm our children's instinct to care, not through a silence that too easily connotes indifference, but by helping them make sense of the troubling aspects of the world—instead of pretending that they don't exist or don't affect them. When they worry about the environment, urban violence, or people sleeping on the streets, they do so because they feel the empathy and compassion that we want to nourish—or, at times, because they're legitimately afraid, for reasons we should hardly dismiss. Rather than wrapping them in a domestic cocoon, we can explain an adult society that might otherwise induce despair or callousness. The more they see us responding to the world's problems, the more they gain a sense of hope and purposefulness. Without our guidance, they may be moved and disturbed by such crises, yet remain silent to protect us from questions they sense we'd rather not face. This collaborative silence can become like the denial in alcoholic families, where people offer rationalizations like, "Oh, your mother's just taking a nap on the floor." Everyone knows that something is wrong, but no one will say it.

PASSING THE TORCH

Beyond shaping the world that we will pass on to our children, our actions and choices offer models for their lives. As writer James Baldwin said, "Children have never been very good at listening to their elders, but they have never failed to imitate them." Socially engaged parents don't automatically turn their kids into social crusaders. But I've met countless individuals involved in important issues who referred to adult examples as key: "Our church has always worked with the homeless." "My first demonstration, I was in a baby stroller." "My mom's been going to marches and meetings ever since I can remember." Meredith Segal, the founder of Students for Barack Obama, often drew inspiration from her father, who'd spoken out against the Vietnam War when he was young, and later ran a national organization devoted to providing counseling services to people who couldn't afford them. When an activist friend in Minneapolis was complaining to his wife about the chronically late garbage pickups in their neighborhood, their five-year-old piped up, "Well why don't you call the City Council?" She was used to people who spoke out.

Young women and men whose parents remain actively engaged are far more likely to view social action as a natural human activity. Early on, many learn to reflect on their personal choices and those of society, to challenge misleading authorities and institutions, and to think about the kind of America they want to help create. They also learn skills needed in public life and indeed in adult life generally, like the ability to articulate beliefs, engage differing perspectives, and enlist new allies. It's worth trying to make society live up to its highest ideals, they learn, even when doing so is difficult. Steeped in traditions of engagement, they know from experience that human action can make a difference.

"Families need to both protect their members," writes psychologist Mary Pipher, "and connect with the world." She describes how she and her thirteen-year-old daughter, Sara, volunteered at a local soup kitchen for a year. Spending time with adults who were doing work they believed in, Sara found a respite from what Mary called "a shallow and mean-spirited peer culture." She saw the value of her own efforts. In the process, mother and daughter renewed their own common bond through a shared sense of meaning and purpose.

By contrast, children who grow up in politically detached households learn to fear and mistrust civic involvement, to regard it as the task of "some other kind of person." They're taught to focus on personal survival or advancement. The absence of family models for social action can also feed cynicism by encouraging the view that such efforts are futile, generally make matters worse, or are the domain of crackpots and crazies. If these children are ever to take on public issues, many will first have to question the values they grew up with, resolve conflicting loyalties, and find new mentors outside their family. The barriers are that much greater.

Not all socially engaged citizens inherit their commitment, of course. But being part of such a lineage can give us confidence, direction, and encouragement. Marian Wright Edelman's father, a minister, built the first home for African American elders in their segregated South Carolina town. He also constructed a playground and canteen behind his church, so that the community's African American children would have a place to play. "I have always believed that I could help change the world," she recalls, "because I have been lucky to have adults around me who did."

YOU FORGOT MY BOOK

Children will always be children, of course, as well they should be. When my stepson, Will, was eight, my wife, Rebecca, and I participated in a largely Jewish vigil challenging Israeli prime minister Benjamin Netanyahu's obstruction of the Middle East peace process. We took Will but forgot to bring extra snacks and a book for him, and he was sullen and cranky the whole time. "But it's for peace in the Middle East," Rebecca explained plaintively. "I don't *care* if there's peace in the Middle East," he said. "You forgot my book," Finally, Rebecca took him to get pizza.

In a similar vein, Marianne Williamson describes a terrible argument with her six-year-old daughter about Barbie. Marianne said the doll was impossibly skinny, cared only about shopping, and was a terrible role model. Then she discovered this note from her daughter: "Dear Barbie. I love you so much, but my mommy hates you." Marianne gave up, recognizing that her daughter was learning to stand up for her own choices. The fact that she happened to choose Barbie at that moment probably wouldn't ruin her.

Marianne made the right choice by backing off from an ultimately unwinnable battle. If we want our children to feel confident enough to develop minds of their own, we need first to love and care for them, and let them develop according to their own needs, interests, and approaches. As psychologist Alice Miller has stressed, they need to be loved not for how they perform or whether they agree with us, but simply for who they are. If we're involved in our community, speak openly about what we believe, and invite our children along when appropriate, they'll get the message. We can't compel them to be concerned about others, anymore than we can compel them to love us.

Nor do we want to create clones that blindly follow us. Planned Parenthood's longtime head, Faye Wattleton, differed strongly with her mother on abortion. Both drew from their lifelong experience in the church. Wattleton's mother prayed that her daughter would change her mind. But they maintained a bond of love and respect, and Wattleton credited her mother's integrity with helping to inspire her. Our kids need to think for themselves, learn from our limits and strengths, and find their own causes and commitments, in personal and public life alike.

AN ETHIC OF FAIRNESS

In *The Little Virtues,* Italian essayist Natalia Ginzburg argued that we should teach our children "not the little virtues but the great ones. Not thrift but generosity and an indifference to money; not caution but courage and a contempt for danger; not shrewdness but frankness and a love of truth; not tact but love for one's neighbor and self-denial; not a desire for success but a desire to be and to know."

The little virtues have their place, Ginzburg said, but "their value is of a complementary and not of a substantial kind; they cannot stand by themselves without the others, and by themselves and without the others they provide but meager fare for human nature." Only the great ones, which we hope our children will spontaneously develop someday but which in fact must be taught through example, can inspire a deeper sense of purpose.

Sometimes the models we provide are less public and more personal. It matters if we parents pass on an ethic of fairness, encourage our children's voices, and help them reason through complex issues. Morris Dees, the founder of the Southern Poverty Law Center, grew up in Alabama, the son of poor tenant farmers who were not politically engaged. But Dees's father was highly egalitarian. He was the only white farmer in the area who invited blacks over to share meals, or who drank from the same bucket in the fields. The way he lived conveyed in vivid terms a moral perspective that, Dees says, continues to motivate his own life work.

As we struggle to move beyond a culture where people wonder whether our national motto had become "Invest in America: Buy a Senator," our children need more than general encouragement of ethical behavior. If we want them to lead lives of commitment and compassion, they'll need tangible examples of people who act on their convictions with courage and integrity. They'll need a connection to history, so they'll know what it means to persist. They'll need to feel confident speaking out on controversial issues, negotiating conflicts, and cooperating with others. All adults provide examples, whether we mean to or not. Therefore we all are responsible. But by the same token, we're also all in a position to make a difference, by giving children the models that can inspire them.

OTHER PEOPLE'S CHILDREN

Ultimately, children give us the best reason to stand up for what we believe. Again and again, activists describe them as their living links to the future. David Lewis, trapped in his cell during the Bay Area earthquake, wondered whether he and his son would both die in jail. Alison Smith worked for campaign reform so that her children wouldn't have to grow up in a cynical world. Suzy Marks first began to duck out from behind her sign because the arms race seemed the ultimate issue in her kids' lives. Pete Knutson's oldest son now fishes alongside him, while his younger son runs their marketing operations and Pete fights to keep the possibility of such family fishing operations alive. "That means holding the line," he says, "against the giant processors who would drive the prices down to where we can't make a living, against the real estate interests that would like to make us like quaint animals in the zoo, and against the mining and timber interests that would destroy the watersheds where the salmon need to breed." Pete works "so that everyone's kids can inherit a healthy planet."

I've mentioned how activists use the image of looking into a mirror, to take stock of their lives and choices. Our children serve as this mirror as well, reflecting who we are—and who we might become, if only we make the effort. We want them to be proud of how we live, and what we stand for. "The young man who stole from my store," said Chris Kim, "could have been anyone in a desperate situation, even one of my kids. If I set myself a standard of how to love people, I believe my own children will follow."

We live up to that standard best when we act in common, and for the common good. Many of the white people of Jackson, Mississippi, responded to desegregation by sending their children to private schools. As a result, the political base for school taxes shrank and public funding declined precipitously. Without a strong educational system, those left behind seemed doomed to a future of despair. But in 1989, a group of white professional parents, convinced that their children needed to learn in real-world classrooms among children whose diversity reflected that of America, decided to send their kids to public schools and to recruit other families to do the same.

The group they formed, Parents for Public Schools, enlisted 600 families like themselves who would normally have fled the system, then approached middle-class African American parents who'd similarly fled to the suburbs. They helped pass a $35-million school bond issue, Jackson's first since desegregation, and created a model for parents in other cities. Though they had fears about their decision, they felt that abandoning the public schools would shortchange their children by passing on a meaner society. Also, as one parent said, "I want my children to know kids of different backgrounds, not just those who are white and middle-class. I want them to be educated in a world like the world that they're going to live in." Twenty years later, Parents for Public Schools has grown into a national organization with chapters in eleven states, helping parents engage with local schools and to influence the local, state, and national decisions that affect their children's futures, like the high-stakes, one-size-fits-all testing regime created by the No Child Left Behind act.

As these parents recognized, our most fundamental responsibility as citizens is to love not only our own children, but other people's children as well—including children we will never meet, who grow up in situations we'd prefer to ignore. To be sure, we'll always listen most attentively to the cries of our own sons and daughters. But if we don't heed the cries of others' as well, America will be lost, and we'll risk losing our souls. As the Buddha said, we need to "love the whole world as a mother loves her only child." For only then do we honor the ties that bind us together—that make us human.

SEASONS OF A CITIZEN

The life of Atlanta activist Sonya Vetra Tinsley exemplifies the balancing act—attending to both work and family, private and public concerns—that many of us try to perform at different moments in our lives. Her community music project, Serious Fun, had a powerful impact, accomplishing pretty much everything she'd hoped for it. But after three years, Sonya decided it was time to move on. Having performed her own songs in clubs and at political benefits, she decided to risk making her musical career her priority, trying to combine social involvement and artistic passion, "like the musicians I've always most admired." She still "went through lots of soul-searching and guilt about backing away from direct organizing. But if I didn't give it a try at some point, I'd always wonder."

Sonya liked the idea that "people like myself may end up listening to my music, but also ten-year-old girls who are just beginning to think about how they fit into the world, so I can help teach them how to keep going when the odds look worse than ridiculous." Working with musicians she'd met through Serious Fun, Sonya began performing around Atlanta. She got some promising reviews, and with the help of an experienced producer, cut a CD of wise, funny songs about life, politics, and love, with a voice that fell between Whitney Houston and Sheryl Crow. Although she received some major-league bites (including being signed by the manager of Hootie and the Blowfish), a recording contract never came through. Gradually, she started thinking about more personal dreams. She'd gotten married a couple years before and was helping raise a now-teenage stepson. But she decided that she wanted a child of her own.

For the next few years, Sonya focused on her daughter, Sophia Joi, as well as her regular day job, while continuing to work with some local projects, like hosting house parties and canvassing Atlanta neighborhoods for Obama. "I felt bad that I couldn't be as involved at this stage of my life as I had been earlier. But sometimes all you can do is get by day to day, and suddenly two years have gone by."

"The biggest lesson," Sonya said, "was realizing that all this other work I want to do will still be there, but there's really only one opportunity to be Sophia Joi's mom when she's a year or two years old, and to help her become an engaged, compassionate, and joyful person." Motherhood also grounded Sonya, "making it much more personal to help create a certain kind of world for her, and not leaving that for someone else to do."

Being a parent, Sonya said, "has made me realize we're in this for the long haul. We'll have seasons where we're more actively involved in organizations and public life, and seasons where we focus more internally, on home and hearth. Each moment shapes the other. When I can't attend a meeting because I have to pick Sophia Joi up, or worry about whether she has adequate education and health care, or have to take care of my mom if she's sick—these are the issues that the majority of people on the planet are dealing with. If I stay in a bubble where I think these things are just obstacles or inconveniences getting in the way of my real work, then I'm probably missing the point."

As Sophia Joi grew, Sonya found more time. "By the time she was three, I began to come out of my cocoon. I joined the board of a nonprofit that sponsors weekly programming on women's issues, race, class, homophobia, you name it. I organized a 'baby shower' for an organization that helps care for homeless children who get sick or don't have anywhere to go once released from the hospital. But my main project I call Strengths for America, an idea to bring coaching approaches to community service and social change groups."

The project emerged from Sonya's day job for the international accounting and consulting firm Deloitte Touche Tohmatsu. At first it was just a way to pay the bills and get health insurance, but she ended up in their career coaching division. Deloitte's coaches worked with company staffers at every level, from mail room employees to top managers and potential partners. They helped them assess their gifts and skills through reflective conversation and standard tests like Myers-Briggs and StrengthsFinder, then explored ways to best match what they liked to do with the needs of the organization.

Seeing the value of this approach, Sonya thought about using it for social change work. "I felt like this is too useful just to be used to help executives climb in their careers. It's all over the corporate world because it works. We've learned a lot about how to help people become more productive with the right kind of support. We don't blink an eye about corporate managers using it, but what about people who can't pay two hundred dollars an hour? What about social change groups?"

Sonya had learned a lot about listening and building relationships through a training she'd taken from the Industrial Areas Foundation, the network that sponsored Virginia Ramirez's COPS group. "But most social change organizations are so overloaded and stressed, so caught up in their day-to-day struggles, that all they can do is think 'Here are the tasks we need. How can we fill them?' Sometimes you do just need whoever you can get to make phone calls or canvass, but you also lose people who might love to do something else. I'd like to help plug people in where they have a passion and a gift."

Sonya began to assemble a team of people to help her launch an Atlanta pilot project, drawing on both her coaching and activist networks. She envisioned getting professional coaches to volunteer or work at reduced rates with community groups, as well as to train lay people as peer coaches, "because even if they won't be as expert, they can still play a powerful role without breaking the bank financially. I'd love to get every PTA, church group, and social action campaign looking at people in the room, finding out who they are and what are the things that light them up inside, then involving them in ways that fit them best." She thought this would increase the effectiveness of the groups as well as their active supporters, and make it easier for people to stay involved for the long haul. After working out the bugs locally, she planned to approach national social change groups and funders to extend the model to other cities and states.

"Sometimes your life path isn't a straight line," Sonya says. "You can approach the same destination, but with detours. Sometimes you have to go around the back way. I'm still focused a lot on being an available and attentive mother to Sophia Joi, but an essential component of being a good mother is giving her the opportunity to see me pursuing goals that make a greater difference in the world."

CHAPTER EIGHT

Village Politics

To carry the message of a cause in a community when you are a generally respected neighbor is far better than when you do it as virtually your sole activity in public.

—*KARL HESS*

Virginia Tech freshman Angie De Soto didn't vote in the 2004 election. The president, she thought, had nothing to do with her life. She didn't care who won. Instead, she and friends played a drinking game in one of their dorm rooms. They divided into random "red" and "blue" teams, and chugged a beer each time new results on TV favored their team. Angie woke up the next morning hungover and with no idea of the election outcome, but it hardly seemed to matter.

When Angie started college, she focused mostly on her social life and picked her classes almost at random. But midway through a resources geology lecture course, her professor told the students, "I'm going to talk about an issue that's going to change your whole future." For two days, he discussed global climate change, and Angie, who'd never heard of it, was stunned. She called her mother, who worked as a teacher, and said "Mom, I just learned about global warming. What is this? Have you heard about it?" Her mother had no idea what Angie was talking about even after she tried to explain it. "Neither did any of the girls on my hall," Angie said. "I just kept asking myself why I hadn't heard about something this

important, and why more people weren't doing anything about it.
Didn't they know? Didn't they care? Did they just not know what
to do?"

Virginia Tech had a nascent student group called the Environmental Coalition, but Angie had never encountered them. The group's
presence was negligible on the school's largely politically disengaged campus of 28,000. Angie was too shy to approach her professor, and she didn't know what to do beyond trying to learn more
through searching out related Web sites and taking an environmental policy class the next term. Then, while Angie was walking across
campus one day, a young woman from the Environmental Coalition
approached her to sign a petition for a green fee, by which "students
would pay a bit extra to support the campus recycling program and
small efficiency projects." Angie started going to EC meetings. Although she liked the people, their ideas, and the effort they were
making, she felt they weren't making the impact that they could;
they did little to bring in new members, and administrators wouldn't
return their phone calls or e-mails. "We'd talk about the same things
each week without making much progress." All that changed when
Angie received a scholarship to attend a student climate conference
at Yale. "They taught us everything about how to organize: how to
recruit people, plan events, run effective meetings, develop leadership, raise money, and lead large-scale campaigns. I came back incredibly charged up, eager to teach as many other students as I
could what I'd learned. For the first time, I began to feel like this
was my calling, what I'm supposed to be doing on this planet. That
one class changed my life with a sense of what we're facing. I felt I
finally had the skills to do something about it."

Through her involvement, Angie learned about the Public Interest Research Groups (PIRG). The PIRGs combine campus organizing with neighborhood canvasses and legislative campaigns, and
Obama worked for them for three months before his Chicago organizing job. After finding a Sacramento, California, PIRG office that
was working for a state cap on climate emissions, she accepted an
aunt's invitation to stay with her there. Angie worked thirteen hours

a day for the PIRG as a field manager, which included knocking on doors to talk with people about the issue and why their voices mattered. Angie had been working since her first year of high school, including fifteen hours a week in the Virginia Tech dining halls, and "this was more hours for less money than any job I'd had. But I loved it. It was one of the best experiences of my life."

The PIRGs helped pass the California state climate change bill, and Angie returned to Virginia "on top of the world. Before, I was too intimidated to approach people because we just didn't talk about environmental issues on our campus. Now I'd go up to everyone, because everyone needed to get educated and involved." She kicked the EC into high gear, setting up a major concert with local bands and training members to approach local media, gather names for the e-mail list, and table at the student center. "We'd approach people as they walked by and ask if they wanted to stop global warming. Then we'd talk about the issues and try to get them involved. I had grown a thick skin from getting the door slammed all those times when I was canvassing, so if they didn't respond I just asked the next person."

As Angie's involvement deepened, she found more ways to act on her newfound convictions. She organized with her campus group to bring over a hundred Virginia Tech students to Power Shift, a national student climate change conference held at the University of Maryland. Angie helped plan the entertainment, and as she looked out from the stage at 6,000 students, she "felt for the first time like we really have a movement." Her group came back highly energized, and the next year hosted a local Power Shift for other Virginia schools.

Working with eighteen other student groups, the EC built a Coalition for Campus Sustainability. It included the college Republicans, which delighted Angie because, as she stressed, "this was an issue that should transcend political parties." Meanwhile, the campus recycling department hired her to coordinate and train a team of thirty student volunteers who educated dorm residents on environmental issues and ways to reduce their individual impact. The young head of all the residence halls was highly supportive, and also invited her to sit on his sustainability task force and promoted her as a resource to other administrators.

As the EC continued to build its base of support, it became one of the school's largest student groups, with a 1,600-name listserv. And they finally got a meeting with college president Charles Steger. "We went in very organized," Angie said. "We dressed professionally, were professional in our tone and word choice, and brought thoroughly researched proposals." The group members asked Steger to join 600 of his peers who had signed the national Presidents' Climate Commitment. Steger balked at just signing a statement and instead offered to create a comprehensive campus plan, which he said would mean far more. He commissioned a committee of administrators, faculty, and students to draft a plan by fall. The committee hired Angie as a temporary staffer, and she spent the summer pulling together ideas and highly specific implementation plans from the EC group and from other schools. "This issue can be so overpowering," she said, "but if we bring it down to what we can do as individuals and as a campus, people feel they can make a difference." Although administrators initially said no to some suggestions, "we didn't freak out. You have to keep approaching them, coming up with new ideas, offering reasonable and feasible solutions."

The group completed the plan, and Angie was hired to carry it out as university policy. Among the many changes, the school enacted comprehensive recycling procedures, switched to high-efficiency light bulbs, installed energy-saving occupancy sensors in the classrooms, and took steps to ensure that new buildings would meet strong environmental standards. The campus saved $200,000 in just one month by lowering winter thermostats to a still-comfortable 68 degrees—and would save more by slightly raising the summer settings. The dining halls decreased food waste by 38 percent by eliminating trays and developed a plan for composting the rest. The university also pledged to explore alternative fuels, make environmentally responsible purchasing a priority, and look into additional efficiency gains, including phasing out their aging coal-fired boilers.

"I started out just an apathetic drunken party girl, with no clear path in my life," Angie said. "Now I'm implementing our campus sustainability plan. People change and even massive institutions can change."

BAPTISTS TO REACH BAPTISTS

The central strategy that Angie and her group adopted—using the face-to-face networks within their community to reach out to fellow students and administrators, gain allies, and address larger issues—could be characterized as village politics. This approach taps into the web of independent organizations that political theorists call civil society. At Virginia Tech, these organizations included the dorms, the fraternities and sororities, the student government, and other campus organizations, activist or not. In the community, they span schools, churches, temples, bicycle clubs, softball leagues, PTAs, Rotary Clubs, babysitting co-ops, unions, and other groups like Pete Knutson's fishermen's association. At times, these networks insulate us from difficult social problems, segregating us by class, race, and belief system. Yet they can also provide a powerful structure for raising critical public issues with the people likely to take our perspectives most seriously: colleagues, coworkers, neighbors, and friends.

The more these groups are independent of governmental or corporate power, the more latitude their members have to think through ideas and act on them together. "In such *havens*," writes sociologist Eric Hirsch, "people can easily express concerns, become aware of common problems, and begin to question the legitimacy of institutions that deny them the means for resolving those problems."

I first thought about the power of these institutions after meeting Bill Cusak, a Baptist preacher in Florence, South Carolina. Although Bill had never organized anything more controversial than a revival meeting, he became concerned that the Reagan-era nuclear arms race was risking his granddaughter's future. The issue challenged him "like a crowbar to my soul." Bill approached a community college biologist who'd written a letter to the local paper, and they began building an activist community from scratch. They spoke and showed a video on the arms race at every church, PTA, and garden club that would have them. They enlisted a key African American pastor and asked younger church members to enlist their friends.

One of the first groups Bill addressed was the local Rotary Club, where he was a longtime member. "They kind of treated me like I had the plague," he recalled later. But eventually some responded. "Basically," he said, "it takes like to reach like: youth to reach youth; blacks to reach blacks; Catholics to reach Catholics. I even think," he added with a sly smile, "it takes Baptists to reach Baptists." Moving from this issue to others like homelessness, Bill began to change his community.

When dialogue begins to take place in the ordinary domains of daily life, previously uninvolved people can find new ways to speak out and influence common choices. As political scientist John Gaventa points out in his book *Power and Powerlessness,* power isn't only a question of who prevails when issues are contested. Power also hinges on the rules and institutional structures that allow access to debate, and the mechanisms that "prevent conflict from arising in the first place."

Village politics can give us a way to challenge these mechanisms by building on already-existing relationships to raise national or even global issues. Granted, some contexts are more intimate and approachable than others, like the Virginia Tech campus or a small town like Florence. But even cities such as Los Angeles, New York, or Chicago are vast patchworks of smaller communities. Each neighborhood, business, fraternal organization, or church group represents a potentially fertile field for public discussion. We each have access to some of these communities. When we use these networks to promote humane social visions, we can build on existing bonds of human conviviality and connection, and we have the advantage of acting where people know us. As Karl Hess, a former Barry Goldwater speechwriter turned Vietnam War opponent, once wrote: "To carry the message of a cause in a community when you are a generally respected neighbor is far better than when you do it as virtually your sole activity in public."

Neighbor-to-neighbor outreach has long been crucial to the growth of successful citizen efforts. We saw this when COPS worked within congregations and neighborhoods in the San Antonio barrios. When citizens in Maine reached out to every conceivable community organization to pass their pioneering Clean Elections initiative. Or when Mothers Against Drunk Driving sought the assistance of local PTAs. We've seen it in church-based engagement representing all political perspectives, from opposition to the Vietnam and Iraq wars to mobilizing against abortion and gay rights.

I've mentioned a University of Michigan student group, Greeks for Peace. They brought critical social issues into the traditionally disengaged domain of their university's fraternity and sorority system. As a result, people who otherwise would never have taken an interest began to respond. While these students wouldn't have walked across the quad to hear the exact same speakers discussing these issues, they responded when peers invited them to events held in safe and familiar environments, like the lounge of a major sorority. "So much politics," said one of the founders "is geared for those already involved. We wanted a vehicle for people to be with their friends and learn to take a stand together."

A similarly intimate community helped engage me as a Stanford freshman. Although I'd been politically active in high school, I didn't do much my first quarter at college. Then I joined a Vietnam study group in my freshman dorm. I'd felt intimidated by similar courses, but this one was pass/fail, taught by a grad student, and in a safe environment. Along with the other students who'd signed up, I soon got involved in trying to stop the war. The experience moved me so much that I resolved to replicate its model the following year, enlisting graduate students to teach similar courses, hooking them up with sympathetic faculty sponsors, and canvassing freshman dorms to find willing students to host them. We ended up with 500 participants, many of whom also got involved in the anti-war effort.

ENGAGED COMMUNITIES

Mobilizing our villages can give us both the confidence and means to address common political and economic problems. The community of support we build can also ease the inevitable frustrations of working for social change, helping us endure the endless phone calls, meetings, and other repetitive tasks needed to galvanize people to act.

Mary Catherine Bateson describes how this process unfolded in the feminist consciousness-raising groups of the early 1970s. "Here, women gave one another mutual support and pooled their experience, adding an analytical process of mutual comparisons to move toward insight. . . . For many women, the greatest discovery of these groups was that other women could be companions rather than rivals. They learned the value of shared experiences and the benefits of solidarity, becoming friends." A comparable process occurred in Latin America's Basic Christian Communities. Peasants read the Bible together and discussed their common economic suffering. These communities created profound democratic ripples both in the Latin American Catholic church and in their societies as a whole. As part of the civil rights movement, Freedom Schools employed a similar model to teach people basic literacy and political skills, and to nurture their spirits.

Perhaps the greatest immediate benefit of engaged communities is that they remind us that standing up for our beliefs is a great deal easier when we're standing shoulder to shoulder with others. "How hard it is to go on singing when one sings alone," writes prison poet Tim Blunk. Engaged communities teach us that change comes only when we climb the mountain together. At their best, their purposefulness, generosity, and reciprocity anticipate the world we seek to create.

Engaged communities span all political perspectives. Think of America's megachurches, which have congregations of as many as 47,000 members. These all-encompassing institutions satisfy nearly every human need, offering groups for parenting, teens, singles, singing, and soccer. They build a sense of purpose in a time when that feeling is scarce, and speak to people's longing for community.

Those who attend these churches experience the same time crunches as everyone else does in our society, but their religious village gives them both practical support and spiritual nurturance. You have more free hours if you're part of a group that helps look after your children, visits you when you get sick, and shares a car pool on the freeway. Consequently, many of their members have gotten politically involved, primarily with conservative causes like opposing abortion and gay rights (although prominent megachurch leaders like Rick Warren and Joel Hunter have also begun to take on issues like poverty and climate change). If more of us had such supportive structures, we'd be less likely to view political involvement as just one more imposition on our already overburdened and fragmented lives.

What is there for those who are more secular, or who attend smaller churches that are less focused on meeting every practical need? The political movements of the 1930s built a cultural infrastructure that made it easier for people to be politically active and win major victories like Social Security, unemployment insurance, a national minimum wage, and the eight-hour workday. These movements flourished not only because they addressed acute needs in the context of an urgent economic crisis but also because they also helped participants fulfill their needs for cultural expression and community cohesiveness within an activist context. Drawing on traditions developed by earlier populist, labor, and socialist movements, activists in certain cities could conduct almost every aspect of their lives in politically supportive environments: They could read a sympathetic newspaper; go to work in a shop represented by an engaged union; participate with fellow activists in a softball league, chorus, or theater group; send the children to a progressive summer camp or join kindred spirits at a resort; get medical care through a medical co-op; attend political lectures, concerts, and rallies; live in a labor or socialist retirement home; and be buried by a progressive co-op funeral society. Of course, these supportive worlds could also breed a dangerous insularity, encouraging members of the American Communist Party, for instance, to deny the horrors of the ghastly Soviet system. But overall, the interlocking cultural and economic institutions of the time created a powerful base for change.

Throughout the civil rights movement, black churches met similar needs for a community independent of the dominant culture. Although they didn't provide such all-encompassing systems of support, they did offer activists a practical, social, and spiritual refuge that supported their immensely difficult struggles. The largely white youth movements of the 1960s tried to build their own oppositional counterculture, as did groups like the Black Panthers, with their community schools and free breakfast programs and health clinics (leaving aside the Panthers' more unsavory aspects). The youth movements and their slightly older supporters didn't sponsor old-age homes, but they did create countless food co-ops, low-cost law and medical clinics, and back-to-the-land efforts, and nurtured their engagement through politically oriented music.

Leaving aside online villages, which I'll discuss later, the most success in building on-the-ground social-justice subcultures has come from activists who are rooted in religious traditions and communities. Churches, synagogues, and mosques offer an institutional base, a common moral framework, and a community with the avowed goal of serving others. At their best, when religious social-justice activists take on common problems, they do so with a vision that sees God—and therefore hope—in every person they meet. "Going to church helps me re-evaluate myself," says Virginia. "It reminds me why I'm doing what I'm doing, and gives me the strength that I need. If I wasn't close to the church, or to God, I don't think I'd be able to continue."

BOWLING ALONE

Creating any kind of engaged community is harder when many institutions that might once have offered a foundation have themselves eroded. In a highly influential book called *Bowling Alone,* Harvard political theorist Robert Putnam observes that since the mid-1960s, Americans steadily reduced their participation not only in voting, but also in traditional forms of community involvement, such as the PTA, the League of Women Voters, unions, mainstream churches, the Boy Scouts and Campfire Girls, and service clubs like the Lions and Kiwanis. Participation in these groups, Putnam suggests, creates what he calls "social capital," webs of connection that help people to work together to pursue shared objectives. But his work explored ways that American's social capital has declined. As an example, Putnam noted that local bowling leagues had seen a 40 percent decline in membership since 1980. During the same period, however, the number of individuals who actually bowled rose (to the point where it exceeded the number who voted in most congressional elections). Putnam and his Harvard colleague, Theda Skocpol, also decried the shift of many advocacy groups from local grassroots participation to a large inactive base whose members did nothing more than writing checks to support researchers, media spokespeople, and Washington, D.C., lobbyists, a trend Skocpol called *Diminished Democracy* in her book on the topic. As both argued, these shifts boded ill for America, because the more socially isolated our citizens became, the fewer chances they'd have for the kinds of conversations that fuel public involvement.

Putnam examined various likely causes for the decline, including the increase in working hours, the fact that women who once would have volunteered now had to pull double shifts by working outside the home while still doing most of the housework and child care, and a trend toward suburbanization that left people more physically separated. While Putnam thought these factors all played some role, the declines he chronicled cut across cities and suburbs, the married and the single, working men, working women, and stay-at-home moms. The key change, Putnam concluded, was the steadily increasing influence of television, to which he would later add all the other screens in front of which people sat, passively entertained. Regardless of background or current circumstances, the more people watched TV, he found, the less they involved themselves in civic activities of any kind, and the more mistrusting and pessimistic they become about human nature. As their sense of connectedness and common purpose eroded, they found it easier to scapegoat others, to view the world in unforgiving terms, and to believe that ordinary citizens could do nothing to shape our common history. This is all the more troubling given that extensive TV watching now begins in early childhood, and that the average American now spends four-and-a-half hours at it every day—not even counting the time we devote to playing video games and randomly surfing the Web. Hours spent staring at screens can indeed breed isolation, although Putnam could not have predicted how online technologies can also reconnect and empower us, a development I'll address shortly.

Critics of Putnam mentioned exceptions like the megachurches, booming youth soccer leagues, self-help associations like Alcoholics Anonymous, and robust political organizations from the Sierra Club to the National Rifle Association and the Christian Coalition. They also pointed out, as Russell Dalton has stressed in *The Good Citizen,* that while this seeming disconnection from common life seemed to have affected voting, other measures of citizen participation in public issues have been increasing, like the willingness of people to sign a petition, participate in a boycott, contact a local official or community leader, or try to convince others to vote for a candidate they support. But most analysts agreed that community in general was declining.

FISHING TOGETHER

This erosion means that we often need to rebuild our villages and direct them toward engagement with the world at the same time. Pete Knutson took this approach with his fellow fishermen: First he helped bring them together; then he helped involve the community in larger public issues. The son of a plainspoken Lutheran minister, Pete grew up in the hardscrabble mill town of Everett, Washington.

He had a Barry Goldwater poster on his wall because, as he said, "Goldwater spoke his mind." At first, Pete supported the Vietnam War and even got a jingoistic letter published on the youth page of the local paper. His views changed as friends who'd fought in the war came home feeling betrayed, and told him, "Don't believe anything the military tells you. They always lie." Before long, Pete was organizing an antiwar moratorium at his high school; then he went off to Stanford, and became the only draft-age man to testify before Congress. He even got his fifteen minutes of fame on the national news, after Senator Strom Thurmond stormed out when Pete had the audacity to ask a Senate committee, "If you're so eager to fight this war, why don't you pick up an M16 and lead the first wave?"

Pete began fishing to work his way through college. Soon, fishing became a way of life, as he bought his own boat to support his wife and two young sons. At the same time he helped build the Puget Sound Gillnetters' Association, which enabled members to market fish jointly, lobby on laws that affected them, and gain leverage against the giant canneries. "I felt we had to trust each other," he says. "If we didn't, we had no chance." The association became a base through which fishermen gradually became conversant with large ecological issues, such as the destruction of salmon habitat, upon whose outcome their livelihoods depended.

Pete worked steadily to bridge the gap between fishermen and the generally more middle-class environmentalists. That was no easy task, given longstanding mutual mistrust fed by class divides and stereotypes. Yet a coalition did in fact emerge, and the fishermen brought a powerful blue-collar presence to issues like the Endangered Species Act and habitat protection. Both Pete's ethical stand and pride in craft were evoked by the bumper sticker on his truck: "Jesus Was a Gillnetter."

This hard-won and unexpected alliance proved critical when Initiative 640 threatened to shut down the gillnetters' operations by banning the nets they used. The fishermen held joint press conferences with environmental groups, picketed a pleasure-boat company that was a prime initial backer of the initiative, and generally

refused to succumb quietly to their opponents' well-financed campaign. They survived because Pete, along with a few others, had
helped change their vision from one of narrow self-interest to a
more complex and sustainable ethic, best summed up when he spoke
of nurturing the salmon habitat "so my kids can fish, too, and everyone's children can inherit a healthy planet." More recently, Pete
has shifted his focus to defending Fisherman's Terminal as a working industrial community, against the Port of Seattle's repeated attempts to replace it with high-priced real estate developments. First
the fishermen learned to work together, then to reach beyond their
own ranks. Building their association's internal cohesion made it
easier for them to tackle difficult issues later on.

COMMUNITIES OF THE VOICELESS

Veteran community organizer Arnold Graf described the challenge
of trying to pull people together in a time when individuals are often
isolated. "When I'm out organizing in a community, I always feel like
I'm in a vacuum. There's nothing to hook up to." Graf works with
the Industrial Areas Foundation (IAF), the parent organization of
the COPS group that changed Virginia Ramirez's life. Their network
promotes some of the most systematic attempts to practice village
politics in low-income communities.

COPS began with straightforward issues like bringing more city
services to desperately underserved Latino neighborhoods. The organization then moved on to address education, job training, and
community economic development. They focused in particular on
the invisible leaders who'd long held together local churches and
PTAs. Other IAF affiliates in such places as Houston, Baltimore,
and the Brooklyn neighborhood of East New York have experienced similar successes. Critics note that local affiliates still hesitate
to join coalitions on national issues that affect their largely low-
income constituencies—budget priorities, equitable taxation, welfare
politics, campaign reform, and environmental justice. The affiliates
have also had a hard time enlisting people who don't already belong

to existing institutions. But they've made tremendous strides in helping people like Virginia Ramirez reclaim their voice, change their
lives, and empower their communities.

This kind of empowerment is particularly important for those
who inhabit the bottom of the economic pyramid. People who occupy a comfortable professional position face their own constraints:
Involvement is discretionary, and the wounds of others can easily
fade to abstraction. But if we're coming from the bottom, common
action is both essential and also more difficult. We're far more likely
to be overwhelmed by day-to-day survival. If we do have extra energy, we're tempted to use it to work toward escaping our impoverished community. And if we do stay, by choice or necessity, our
friends and neighbors face greater despair, wield less institutional
power, and have less room to maneuver than individuals coming
from more privileged circumstances. We're also more likely to be
disconnected from the skills, connections, even the information
that we need to change our communities. This makes efforts like
those of COPS and similar groups all the more important—and
admirable.

LET'S NOT TALK ABOUT THE BAD THINGS

I've discussed ways that our everyday villages can help us get involved. But they can suppress as well as expand civic dialogue, reinforce our moral cocoons as well as dissolve them. They can breed
parochialism, which can easily become complacency. In my time at
the massive Hanford nuclear complex, for instance, I visited churches
and schools, bridge clubs and bars, virtually every domain of everyday life. Participants in the nuclear enterprise rarely discussed the
downside of their work—neither the potential for global annihilation
from bombs created with the plutonium they produced, nor their
enterprise's major environmental consequences. As one Hanford
wife said, when I raised these questions, "Let's not talk about the
bad things."

Hanford may be an extreme example, but I see a similar culturally and economically reinforced silence in other domains. Corporate whistleblowers often risk their careers. Southerners resisting the civil rights movement fired blacks who spoke out, and they used social pressure to isolate whites who supported integration. In Amarillo, Texas, the local United Way cut off all funds to Catholic Family Services because Bishop Leroy Matthiesen had suggested that workers who assembled nuclear warheads at the nearby Pantex plant should consider the moral implications of their work.

The desire for community approval can make it harder to bring up urgent social concerns, especially among people who know and respect us. We may fear being branded as dissenters merely for raising controversial ideas. Occasionally, our passivity is the result of misplaced politeness: We don't want to discomfit people we care about. We fear the tension that emerges when we switch from discussing the latest movies or the fate of our favorite sports team to voicing emotionally loaded issues. We're afraid of triggering family fights or jeopardizing our friendships.

"It's always harder to take a stand in your own neighborhood and community," says Suzy Marks, "to leaflet at your own local market or synagogue. Most of us got involved after being approached by someone we knew. But that doesn't make it easier. If I'm really brave, why was I so hesitant and ashamed to talk about these issues with my friends? It's simpler with people who don't know you. You can always raise hell in a strange town."

Shortly after the 2004 election, I met a community activist who ran a hair salon in conservative rural Washington. When talking with her clients she'd raised her reservations about President Bush and the war in Iraq. Although she lost some customers as a result, and consciously held her tongue with certain others, she kept speaking her mind as much as she could. A couple of years later, she e-mailed to tell me that some who'd left had since returned and now shared her perspectives. It reminded me that large political changes can be fed by millions of small conversations, where people talk with neighbors, coworkers, and friends, and shift public sentiments one-by-one.

French philosopher Michel Foucault and other social theorists in his tradition view daily life as a web of domination that suppresses critical dialogue at every turn and can be challenged only through "transgression" at the margins. I'd argue that the actual picture is far more complex and more promising. True, social norms can discourage open dialogue regarding the most important questions that we face. But the networks and associations of civil society can serve a broad range of purposes, either hampering or promoting an ethic of common responsibility. It's up to us to move them toward the latter by building on community-oriented values that are often given lip service but not always carried out in practice. That's what Angie did at Virginia Tech, and what Pete did with his fellow fishermen. To be sure, it's a risk to "talk about the bad things" within these networks. But if we act with enough courage and vision, we can transform them into conduits for addressing our most critical public concerns.

A NEW THREAD IN THE WEAVE

Here's an example of changing the culture in a community that seems an unlikely venue for change: A surfer (and computer scientist) named Glenn Hening began worrying about the pollution and deterioration of the California beaches near his home. He'd just become a father and wondered whether his daughter would be able to enjoy the beaches when she was older. He was also increasingly angry at the stereotype of surfers as dumb blond party animals "whose total vocabulary consists of 'hang ten,' 'cowabunga,' and 'far out.' " He decided to counteract that image by persuading his fellow surfers to "use their skills to protect the marine environment for all of us."

Glenn first talked to surfer friends who were similarly concerned. Their inaugural effort addressed a Malibu lagoon where spillage of polluted water was damaging the shape of the waves on an adjacent beach. The group, now called the Surfrider Foundation, next challenged the dumping of contaminated waste into that same lagoon. Fellow surfers enlisted in droves.

Surfrider went on to win the second-largest Clean Water Act

suit in American history, stopping pulp mills from polluting northern California's Humboldt Bay. Members testified at hearings, filed
lawsuits, educated schoolchildren about marine ecology, challenged
destructive developments, and monitored coastal water pollution
levels nationwide. They enlisted swimmers, divers, beachcombers,
windsurfers, and sympathetic environmental scientists. The organization now has 50,000 members in chapters throughout the United
States, plus affiliates in eighteen other countries on five continents.

Glenn believes he's helped change the culture of his community.
"Thirty years ago, a beach full of surfers would end up being a
beach full of trash. We let developers wreck some of the finest surfing areas on the planet. That doesn't happen anymore. By now, the
issues we've raised have gained the attention of surfers everywhere.
They think about water quality, the impact of development, the need
for government agencies to protect the environment. We created a
new thread in the weave of what it means to be a surfer."

Wherever we are, we can apply a similar ethic of responsibility,
engaging our local villages to take on even the most daunting global
issues. In the spring of 2005, Seattle Mayor Greg Nickels saw in a
report that the snow-pack that fed Seattle's hydroelectric power
had been steadily declining in recent years. He "realized that climate
disruption wasn't something a long time in the future or far, far
away but here and now." He also realized that he could do things
as a mayor to tackle the problem, regardless of what might happen in Washington, D.C. Nickels proposed that the city government decrease greenhouse gas emissions to 1990 levels, as the Kyoto
Treaty mandated, and challenged the city's major employers to do
the same. In less than three years, the government lowered its greenhouse emissions below the initial target. Some of Seattle's largest
companies did the same. Meanwhile, Nickels and seven other mayors sent a letter inviting even more of their counterparts to join in
the effort.

A thousand cities have now signed the U.S. Mayor's Climate
Protection Agreement, and many of them have moved even faster
than Seattle. In Salt Lake City, mayor Rocky Anderson reduced his
municipal government's emissions by a staggering 31 percent in three

years through such measures as retrofitting traffic lights, radically expanding public transportation, and converting methane gas from the city's wastewater plant and landfill to electricity. Every participating city can tell stories of similar initiatives, often galvanized by grassroots efforts.

VIRTUAL VILLAGES

We've been talking about traditional communities. But most of us also inhabit newer virtual villages that have become so woven into the fabric of our lives that we take them for granted, almost as much as the air we breathe. When Robert Putnam first described the decline of American community in 1995, the Web as we know it was only three years old. Neither Putnam nor those who disagreed with him could foresee how much online forms of connection would provide both new kinds of community and new ways to take action. We routinely keep in touch with far-flung friends and colleagues through e-mail, text messaging, and social networking sites like Facebook. When one of my closest friends contracted throat cancer, he blogged about his progress on one site and used another to enable friends and relatives to coordinate delivering meals and driving him to daily radiation treatments. We rely on our online world for information, entertainment, and even romance. It's become so familiar that if our high-speed Internet access is disrupted it almost feels like we've suffered a stroke—like something has blocked the commands we issue from our brain.

We now also rely on our virtual villages when we act politically. If we want to research an issue or connect to a cause, we do so with the click of a mouse. Organizations that would once have reached their members through expensive mailings or time-consuming phone calls now routinely communicate instantly, with minimal cost. As e-mails from MoveOn, the Sierra Club, or the National Rifle Association arrive in our inbox, we simply click and sign, and our Congressional representative receives the letter or petition du jour. Or a group we support sends out a video of an ad it wants to run on national television, we donate $25 (along with 10,000 others), and it shows up in its audience's living rooms two days later.

Newer social networking technologies let individuals connect and take action in even more fluid ways. Meredith Segal started her Students for Barack Obama Facebook group without leaving her campus in Maine. A University of British Columbia freshman named Alex Bookbinder returned from traveling through Burma and created a Facebook group devoted to challenging that country's dictatorship. After membership grew to a quarter million, Burma Campaign UK, Amnesty International, and the international online group Avaaz used Bookbinder's network to launch a Global Day of Action, with major rallies in one hundred cities and thirty countries. When brave Iranians protested a stolen election in 2009, they coordinated and communicated with the world through Facebook, texting, and, as those platforms were blocked, Twitter; in fact, Twitter's role became so critical that Obama's State Department asked the company to delay a scheduled maintenance outage so the network wouldn't interrupt service amid the protests.

Online networks build social capital differently from Putnam's bowling leagues, but their connections can nurture similar bonds of community. People talking about their lives at a Rotary Club meeting aren't so different from individuals networking on Facebook, passing on jokes, videos, photos, and news stories via e-mail, or texting with updates on their daily activities. All build horizontal relationships that can foster public involvement. Online networks can then spread calls to action farther and faster, linking overlapping circles of friends and acquaintances in a manner that was impossible twenty years ago.

For many of us, these electronic communities have become our prime sources of information, our windows onto the larger world for framing the arguments that we make to friends, neighbors, and coworkers. They also create new forms of dialogue. Sarah Brylinsky, a student sustainability coordinator at Ithaca College, recalls a class assignment in which she analyzed news reports on Afghanistan, then posted her analysis as a blog. Within weeks, she had people logging in from Iran, Istanbul, Mexico City, Montreal, and

Afghanistan itself. "I'd analyze a piece on women in Afghanistan, and an Afghan woman would respond, 'I agree with you on this point, but did you consider these other points?' I was getting feedback from people I'd never meet in my life." Of course, this dialogue is only beneficial if the stories we forward or the comments we post do justice to the questions we address, as opposed to passing on lies or furthering an omnipresent culture of distraction.

Once we do get interested in public issues, it's become far easier to invite others to share our concerns. Joe Green, the developer of Facebook Cause, points out that the process is anchored in personal recognition and trust, as in traditional civic organizations. People are more likely to respond when someone they know asks them to donate, sign a petition, or participate in a campaign. In this context, the more we draw on existing networks of connection, the more likely our engagement efforts will succeed. Sarah Brylinsky describes a project in which she and other students placed lines of red removable duct tape on campus buildings, along with explanatory signs, to mark the projected water-level rise at various degrees of global warming. "We asked everyone we knew and every organization to post on their Facebook pages, and to e-mail, Twitter, and text their friends with an explanatory link and the message, 'Are you interested in a guerrilla climate change action? Meet at the flag pole at midnight and bring a friend.' We got two hundred people, most of whom I didn't know. The technologies vastly broadened our base."

Since its inception, online activism has taken advantage of the Internet's viral reach and speed. With 5 million members, MoveOn is the 600-pound gorilla of liberal organizing. But it began accidentally. In September 1998, Joan Blades and Wes Boyd, a previously apolitical Berkeley couple who'd run a software business, became frustrated with the endless circus of the Monica Lewinsky affair. They sent an e-mail to about eighty family members and friends with a link to a one-sentence petition, with space for personal comments, that asked Congress to formally censure President Clinton and then move on to the real problems facing the country. The recipients passed it on to their friends, who then forwarded it to others. Within a week, their petition had generated over 100,000 online signatures, and within a few weeks 300,000. Joan and Wes had intended it as a one-time statement, but given the massive response, they felt a responsibility to use it to help people get involved. Improvising as they went, and drawing on the help of their friends, they sent out follow-up e-mails encouraging people to phone their representatives. Wes then flew to Washington, D.C., to help deliver boxes of petitions, with the help of volunteers he'd recruited online.

After Congress voted for articles of impeachment, Wes and Joan created a political action committee to give those who'd responded another way to act, and circulated additional online petitions and action alerts that let people e-mail their representatives. They pioneered an immensely convenient way for people to participate from the sanctuary of their homes.

Following the 9/11 attacks, a twenty-year-old student named Eli Pariser launched his own petition urging "moderation and restraint" that started with thirty friends and generated a half million names. MoveOn's new executive director began informally advising Pariser, then hired him; within four years, Pariser was running the entire organization, whose membership reached 1.6 million during the lead-up to the Iraq war. MoveOn developed some of the first Web-based remote voter calling programs, and it created local councils so members could undertake their own initiatives in their cities and states. The organization had nearly 2 million members by the time George Soros donated a $2.5 million matching grant for its 2004 electoral work, thus, contrary to right-wing mythology, it was hardly Soros's Machiavellian creation; it has more than doubled since then. And by 2008, MoveOn's small donors contributed $88 million to Obama and millions more for other candidates they supported. Because the core of the group's work takes place online, it is run by only twenty-three staff members who work from home and coordinate via e-mail and conference calls. I remember visiting Joan and Wes at their house, with *Captain Underpants* books on the floor and their daughter running through a backyard sprinkler with a friend—an unlikely but nonetheless effective base for the largest progressive organization in America.

MoveOn achieves its impact primarily through e-mail. Technologies like Facebook draw a younger demographic, while creating more fluid avenues for social involvement. "A college student is much more likely to visit a Facebook group that a friend invited them to," Meredith Segal stressed, "than to browse CNN.com. You build on the connections with people you know, even peripherally."

These advantages, Meredith believed, weren't restricted to campuses. Facebook and whatever technologies would succeed it were stronger, she thought, because they were "structured around natural groups, like schools, places of work, and geographical regions," and they facilitated involvement at various stages of commitment. Facebook also drew on the strengths of an open-access bulletin board. "When you're sending e-mail," said Meredith, "you're still targeting individuals. A bulletin board, like Facebook, is less intrusive and easier to compartmentalize than having everyone send you e-mail and swamping your inbox." You can post information on your Facebook site in a way that would overload other platforms, and you can adjust the settings to target specific groups."

Facebook's loose connections, Meredith stressed, were critical. "Eighty percent of your Facebook friends you don't know well. Maybe you had a class with them, shared an activity, or met at a party. But when they see something that's cool, exciting, or inspirational, they'll share it with all their Facebook friends, and that's how word travels. Each person creates new pathways to engage others, in ways that are inviting, interest provoking, and nonthreatening."

Put differently, online social networks build on what sociologist Mark Granovetter called "the strength of weak ties." Gideon Rosenblatt, who heads ONE/Northwest, an organization that advises environmental groups on the new technologies, says, "The old world that Putnam describes had those weak ties to some degree, but it was based primarily on 'strong ties,' where people stayed in their local familiar networks, and found it hard to bridge out of them. The new tools make it easy to maintain much looser networks that we continue to nurture in easy small ways. And these networks of weak ties can be put into action on a moment's notice, enabling online social change efforts to go viral at a speed and on a scale never previously possible."

New information technologies have also expanded the reach of established organizations and allowed them to collaborate in more fluid ways. Groups from the Sierra Club and NAACP to the NRA and Christian Coalition continue to play a key role in helping citizens create an effective voice, but it's become easier to work with them from the outside, as when the University of British Columbia student helped initiate the global Burma protests. Bill McKibben has been a leading writer and advocate on global climate change since his 1989 book, *The End of Nature*. But he was not an organizer or activist until October 2006, when he and seven of his Middlebury College students got the idea of initiating a day of decentralized rallies and other events around this issue. Rather than continuing to wait for the national environmental groups to create a grassroots presence, they simply picked a date, created a Web site and network called Step It Up, and began inviting everyone they could think of to do whatever they could to help, through an open-source "assign yourself" approach. McKibben enjoyed strong working relationships with major organizations like the Sierra Club and National Resources Defense Council, and they quickly signed on and began passing the word. The students took care of the tech side, media outreach, and logistics. The campaign's centerpiece was a Google Maps site where people could register as they signed up to create local events, with little flags designating their locations across the United States. This allowed people to coordinate directly with others in their communities, while receiving national updates and using the national blog to post their own stories and photos. Besides connecting people, the map tool helped reporters follow the building momentum, thus encouraging major media coverage that engaged even more people. Step It Up eventually organized 1,400 events in every state in the country.

The most sophisticated example I've seen of blending virtual and on-the-ground organizing was the 2008 Obama campaign. Building on approaches pioneered by Howard Dean in 2004, the campaign continually provided new opportunities for volunteers to channel their passion and enthusiasm. People signed up online or by texting at rallies, then received updates, videos, donation requests, and opportunities to join phone banks and door-to-door canvasses. 24-year-old Facebook co-founder Chris Hughes helped the campaign develop its own social networking site, MyBarackObama.com, which allowed supporters to self-organize by establishing or joining local groups, setting up personal fundraising pages, creating independently initiated events, and encouraging people they knew to join the on-the-ground outreach. Although the campaign failed to use its massive list to help volunteers stay engaged after the election, it remains a model for melding online and face-to-face involvement. Obama also benefited from independent online efforts like Meredith's and the will.i.am video, "Yes We Can," which was seen over 22 million times on YouTube and other sites without the campaign spending a dime.

THE SEDUCTIONS OF CLICKING

For all its strengths, online activism has its limits. True, we can pass on information to friends who are on the fence about issues or haven't yet gotten involved, but most of what we do with the new tools reaches the unconvinced only fleetingly, and in a way that's often too peripheral to engage them. Because the threshold of response is so low, the representatives to whom we send our online petitions and automated e-mails can readily discount them. Even those who know us can become so saturated that they dread hearing from us. So while our forwarding, clicking, and networking can help us reach out and be heard, the Internet furthers social and political engagement only when it's used alongside other approaches.

MoveOn's 2006 election efforts illustrate the challenge of persuading people to act offline. The organization mobilized roughly 100,000 members to call Democratic-leaning voters who had a history of only showing up intermittently at the polls. Follow-up studies suggest these calls made the difference in many of the close races that helped shift control of both the Senate and House. But the organization brought about that outcome through the efforts of only 3 percent of its members. The impact would have been even greater had more participated, yet most members didn't make the leap from clicking and sending to picking up the phone or knocking on a door.

This resistance isn't limited to MoveOn or to liberal groups. Citizen organizations of every political persuasion face similar hurdles when attempting to translate online engagement into on-the-ground activism. The reason, I suspect, is vulnerability. We're invisible when we click, even if our name is attached. If people disagree with us or even attack us, we don't see their faces or hear their voices. When we call or knock on someone's door for a cause, we're far more exposed, not to mention ambivalent about intruding on private space. We're even more vulnerable when we raise contentious issues with people who know us. While the new tools can help people take non-threatening first steps, it's a far greater challenge to get them to act in ways that involve more personal outreach.

New technologies have also introduced new ways for us to scatter our attention and to eat up more of our already-burdened time. We can waste entire days and nights clicking on endless strings of Web links, texting, or tweeting about the minutiae of our lives, or being so focused on our Facebook friends that we have little time left for flesh-and-blood relationships, much less larger causes. As repeated psychological studies have shown, constant multitasking often makes us less efficient at everything we do, unable to focus on single tasks as our brain shifts gears over and over again, never remaining in one place long enough to accomplish anything of significance.

Reflection on deeper questions of meaning requires internal and external silence, but for most of us that tranquil, creative silence is increasingly hard to find. Just as our elected representatives are besieged by electronic communications, our Attention Deficient Disorder world creates so many competing claims on our focus that it's now almost impossible to escape the noise, and harder still to distinguish the important claims from the trivial ones. Given the potential of technological resources to distract us, we need, in the words of pioneering green-jobs activist Van Jones, to "stop using them as toys and start using them as tools." I'd add that we also need to place boundaries on even the most powerful of these tools, to remember that they are indeed merely a means to more important ends, not the ends themselves.

We'd also do well to remember that all our new technologies work best when we combine them with more traditional mechanisms of engagement. The Obama campaign complemented its new-media tools by establishing on-the-ground field offices in every corner of key states, recruiting and training local volunteers with deep community roots. MoveOn managed to get a fifth of its members involved in the same election by creating a massive phone bank where members invited other members to participate—using this older and more personal technology to give them the extra encouragement they needed to do what they already believed in. One reason those who worked to elect Obama have had less impact than many had hoped since he took office might be that too much of their more recent engagement has been virtual. They've clicked and signed letters of petitions, maybe called their representatives, but have stopped reaching out to their fellow citizens to shift and mobilize public sentiment.

For all the strengths of online engagement, people still need to gather together, eat, joke, flirt, tell their stories, attach names to faces, and ultimately build deeper levels of trust. And we need to keep reaching out in less glamorous ways, like Angie De Soto sitting at a table in the quad, Harry Taylor joining the Sierra Club vigils, or Rich Cizik approaching key evangelical leaders one-by-one. An activist in the PIRG chapter at the University of Connecticut described how she ignored endless e-mail and Facebook solicitations for worthy causes. "Then someone actually called me. I was just so surprised because people almost don't do that anymore. It's easier to get involved when you're actually talking with another person."

If we assume that people will jump on our favorite bandwagon just because they receive our communiqués and agree with us in principle, we underestimate the degree of inertia in our culture—indeed, in life as a whole. For most people who are contemplating taking their initial steps, often a more intimate approach is required, one that will put them at ease one question at a time, take their hesitation and uncertainty into account, and reassure them that the barriers they face are the same ones we once had to surmount as well. That takes more than virtual communication.

MY OWN VILLAGE ACTIVISM

The most effective organizing effort I've ever undertaken drew on the strengths and resources of existing institutions—specifically, colleges and universities—and challenged them to engage their students in the 2008 election. It blended virtual and on-the-ground activism, and needed both to thrive. And it required the multiple leaps of faith essential to any social change.

In the spring of 2008, I reconnected with a former high school history teacher of mine, whose critical and iconoclastic approach had profoundly influenced my worldview. He was now teaching at a college where I spoke, and we shared our excitement about the resurgent political interest of students and talked about how campuses could encourage this. When I returned home, I checked what the national higher education organizations were doing. Several had excellent Web sites detailing how schools had involved their students in previous elections, but none planned any personal follow-ups to ensure that colleges actually used their valuable examples, suggestions, and templates. This seemed like a huge missed opportunity.

For the next month, I approached everyone I could think of, attempting to convince at least one national group to do some serious outreach to help campuses get their students involved in the election, in a nonpartisan way. But I struck out again and again. The people I contacted were too overloaded, weren't in a position to coordinate an overall campaign, or simply thought that they couldn't make a difference. Then I spoke with the new director of Campus Compact, a network that links campus community service efforts to classroom teaching. I'd worked closely with their previous director and they had the best election-related Web site. The national staff couldn't do more because they were about to move their office to another state, but the director suggested, in an afterthought, that I talk with some of their state affiliates. She didn't sound hopeful.

Because I'd envisioned a major national organization spearheading the effort, I felt defeated. I had all but concluded that my plan was doomed when I called the director of Illinois Compact, whom I knew slightly. I was primed for another rejection, but, to my surprise and delight, she loved the idea of working through the organization's state offices. She suggested I call her Ohio counterpart, who was equally enthusiastic. He even proposed a candidate—a just-graduated student body president from the University of Akron named Kyle Bohland—to coordinate our outreach in his state.

When I spoke with Kyle, I sensed he'd be perfect. He'd just started a new job to help support his wife through law school, but said that he'd take on this project if we could guarantee six months' salary. I hadn't yet approached any potential donors, but decided on the spot to personally guarantee the money so that Kyle could start immediately. This was a major risk; the lectures that supported my work were already beginning to decrease because of the economy, and I'd be on the hook for $20,000 if the donors didn't respond. But I didn't want to lose the opportunity. I took some deep breaths, then told Kyle to go ahead.

The fund-raising wasn't easy. It rarely is. I approached every foundation I could think of, every individual who'd ever supported my work, every potentially interested person who might have access to financial resources. In one case, I began with a ninety-one-year-old liberal Texas insurance magnate, who had declined my first approach when I was fund-raising for *Liberation,* a small political magazine I edited, thirty-five years earlier. We'd stayed in touch, and he'd occasionally given $500 or $1,000 to my projects, but never more. Although he liked this project, he said that the stock portfolio of his family foundation had recently significantly declined in value (this was shortly before the major crash in the fall of 2008), and he'd have to see if it recovered. I was disappointed, but then I e-mailed the material to his son, a political scientist who was on the Foundation board. When we finally spoke on the phone (while he and his family were vacationing in North Dakota), he suggested that I talk with his daughter, a strong student activist who'd just graduated from college. After a few more delays, she and I had a great conversation about how to reach out to traditionally underrepresented schools like community colleges. Thanks to her backing, the family contributed $20,000.

A Florida woman who was battling terminal cancer e-mailed from her hospital bed to donate $4,000. A San Diego hunger action activist gave $15,000 so that Colorado could participate. A group of Ohio foundations came through to support Kyle. I raised $10,000 in mostly smaller donations from the 20,000-name e-mail list of people who receive my monthly articles—my own virtual village. I also decided to contribute $13,000 of my own. Together with money I'd already donated to various campaigns and causes, it was well over a quarter of my income in a year when I was already watching my savings melt away with the plummeting stock market. But the project felt that important, and my donation inspired others to increase their contributions. I ended up raising a total of nearly $200,000, enough to hire staffers in fifteen states.

As more money was pledged, I added new states, allowing their state Compact offices to hire additional staffers to take on the project. They called and e-mailed the schools in their areas, building on the organization's existing relationships. Our ideas drew on national Compact's existing Web site, but also on what we were learning through all our outreach conversations. Just as Angie De Soto figured out how Virginia Tech could make an impact on climate change, we helped campuses use their existing networks and resources to get students to discuss political issues, volunteer in campaigns of their choosing, and turn out at the polls. We also helped schools work with local and state elected officials to steer their students through the Byzantine voting and registration rules—an area where we may have made our greatest impact.

Building on an approach initiated by North Carolina Compact, we also passed out mini-grants to cover things like pizza for debate-watch parties, vans for shuttling students to vote, and publicity for "parades to the polls." Our final grants paid for posters that reached every Minnesota community college, including tribal colleges, to tell students how they could still register on Election Day. Their participation likely decided a Senate race in which the final margin was 312 votes.

Even as we provided suggestions for local staffers, ideas flowed in every possible direction in a way that would have been impossible without the new technologies. Local groups created state-specific Web sites and listservs. They mentored each other, with Kyle taking the lead. They passed on great ideas that emerged from the schools. Other higher education groups, academic associations and youth involvement projects also used our materials, and we helped people connect with each other through our own Google mapping tool, created by a volunteer from my e-mail list. That list also made possible our Virginia effort, after the field director of Youth Service America received my descriptive e-mail and offered to donate the time of two interns. With the help of my assistant, a veteran community organizer, we exchanged resources, tools, and weblinks with these other organizations; helped individual staffers navigate resistant bureaucracies; and kept suggesting new approaches, with a final checklist of last-minute ways schools could turn out their students—like Halloween "trick or vote" efforts, where students dressed in costume to canvass their dorms or staff visible tables in their campus student unions.

Some schools came up with wonderfully creative ideas. North Carolina A&T, a historically black university, combined off-campus service projects with voter registration in low-income neighborhoods. Eastern Michigan University students wore orange arm bands listing issues they cared about. University of Michigan Dearborn created a Web site in partnership with Detroit Public TV, where students across the state uploaded their own election-related videos. At Lorrain Community College, outside Cleveland, volunteers held a "Spray Paint the Vote" event where students painted a statement on T-shirts about why they were voting. Florida State University students formed a flash mob, coordinated by text messaging, where they suddenly gathered in the student union wearing T-shirts saying "I vote for peace" or "I vote for health care." The mob would freeze for five minutes, long enough to let their peers take notice, then disband, reunite elsewhere on campus, and repeat the process.

My favorite project came from the combined campus of University of Colorado Denver, Community College of Denver, and Metro State University, urban commuter schools whose predominantly low-income and minority students were often too overloaded to get involved. But the leader of a student group called the Hip Hop Congress came up with the idea of buying rubber McCain and Obama masks and giant inflatable boxing gloves. His group wore the masks in break-dancing and mock-fighting contests throughout the campus, and in a march to early voting stations. The other students loved it. Colorado Compact distributed masks and boxing gloves to practically every school in the state. And schools in other states bought them as well. It was a wonderful example of the power of imagination to inspire, with the effects rippling ever outward.

By Election Day we had enlisted the participation of more than 500 schools, with a combined undergraduate enrollment of nearly 3 million. In state after state, we helped colleges get students registered, educated, and motivated to vote—then saw these students help shape a watershed election. We broadened the horizons of what seemed possible for both the schools we worked with and participating organizations like Campus Compact and Youth Service America.

Granted, I had some advantages initiating the project. I'd worked long enough for social change that I knew potential donors and staffers in organizations like Campus Compact. And I had a track record helping campuses engage their students. But the project also embodied key aspects true of any engaged effort—even for someone completely new to such endeavors. Encouraged in part by Bill McKibben's Step It Up campaign, and his transition from engaged journalist to organizer, I took the leap even though I'd never done anything like it. I persisted despite initial rejections. By committing my own time (and money), I encouraged others to stretch and give more. I trusted my instincts but stayed flexible enough to shift gears when my initial approaches stalled out, or when new possibilities emerged. Once I enlisted enough skilled people through the Campus Compact networks, I let go of the impulse to control their every action and tactic. While we used the new information technologies whenever they helped, our prime tool was that amazing 130-year-old device known as the telephone. Our efforts worked best when we listened closely to the specific needs and possibilities of each campus—the local villages we worked to engage—and then passed on the best of their ideas so that others could run with them further.

CHAPTER NINE

Widening the Circle

I do not forget that my voice is but one voice, my experience a mere drop in the sea, my knowledge no greater than the visual field in a microscope, my mind's eye a mirror that reflects a small corner of the world.

—C. G. JUNG

When it comes to protecting Internet freedom, the Christian Coalition and MoveOn respectfully agree." So read an ad in *The New York Times* that helped save the Internet as we know it. MoveOn was the largest progressive organization in America, and the Christian Coalition had long been the major grassroots group for conservative religious activists. That they'd team up on anything made national headlines.

The ad would never have run if not for a former Army Ranger captain, Republican congressional candidate, and Christian Coalition activist named Joseph McCormick. After falling short in his campaign and being a Bush delegate in 2000, Joseph began to recoil at the polarization of American political debate. He dropped out of active politics and took time off to retrace Alexis de Tocqueville's journey across America, interviewing a mix of ordinary citizens and political leaders across the ideological spectrum. The discussions were so rich that Joseph decided to create gatherings that would bring together key organizational leaders of differing perspectives, to get them listening to each other.

Christian Coalition president Roberta Combs got involved early on, cosponsoring the second gathering of what would be called Reuniting America, in December 2005. The other main cosponsor was MoveOn co-founder Joan Blades, who had worked as a mediator and was strongly drawn to the idea. The retreat drew together leaders from organizations representing 70 million Americans, including conservative groups like the American Legion, the Club for Growth, Americans for Tax Reform, and the Christian Coalition; liberal ones like the Sierra Club, MoveOn, Common Cause, the National Council of Churches, and the League of Woman Voters; and the massive seniors' organization, the AARP. Roberta and Joan quickly hit it off and became friends.

Four months later, Roberta couldn't make it to a Reuniting America steering committee meeting, so she sent her daughter, Michele Combs, a former head of the South Carolina Young Republicans who served as the Christian Coalition's communications director. Michele and Joan, who sat next to each other at breakfast, also connected immediately. Michele was going through a divorce, and Joan had written a book on cooperative custody arrangements. Both were moms, so they talked about their children. Despite vast political differences, they instantly became friends and continued building their friendship by phone and e-mail. "We connected just talking the way women do," said Michele. "We have lots of commonalities. Plus most women agree on 85 percent of everything, and even where we disagree, like abortion, we can still see both sides."

At the next retreat, which focused on energy security, Michele connected again with Joan, as well as with Al and Tipper Gore, who participated, along with scientists, energy industry leaders, and activists of diverse perspectives. "It was in a little hippie town an hour north of Denver," said Michele, "with peace signs everywhere. I was a little shocked. Then I walked in and the first people I met were Al and Tipper Gore. But Tipper was just a very kind person, compassionate and honest. I liked Al, too, even though I didn't vote for him. When you meet someone intimately with just thirty other people, you have a chance to see the good in them. They went through a lot."

Later Michele participated in Gore's global climate change training sessions, where she met Sir James Houghton, the prominent

British scientist and evangelical who played a key role in Rich Cizik's journey. "I'd been thinking about environmental issues since I was pregnant and was told 'don't eat shellfish because of mercury.' If it's such a problem when you're pregnant, I thought, isn't it a problem when you're not? Thinking about climate change was a logical next step." After learning more about the issue, she and her mother Roberta started a Christian Coalition project promoting alternative energy, together with the National Wildlife Federation. Michele described the head of that group, Larry Schweiger, as "a very strong Christian, passionate on this issue, with lots of evangelical hunters and anglers in his organization." Michele liked joining Schweiger to lobby Republican Senators, "because when he goes in with the Christian Coalition, they can't accuse him of being liberal."

Joan always gained something from talking with people she disagreed with. "But with Michele and Roberta, it went deeper. We formed a friendship. We'd talk on the phone about our families and who Michele was going out with since her divorce. Kind of a girl-friend thing. We bonded further at another retreat just for women. We figured if we got along so well, our friends and political allies would, too, which turned out to be true."

The retreats fostered their friendship, and more. Roberta and Joan were looking for ways to work together from the start, but soon after meeting Michele, Joan got the idea of a joint political effort to save what was called Net Neutrality—the right to keep the Internet available as an open commons for all. The Internet had developed that way from the beginning, on the assumption that all content would have equal access and that while phone and telecom companies supplied the physical media through which data traveled, they wouldn't be allowed to favor or disfavor particular Web sites, applications, or data transmissions. But as high-speed Internet use took off, telecom companies like AT&T, Verizon, Comcast, and TimeWarner lobbied for the right to control everything that traveled via their media, which would mean that they could auction off the right for Web sites or applications to load faster, thus relegating other sites to second-class service. Such a shift would have devastated nonprofits, small businesses, and all kinds of political advocacy groups, which couldn't afford the rates that the most lucrative sites could pay. As Joan said, MoveOn had become large enough that it would have survived, but for any organization just starting up, it would have created impossible barriers. The telecom companies would also be able to control any content they chose, as when Verizon refused to distribute a text message alert from NARAL Pro Choice America and AT&T muted singer Eddie Vedder's criticism of President Bush during a live Pearl Jam webcast. In August 2005, the telecom companies succeeded in getting the Federal Communications Commission (FCC) to eliminate the requirement that all content providers be treated equally.

The next spring, the battle moved to Congress, with the telecom companies spending millions to change the rules permanently. The House passed a bill that would have confirmed the elimination of Net Neutrality. It looked as if the battle was lost. But a word-of-mouth revolt began working to block similar legislation in the Senate. Prominent bloggers of all perspectives took up the cause, including apolitical ones covering food, sports, and technology. In April 2006, the media reform group FreePress.net launched a new Save the Internet Coalition including the AARP, MoveOn, Gun Owners of America, the American Library Association, the National Religious Broadcasters, Common Cause, the Service Employees International Union, and key individuals like many of the people who'd first developed the Web. Online video gamers also joined in. So did prominent musicians. Opponents delivered petitions to swing Senators. But they were running out of time.

Then Joan proposed to Michele that their two organizations work on the issue together. MoveOn had already taken a leading role. The Christian Coalition had done some low-key lobbying but had issued no public statements. When Joan broached the subject, Michele promptly got the go-ahead from her organization to participate. They ran *The New York Times* ad, as well as a joint opinion piece in *The Washington Times*. Roberta also wrote a separate op-ed in *The Washington Post* with the head of NARAL, the leading pro-choice group. Michele and Joan then delivered a petition with over a million signatures at a Washington, D.C., press conference, together with Democratic Senator Byron Dorgan and Republican Senator Olympia Snowe. Michele also testified four times before Congressional committees and worked with MoveOn's media person. Because the groups were such strange bedfellows, their joint efforts attracted far more attention than if either had acted on its own. "If we'd just done this with other conservative groups," said Michele, "it wouldn't have had nearly the impact."

Joan agreed. "It's nice to not always be predictable," she said. "When MoveOn shows up, people expect what we're going to say. But when MoveOn and the Christian Coalition show up together, people think, 'If these guys can agree on this, maybe it's something I should pay attention to.' You get a totally different response."

Although the Christian Coalition took heat from some usual allies, the two groups persisted, and the regressive legislation deadlocked in the critical Senate committee. Political momentum shifted further after the 2006 election—and also two years later, when avowed Net Neutrality supporter Obama won the presidency, and the FCC Commissioners he appointed enshrined the doctrine as policy. Without the friendship and unlikely political partnership of Joan and Michele, an equal-access Internet might well have vanished into cyberspace.

Both women found value in what Joan described as "working outside our regular neighborhoods. It was wonderful to make a difference on an issue that not a lot of people are thinking about, but is very big in terms of maintaining a public square that benefits everybody. It was a very happy ending."

"I think it's America at its best when you come together like this," said Michele. "At the end of the day everyone wants to make a better country for their families, for the future. When we talk basic values, there's a lot we come together on." Working with new allies also energized her. "When people on either side of the aisle work with others who feel the same way as they do, there's often in-fighting and egos. When you work with a group you normally disagree with, you're coming together without common baggage. You're both passionate, and you get a lot done. Not that I don't appreciate the organizations I usually work with, but when a group like ours comes together with

MoveOn or the National Wildlife Federation, it shows that we really can find common ground."

CLIQUES AND ENCLAVES

Social involvement helps us enter new worlds. We may build on our existing values and knowledge, but we also develop new priorities, gain new skills, meet new people, hear and heed new stories. Issues once at the margins of our vision become the focus of our lives. Upon accepting the challenge of trying to shape a different future, we feel a sense of larger purpose. We become linked to others who share our vision.

As I've discussed, engaged communities are essential if we're going to remain committed over the long haul: They can give us a sense of shared purpose, help us pool our individual energies, and provide opportunities to develop friendships and learn from mentors. At the same time, they can become insular, even cliquish. It's tempting to retreat into the domains where we feel most comfortable, commiserating about the difficulty of our task with our fellow kindred spirits. I've seen too many well-meaning groups whose members send out their e-mails, hold their vigils, and put together impressive paper coalitions—yet never take the trouble to talk to anyone except those who already agree with them.

In the words of a longtime peace worker, we activists too often spend our time "bemoaning why no one understands our positions, clinging to our isolation as if it proved our rightness. If we want peace in the Middle East, we need to do more than berate the extremists. We need to reach new people and help them understand why we hold the views we do."

Granted, reaching out to people who don't share our assumptions entails risk. They might challenge our motives or arguments—or even reject us outright. We might feel unprepared and inadequate, unable to change their minds. Our visibility might bring economic or social penalties. When we do try to enlist others in our causes, it requires us to meet them where they are, not where we might like them to be. And we don't always get a favorable response. Virginia Ramirez might have turned away the nun from COPS who visited her after that first meeting. Angie De Soto and Meredith Segal became inured to hearing people say that they were uninterested, or to having them dismiss their efforts as futile. Sometimes involvement can even require physical risks, as when environmental activists in certain fights have been attacked by police or right-wing vigilantes, or when David Lewis goes to crack houses and bars to enlist desperate addicts in his Free at Last programs.

It's safer to stay hunkered down with our fellow believers. After a while, we may regard ourselves as more virtuous than those lesser souls who remain uninvolved. Why risk having our visions attacked?

But without outreach, isolation becomes self-perpetuating. Like *Dr. Strangelove's* General Jack D. Ripper, who launches a nuclear attack because he fears the Russians are corrupting his "precious bodily fluids," activists caught in the enclave sensibility can become obsessed with purity, taking refuge within their movement's familiar language and values; fearing contamination from outside interlopers with less than perfect political consciousness; ending up, as a longtime Australian labor activist said, "run by what we dread instead of by what we want."

ARMORED WITH LANGUAGE

The further we get into our causes, the more likely we are to start believing that everyone shares our knowledge and assumptions, and that can be dangerous. We may armor ourselves with language, talking of "hegemony" and "patriarchy," "imperialism" and "oppression," as if everyone assigns the same meaning to these words that we do, and as if everyone enjoys indulging in rhetoric. Used appropriately, the words, phrases, and acronyms we adopt can serve as a useful shorthand among those already in the know, like the specialized vocabulary of scientists. But our language can easily exclude others who haven't learned the right phrases and feel less confident in their beliefs. And this can leave us more isolated.

It's especially important to explain ourselves clearly to those just getting involved, to walk them through the process that produced our perspectives—as the COPS trainers did with Virginia, or Angie did with the new Environmental Coalition members—so they can find their own voice and take their own stands. Often we fail to appreciate how foreign social engagement seems to those who haven't made it part of their lives yet. We forget that we were hesitant and doubtful at first. We risk portraying ourselves as the experts to whom newbies should defer, creating our own unreachable perfect standards.

I've mentioned the University of Nebraska student group that addressed the crisis of family farms. They worked hard at continually enlisting new members, many from the same beleaguered farming communities as themselves. Yet even there, a rift grew between the initial participants, who quickly became highly knowledgeable about the larger related issues, and those who joined later on. "It becomes hard to relate to someone with a different level of understanding," said one of the founders. "Our efforts to educate people often blow them out of the water instead of painstakingly taking them along. It's almost like we have to create another organizational level for those just coming in."

Movements flourish, as I've suggested, when discussions in thousands of ordinary communities bring issues to public attention. They decline when activists talk to no one but themselves. But the conversations with "outsiders" must be real. They must be give-and-take exchanges, accessible, particularized, and compelling. They must include the stories that impelled us to act in the first place, not merely the abstractions and rhetorical shorthand that come to represent those stories.

AN ETHIC OF LISTENING

Whenever we reach across traditional boundaries, we create opportunities for learning and growth. If we've been involved for a while, much of what we do will become familiar, even routine, whether calling our phone trees, posting fliers, updating Facebook alerts, or holding signs at vigils. These actions are necessary, to be sure, but they rarely renew or expand our vision. That happens only when we place ourselves in circumstances that require us to view our efforts and ourselves with fresh eyes.

We can prepare ourselves to do this by reaching within. To hear others clearly, we may need to still our own voice momentarily. In his essay "The Spiritual Heart of Service," psychiatrist William Deikman distinguishes between what he calls "instrumental consciousness," by which we view ourselves as separate and distinct from our world, which helps us survive in it, and "receptive consciousness," by which we realize our more spiritual connection to others and the world as a whole. "Both modes of consciousness are needed," Deikman explains. Instrumental consciousness helps us focus, achieve material goals, carry out practical tasks. But it also limits our ability to be part of something larger, makes us feel more isolated than we need be—and, unchecked, leads to blind ambition and greed. Receptive consciousness, practiced alone, breeds passivity. It gives us no way to defend what we believe in against the all-too-instrumental predators of the world. But receptive consciousness helps us view ourselves as part of a larger life process. It gives us a sense of meaning and equanimity. It lets us reach out to our fellow human beings. Without the spiritual self, in other words, we're left disconnected and mistrusting.

At its best, receptive consciousness encourages humility, reminding us that we are imperfect and that others have much to teach us. It helps us acknowledge that our positions on social issues may be flawed, our own motives mixed. As Alexander Solzhenitsyn wrote: "The line separating good and evil runs through the heart of every human being, and who is willing to destroy a piece of his own heart?"

Wholeness requires that we know our limitations. I once ate at a Chinese restaurant with paranoid fortune cookies: "Pay no attention to what others tell you," said one. "You know better than anyone." An ethic of receptivity is based on precisely the opposite assumption—that our knowledge and perceptions will always be partial, and that we learn best from dialogue with others. "I do not forget," wrote psychologist C. G. Jung, "that my voice is but one voice, my experience a mere drop in the sea, my knowledge no greater than the visual field in a microscope, my mind's eye a mirror that reflects a small corner of the world."

This perspective, says battered women's advocate Ginny NiCarthy, is consistent with Quaker and Gandhian views of humanity. "You try to recognize the good in every person and speak to that, while maintaining your own values and goals. My vision of the world is more than the good guys and bad guys, friends and enemies, just and unjust, because all of us have good and bad elements within us. We have to work to understand all people from their own perspectives." That included working to understand the men who abuse women, so we help break the cycle of violence.

Environmental evangelical leader Rich Cizik considers this one of Jesus' core lessons. "He listens to others. He genuinely wants to know what they think. Not to trip them up, have an argument, or embarrass them, but to draw them into a dialogue." Or, in the words of environmental writer Don Snow, "Strange bedfellows make interesting kids. To listen to people who you disagree with most ardently, you come out changed from the experience, from understanding their different beliefs and perspectives."

I recently spent three days watching videotaped dialogues between pro-choice and right-to-life activists—moving, honest conversations where people from both sides explored their beliefs and motivations. Personally, I'm strongly pro-choice. I know caring and compassionate nurses and doctors who work in abortion clinics. Friends and relatives who've had abortions look back on their decisions as essential to having decent lives—including being able to devote enough time and attention to the children they already had or would later have. But I also know and admire people like Cizik who have very different perspectives, and I found the taped conversations fascinating. Participants talked about their concepts of responsibility and their fundamental ethical assumptions. Some found agreement in areas like exceptions for rape and incest, access to contraception or the need to provide resources for low-income families.

But even when participants didn't agree on anything, the discussions were rich and fertile.

In one case, participants met regularly for five-and-a-half years following a shooting at an abortion clinic in Brookline, Massachusetts. They included the head of Massachusetts Citizens for Life, the Catholic Archdiocese's pro-life office, the heads of Massachusetts Planned Parenthood and National Abortion Rights Action League, another major anti-abortion activist, and a prominent pro-choice minister. The meetings were secret, because participants feared adverse judgments from their political allies, and some had initial reservations about getting together at all. But they talked, exchanged their stories, even became friends. They said that the process stretched them spiritually, helping them recognize the humanity and dignity of those on the other side. It fleshed out the ambiguities and nuances of their own positions through what one called "the crucible" of their conversations. None switched sides, but the process brought some practical consequences—like the pro-life leaders dissuading a highly inflammatory Virginia activist from coming to their state. And both sides toned down demonizing rhetoric in their public statements. All considered the conversations among the most powerful experiences in their lives.

As the Boston participants made clear, listening to those we disagree with doesn't mean letting go of our sense of outrage and urgency, or our ability to act. When our heart cries out against injustice, it's wise to pay heed. But we would also do well to cultivate a bit of humility. To hear the souls of others requires silencing the clamor of our own obsessions and our own assumptions about how the world should be. Only when we truly listen to those who don't share our beliefs do we get the chance to discover and celebrate what we actually hold in common.

COMMON AIR, COMMON GROUND

Widening the circle can mean convincing our own team to broaden its horizons. At the suggestion of environmental writer Bill McKibben,

Jim Ball of the Evangelical Environmental Network launched a "What Would Jesus Drive?" campaign that challenged Christians to buy fuel-efficient cars. He and Rich Cizik carried a placard to a pro-life rally that said, "Stop Mercury Poisoning of the Unborn." The two then handed out fliers explaining that one in six babies is born with mercury levels high enough to place them at risk of learning disabilities, developmental delays, and motor coordination problems—and that most of the mercury comes from coal-burning power plants. Both Cizik and Ball opposed abortion, but as Cizik routinely pointed out in media interviews, cutting the poverty rate by 10 percent cuts the abortion rate by 30 percent. "If you care about the sanctity of human life," he said, "then care about whether people live desperate lives and care about the mercury from power plants."

As Cizik said of his role as head lobbyist for the National Association of Evangelicals, "we collaborated with Tibetan Buddhists in passing a bill that put religious freedom at the center of American foreign policy. We collaborated with feminists to pass a human trafficking bill, with the ACLU to pass a prison rape bill, and with gays and lesbians to pass an emergency plan for AIDS relief. If we did all that, then surely it's not heresy to collaborate with environmentalists."

Whatever our politics, it's easy to dismiss those of different beliefs—and in the process lose them as potential allies. When I was writing the original edition of this book, I remembered that a poll by the highly respected Pew Research Center found that most born-again Christians favored universal health care and greater environmental protection, and believed the government should take an active role in improving housing for low- and middle-income families. I couldn't find the survey, so I called up the Center to check. The nice young woman who answered said, "Oh, I'm sure that can't be true. They're just a bunch of bigots." She called back an hour or two later, quite sheepish, and said, "I looked it up, and I guess you're right."

In *The Activist's Handbook*, one of my favorite guides to strategies and tactics for social change, longtime housing activist Randy

Shaw describes a coalition that fought a proposed garbage incinerator in the Brooklyn Navy Yard for fifteen years. The fifty-five-story facility would have produced toxic emissions, including a half-ton of lead per year, further saturating already-polluted neighborhoods like Williamsburg. Leaders in neighboring communities quickly opposed the project. But they'd long been at each other's throats. The hostility was especially fierce between the Hasidic members of the United Jewish Organization (UJO) and the Puerto Rican and Dominican communities, who worked together in an organization called El Puente. They'd fought over issues like control of local public schools and comparative levels of police protection, trading accusations of bigotry and anti-Semitism and building up a tremendous— and seemingly insurmountable—legacy of mistrust.

Yet these communities came together for the health of their children—first in a fight to limit emissions at a local toxic waste facility called Radiac, then in opposition to the proposed incinerator. A Hasidic rabbi, David Niederman of UJO, inaugurated a historic rapprochement by walking into the offices of El Puente and offering to help lead a march against Radiac. El Puente's founder, Luis Garden Acosta, responded by reaching out, not only to the Hasidim, but also to the Poles, Italians, and other white ethnic groups in the area. Along with other allies, they raised complementary issues and spoke from similar passions.

Although they had no history of working together, the groups continued to mobilize their constituencies. In time, Brooklyn borough officials joined in. The coalition enlisted American Legion posts and historic preservation organizations after discovering that the incinerator would pave over a burial ground for Revolutionary War prisoners. It continued to organize and demonstrate, despite hostility from major media outlets and opposition from most of the New York City power structure. Finally, a deal in the state legislature ended the incinerator project for good. As Garden Acosta said, "In our common air we have found our common ground."

As we've seen, Pete Knutson built a similarly disparate coalition that extended from Sierra Club activists and Native American tribes

SOUL OF A CITIZEN 241

to the highly conservative Pentecostal churches of some of his fellow fishermen. When a local affiliate of the fundamentalist Trinity Broadcasting Network broadcast a segment supporting Initiative 640, a gillnetter named John, who belonged to a local Assemblies of God church, called the reporter. "Do you know who Jesus' disciples were? They were fishermen. What do you think Jesus is going to do when he comes back and finds out you've stopped people from making a living by fishing?" he asked. "He's going to rip your head off."

Taken aback, the reporter apologized, as did John for losing his temper. The two prayed together, and Trinity gave the fishermen a half hour to make their case on the show. John also talked about the initiative with his minister, who decided, after dreaming about a related passage from Isaiah, that it was indeed a pressing moral issue. The minister, in turn, helped shatter stereotypes of who does and does not typically support environmental concerns by giving invocations against greed at fishermen's rallies and sending out fliers to the state's 300 Assemblies of God congregations, endorsing the gillnetters' cause.

"We've got to keep approaching the Pentecostals," Pete says, later on, thinking back on the campaign. "Lots of their members are getting economically screwed. They mistrust the giant corporations. But if we don't reach out to them and establish some dialogue, they're going to be pulled into the right-wing coalitions."

An important element in maintaining such complicated alliances is recognizing that certain subjects need to remain off-limits. For example, when a priest wanted to raise the issue of school vouchers during a discussion that COPS was leading about the need to support public schools, the COPS founder told him that the issue would fracture their coalition. The priest agreed to table the matter.

Whatever causes we take on, we need to reach beyond the "usual suspects" in our activist communities. As singer and civil rights activist Bernice Johnson Reagon, of Sweet Honey in the Rock, points out, "If you're in a coalition and you're comfortable, you know it's not broad enough."

THE REDEEMABLE SPARK

Sometimes the search for justice requires us to reach out to people whose actions appall us. In the late 1980s, human rights lawyer Julia Devin joined Quaker physician Charlie Clements and activist Seattle Congressman Jim McDermott to try and negotiate an agreement for medical neutrality in El Salvador. It was the height of the Salvadoran death squad terror; the U.S.-trained military had just brutally murdered six Jesuit priests at the University of Central America, as well as their housekeeper and her young daughter. Earlier on, an assassin shot Archbishop Oscar Romero while he was conducting mass—a month after Romero publicly asked the U.S. Government to cut off Salvadoran military aid. The military and allied death squads kidnapped and "disappeared" more than 30,000 people and carried out large-scale massacres of old people, women, and children. Yet Julia and the others met with the colonels and generals to persuade them to allow the provision of medical care in all areas of the country, from the government zones to those controlled by the opposition guerrillas.

"Many of my friends who worked for Central American peace were outraged that we even talked with the military," recalls Julia. "But we weren't naïve. We knew the generals would use any agreement to look good in Congress and try to get more money in the face of our efforts to cut off the aid that kept them going. But the peace process had to start somewhere. This seemed a logical place. If they went back on their word, we'd have a huge report that we could wave in front of Congress describing all the violations."

Some of the generals gave Julia the chills. "You walked out feeling like you'd just encountered pure evil. They'd done horrible things, helped kill thousands of people." Still, she said, "I tend to believe that everyone has a spark inside them that's redeemable, even if they've never done a single decent act in their lives. Although some people for all practical purposes can't be reached or redeemed, mostly, I kept coming back to the sense that we had to try, and the possibility that this might help end the war. You don't have to like people to talk and negotiate."

Much as Julia hated what the generals had done, the meeting offered "a way to draw them in, give them a stake in the peace process, and create a precedent for addressing other issues, like not bombing hospitals. We kept coming back to our priorities, what people in the Salvadoran villages said would help their situation. Working out agreements like this with both sides seemed a first step, a piece of the puzzle toward something larger." As it turned out, the agreement they helped negotiate became a key building block in finally achieving a lasting peace in El Salvador.

Julia's belief in a "redeemable spark" may seem like wishful thinking, but people who've done terrible things reverse course often enough that we should never lose hope that a particular person can change. We never know when someone whose past may seem abhorrent will nonetheless surprise us. As recounted in Studs Terkel's book, *American Dreams: Lost and Found,* a Ku Klux Klan leader named C. P. Ellis accepted an invitation from the North Carolina AFL-CIO to a public meeting on racial tensions in the state's school system. Ellis, who had worked hard to prevent integration in the schools, accepted because he wanted to see what was going on and to speak his mind. "If we didn't have niggers in the schools," he told the group, "we wouldn't have the problems we got today."

To Ellis's surprise, an African American activist praised him for "being the most honest man here tonight." Later, another black man nominated Ellis to co-chair the group with Ann Atwater, an African American who had led civil rights boycotts and protests. Ellis hated Atwater "with a purple passion," but he was "tired of fighting." He accepted the position, and the improbable partners began "to reluctantly work together." After both their kids came home crying because classmates had accused their parents of collaborating with the enemy, Atwater and Ellis began to recognize a deeper commonality, and they eventually became close friends. Ellis found a new career as a union organizer, bringing poor blacks and whites together against employers who had long exploited their mutual mistrust. This former Klansman had completed one of the longest journeys imaginable—largely because his opponents had reached out across an enormous divide.

A POLITICS OF FORGIVENESS

Whatever we're trying to change, it takes moral imagination to see a redeemable spark in our opponents, particularly if they participate in actions we consider destructive, even reprehensible. When we—or our loved ones—have been wronged, the desire for retribution may almost be instinctive. "I just hope there is a hell," said a South Carolina textile worker I once interviewed, "because that son-of-a-bitch foreman will get his." Think of Pirate Jenny's classic song from Bertolt Brecht's *Threepenny Opera,* in which the hotel maid scrubs the floors under the scornful stares of the rich. Jenny dreams of "the ship, the black freighter," whose pirate crew will burn and ransack the town. Then they'll bring the well-fed gentlemen to her in chains, "Asking me 'Kill them now—or later?' Asking *me.* 'Kill them now—or later?'" It's a powerful vision, and we all know the feeling.

Yet holding on to resentments can be like drinking poison, day in and day out. Eventually it will destroy us. Forgiveness, wrote Catholic theologian Henri Nouwen, "is an act of liberation. . . . We say, 'I no longer hold your offense against you.' But there is more. We also free ourselves from the burden of being the 'offended one.' The great temptation is to cling in anger to our enemies and then define ourselves as being offended and wounded by them. Forgiveness, therefore, liberates not only the other but also ourselves."

Mixing forgiveness with accountability, like South Africa's Truth and Reconciliation Commission did, can offer unexpected hope. "To pursue the path of healing for our nation," Archbishop Desmond Tutu has said, "we need to remember what we have endured. But we must not simply pass on the violence of that experience through the pursuit of punishment. We seek to do justice to the suffering without perpetuating the hatred aroused. We think of this as *restorative* justice." Rather than being idealistic or naïve, Tutu argued that this path was "thoroughly realistic," perhaps the only way to heal a profoundly divided nation.

Restorative justice—that's an extraordinary notion. Fairness *plus* forgiveness. Moral courage *plus* mercy. How can we Americans practice restorative justice, reuniting our own profoundly divided nation? Perhaps by letting go of some of our long-drawn-out resentments. By focusing less on the evils of our enemies and more on the world we'd like to build—with their cooperation if possible; without it, if necessary. And by remembering that even those whom we mistrust most profoundly are capable of good—perhaps even of radical shifts of heart.

In a seminar at a Seattle conference, spiritual writer Marianne Williamson offered a prayer requesting forgiveness for America's deep racial divisions. At one point a gray-haired man in a suit raised his hand. "I know this will probably push a lot of people's buttons," he said hesitantly, "but my name is Egil Krogh. I was the lawyer who headed the 'plumbers' group' in the Nixon White House, hired G. Gordon Liddy, and coordinated the break-in at the office of Daniel Ellsberg's psychiatrist, Dr. Fielding. I pled guilty and went to prison for it as part of the Watergate trials. I've apologized to Ellsberg and Fielding. But those apologies aren't complete enough. I want to apologize publicly now, for what we did and what it caused."

The seminar participants were stunned. Krogh went on to make a full confession. He said that he'd helped demonize the Democrats and those who protested the war. Once, he had vowed, "Anyone who opposes us we'll destroy. As a matter of fact, anyone who doesn't support us, we'll destroy." He'd suppressed his own moral qualms "to go along for the sake of the team," he now said, and damaged the country to the point where "we almost destroyed our democracy. I spent a long time at the Vietnam Memorial, thinking about my actions. Those of us involved have a responsibility to help America heal."

Except in his personal meetings with Ellsberg and Fielding and his response to the sentencing judge, Krogh had not raised this history before. This was his first public acknowledgment that what he had done was wrong and had created profound harm. But Williamson's message about the power of forgiveness had compelled him to come forward. Gestures like Krogh's help us feel more generous—less ready to demonize our own enemies or turn other humans into fodder for our causes. They remind us that individuals and institutions can change, and that when we voice difficult but important truths, we never know who may hear them and respond.

DRAWING THE LINE

It's essential not to dismiss potential allies, or even negotiating partners, because of their lifestyles, belief systems, or the political configurations with which they may have aligned themselves. But that doesn't mean relinquishing our beliefs. Although compromise can be useful, it isn't always the best route, particularly if it means failing to hold political and economic leaders accountable for the damage they cause. Too often, wealthy and powerful interests create sham coalitions of so-called stakeholders, whose pronouncements and reports justify proposals like privatizing the Social Security system or making sure that we do nothing substantive about climate change. In the fight over fixing America's dysfunctional and cripplingly expensive health care system, I've heard endless pronouncements about the need for reform by the very insurance and pharmaceutical interests that helped create and perpetuate the problem. Meanwhile, they do everything in their power to block real change. In the face of such destructive actions, sometimes, as Virginia Ramirez says, we have to "learn to be rude."

At one point, Washington State timber companies ran a series of TV and newspaper ads urging that local salmon be exempted from the Endangered Species Act. As always, they insisted that their position would benefit the environment, transferring the responsibility of habitat management from distant federal bureaucrats to locals, who, according to their self-serving arguments, would be in a better position to know what's needed. Yet as Pete Knutson said at a meeting of area environmentalists, "Everyone wants to hold hands and pretend we're all interested in preserving habitat. But we don't all have the same interests here. Weyerhaeuser says they're interested in preserving habitat. They've sure shown it with their clear-cuts. Trillium [another giant company] also says they want to preserve habitat but they've been just as bad. ITT Rayonier has the largest Superfund site in the state, and they say they want to preserve habitat, too. Maybe we'd better look at their track record."

Gross abuses of power must be challenged head-on. When needless violence or rapaciousness destroys lives or land, we need to express our outrage. Otherwise, we contribute to a climate of complacency. "There are moments," writes poet Charles Simic in *Harper's*, "when true invective is called for, when it becomes an absolute necessity, out of a deep sense of justice, to denounce, mock, vituperate, lash out, in the strongest possible language."

We live in a world where evil exists, where the rich and complex lives of individuals, neighborhoods, communities, entire species, and ecosystems are continually ravaged because of greed, callousness, ambition, and fear. Such destructiveness can't be erased by wishing it away or giving it a politer name. Quite the contrary. Tobacco companies may have sophisticated rationalizations for deliberately targeting teenage kids and using ammonia to make the nicotine in cigarettes more addictive. But they're ultimately responsible for the death and suffering of hundreds of thousands of people. Companies like Lehman Brothers and AIG really did crash the entire global financial system through reckless speculation, destroying lives and livelihoods. Exxon and coal companies like Peabody Energy threaten the habitability of the entire planet when they fund climate change deniers, aiming to block critically needed legislation. When corporate or political leaders make deals that damage communities and lives, we need to hold them accountable for their actions.

But how do we do this? The religious notion of hating the sin while loving the sinner can be helpful in this context. It's sometimes used destructively, as when preachers tell gay people that God wants them to be straight. But it's also a way to challenge unjust political, cultural, and economic systems—what the Bible calls "powers and principalities"—without dehumanizing those who participate in them. Individuals may support unjust systems out of habit, fear, blindness, or the limits of their experience. Their all-too-human flaws deserve our sympathy, even as we do everything we can to oppose their actions.

To use a domestic metaphor, if one member of a family is consistently bullying, abusive, or destructive, he or she must be made to stop. Sometimes patient explanation will suffice. More often, however, other family members have to learn to stop excusing or tolerating behavior that damages the group. The same is true of people whose actions damage the larger human family or despoil the earth. Bearing in mind that, as Julia Devin says, everyone possesses a redeemable spark, we shouldn't give up on them. But we nonetheless need to acknowledge their destructiveness and refuse to cooperate with it. We need to draw a clear line and abide by it, setting limits to their behavior and stopping them from creating further harm.

BRIDGES IN A HOT TUB

When we do draw the line, we can sometimes unexpectedly discover the humanity of those we oppose. In the early 1990s, Rainforest Action Network (RAN) targeted the huge Japanese conglomerate, Mitsubishi, for importing massive amounts of rainforest timber. RAN promoted an international boycott of Mitsubishi cars and electronic products, backed by a major petition campaign and a documentary detailing the company's offences. A button on the RAN Web site provided a link so people could deluge Mitsubishi with comments. Supporters from the United States to Australia and the United Kingdom hung roadside banners saying "Mitsubishi Destroys Rainforests," and a plane towed a similar banner over the Super Bowl at half-time. Campaign participants held demonstrations at car shows and local dealers. A full-page ad in *The New York Times* called Mitsubishi the "Worst Corporate Destroyer of Rainforests."

At first, Mitsubishi attacked the campaigners and denied the destructive impact of its operations. But as pressure built, the company eventually relented, pledging to sell only those wood products certified by the Forest Stewardship Council, and to phase out its use of tree-based paper and packaging products in favor of alternative fibers. More recently, RAN has had similar victories in campaigns targeting companies like Home Depot and Kinko's, and in an effort to persuade Bank of America to stop financing coal-fired power plants or mining companies involved in highly destructive mountaintop removal.

The relationship between key boycott leaders like RAN president Randy Hayes and top Mitsubishi executives had gotten pretty ugly, so Hayes wasn't sure what to expect when he and a senior Mitsubishi America executive later attended the same Santa Barbara retreat on sustainability and business. The two men avoided each other around the coffee urns and at the meals, almost like two negatively charged magnets repelling each other.

When the proceedings were done, Hayes and a friend decided to grab a six-pack of beer and go to a retreat center hot tub that sat atop a hill overlooking the Pacific. But when they arrived there, they found the Mitsubishi executive, sitting naked in the tub with his own cold beer. Hayes and his friend hesitated, then stripped down and settled in the tub as far away as they could.

An awkward silence lasted about five minutes. Then the Mitsubishi man said, "Randy, I want to thank you. I have kids. I want them to see the rainforest. Other executives have kids, too. They also want them to see the rainforest. Until you brought this to the attention of our CEO and our stockholders, we were afraid to speak out, to do the right thing. You brought it to the attention of our executives. I want to thank you." He raised his beer in a toast.

When we cease demonizing our opponents, astounding victories become possible. In concert with the largely youth-led protests that brought down Serbian dictator Slobodan Milošević, citizens converged on the Serbian capital of Belgrade. In a scene captured in the brilliant documentary, *Bringing Down a Dictator,* one particular column of townspeople, headed by an overweight small-town mayor in his green jogging suit, encountered a line of soldiers blocking the road, along with a military bus. "We're sorry," the soldiers told them. "We have orders not to let you pass." The marchers conferred and responded, "We understand you have your orders. Of course you have to obey them. But supposing we went around you? Would that be okay?" After talking among themselves, the soldiers said it would be fine.

The townspeople thanked them and then asked if they could possibly make things easier by moving the military bus out of the way with their tractors. Once again the soldiers agreed; they weren't allowed to move the bus, but if the townspeople wanted to, they'd have no problem. After that small but encouraging victory, the procession continued on to Belgrade, to join several hundred thousand other citizens in protests that brought about the collapse of the Milošević regime.

WORKING FOR WALMART

Sometimes, however, reaching across the divide gives legitimacy to an adversary who may not deserve it. After Adam Werbach left the Sierra Club, he started Ironweed, a subscription-based video club to support social-justice documentaries, co-founded the labor-environmental coalition, the Apollo Alliance, and joined the international board of Greenpeace. He also launched a consulting group to help major companies reduce their environmental footprint. And in the process he was hired by Walmart.

Many of Adam's previous allies were appalled. Walmart is known for destroying local independent businesses and downtowns, and for depressing local wages. It fires employees who try to organize unions, has been fined repeatedly for forcing workers to log in extra hours off the clock, and pays so little that its "associates" often end up on food stamps or Medicaid. It has forced U.S. companies to shift production to low-wage overseas factories, under the threat of being dropped in favor of cheaper competitors. Walmart also donates massive amounts to regressive candidates, and it continues to fight laws that might give their employees the chance to get treated with dignity.

Adam had once lambasted Walmart for precisely these predatory approaches. Now the company was about to use its relationship with him to promote a new green image. After meeting with the company's new vice president of sustainability, he flew to Walmart's Arkansas headquarters and met with other top executives, including CEO Lee Scott. Deciding that the company's leaders were sincere, Adam agreed to work with them.

Assisted by Adam and other environmental consultants, Walmart has quickly become the world's largest purchaser of organic cotton and organic milk, has begun to significantly improve the efficiency of its trucking fleet, and has pledged to invest $500 million in technology to reduce greenhouse gases at its stores. The company has already retrofitted several hundred stores with energy-efficient heating, cooling, lighting, and refrigeration systems, and it has begun to purchase wind energy where available. Meanwhile, Adam designed a program under which two employees per store will attend company-paid retreats to brainstorm ideas for ways they and their stores can undertake more sustainable actions.

Lee Scott and the other Walmart executives may genuinely recognize the planet's massive environmental crises. But as far as I can tell, the company continues to lead a global economic race of plummeting wage scales. Former Greenpeace head Barbara Dudley co-wrote an open letter to Adam called "The Death of Integrity," charging him with abandoning his principles. Sierra Club director Carl Pope believed Adam was acting with good intentions but stressed that unless Walmart addresses its supply chain—the global, carbon-intensive production and transportation system that favors products manufactured at the lowest possible cost in places like China, then shipped halfway across the world to Walmart's stores— even the best energy-efficiency improvements will yield only a fraction of what's needed. Recently a Seattle-area ten-year Walmart employee collapsed at the store after being refused time off to go to the doctor, and died a couple of days later of an aneuryism caused by potentially treatable blood clots. So if some aspects of the company have changed, others have not. I also suspect Walmart would never have undertaken their environmental initiatives were it not for the massive citizen pressure that has challenged its other actions.

To be honest, I'm torn about Adam's choice. Who wouldn't jump at the chance to help reduce the environmental footprint of the world's largest corporation? But we also live in a public relations world, and Walmart is already spinning the partnership with Adam to burnish its severely tarnished image and try to extend its reach, with all the attendant costs. Whatever we think of Adam's individual decision, we need to remain mindful lest any institution's carefully selected good works seduce us into muting our opposition to the indefensible practices it continues in all the other realms where it operates.

A GOOD ATHEIST

I wish I could ask Hazel Wolf, an environmentalist who lived to be nearly 102 years old, about Adam's decision to work with Walmart. Hazel reached out to everyone she could, but she also never held back from confronting injustice. Still, she had a mischievous way of approaching individuals and communities where she was seeking to build bridges. Once, after she gave a talk at a Seventh–Day Adventist college, an audience member asked her why she was an atheist. "Why are you Christians?" she responded. "Because your parents were. If your parents were Moslems, you'd be Moslems. I'm an atheist because my parents were. There are some bad Christians. But most Christians are good. There are some bad atheists. But most atheists are good. I'm just trying to be a good atheist."

A good atheist, Hazel continued, is required to take care of the earth, just as a good Christian is. "And just in case I'm wrong, I have some insurance. Because Jesus said to the man, 'You fed me when I was hungry, clothed me when I was naked, visited me when I was in prison. If you've done this to the least of these, you will be on my right hand in heaven.' Well, I've worked for child welfare, worked for Medicaid to take care of the sick. I've visited the prison up on the hill. So I just might be seeing you guys in heaven." The audience had a very different theology, but they loved this fiery great-grandmother with her white hair, lined face, and playful style.

Reaching out to bring people together came naturally to Hazel. She was born in British Columbia in 1898. Her father, a cook on freighters, died in an accident at sea when Hazel was eight. Her mother belonged to the Wobblies, the Industrial Workers of the

World, and eked out a living scrubbing floors, taking in boarders, and working in a factory making overalls. Hazel grew up strong and energetic, swimming in a slough near her house and outrunning the local policemen.

She also developed a sense of compassion. Early on, she was exposed to the harsh lives of people in her neighborhood, such as the local prostitutes. There was an orphanage nearby, and when Hazel selected softball players for her team, she chose the orphans first, so that "they'd feel wanted." One day Hazel and some friends threw snowballs at the windows of the local Chinese laundry, and took off running when one of the windows broke. Later one of the laundry workers returned a valuable brooch that the parent of one of the children had left attached to a piece of clothing, and Hazel felt terrible for having harassed them. "I realized how hardworking and honest they were, even when everyone taunted them."

Hazel got her start as a rabble rouser in the eighth grade, in 1911. She was always athletic, but her playground, like her classroom in Victoria, British Columbia, was segregated by gender. Basketball was played by boys and watched by girls. After Hazel talked with some of her friends, she approached the principal and said, "We want to play basketball, too." "Girls don't play basketball," he said, dismissing her. "Of course we don't," Hazel responded. "We *can't* if we don't have balls or hoops." Taken aback, the principal agreed to furnish them if Hazel could raise two teams, which she did by that afternoon.

The Canadian economy hit the skids shortly after World War I, so Hazel moved to Washington State. Her first job was pasting "Made in Japan" stickers on plastic Easter bunnies. Then one day a Communist Party organizer circulated a petition for unemployment insurance. The issue touched Hazel's heart, because she'd been in and out of work far more than she wanted, and was struggling to support a daughter from a brief marriage. So she signed the petition and joined the Party. Soon she was writing letters to politicians, demonstrating at the state capitol, carrying evicted families' furniture back into their houses, and occupying Seattle's city hall. She fought for food, housing, and clothing for the poor and unemployed. She also helped the Party organize a Senior Citizens Union, whose efforts helped secure one of the the first public pension program in the country, a model for Social Security. Hazel considered this "one of the most exciting and delightful periods" in her life.

All the while, she was raising her daughter and working as a legal secretary. Having never made it past eighth grade, she enrolled in night school and later entered the University of Washington at age thirty-four. But adult students were rare at the time, and the school provided no support system for single mothers. Eventually, Hazel dropped out and went back to work for a Seattle civil rights and labor lawyer, with whom she stayed for more than twenty years.

She'd left the Communist Party by then, frustrated at the members' insularity. "I liked them in the thirties, when they marched on the state capitol. But I've always been an action kind of person, and it changed when they just sat around talking about Karl Marx, who always bored me. I never got past the first chapter in that big book of his. So I gradually quit going to meetings and paying my dues. I just drifted away."

But Hazel was still a target for those who wanted to stamp out every hint of dissent in America. In 1958, when she'd been out of the Communist Party for thirteen years, the FBI tried to deport her. Hazel resisted, "while those stupid characters bent heaven and earth to send me back to Canada." Along the way, she stopped the deportation of other radicals who had committed the same unpardonable sin of speaking out. Finally, after sixteen years, the government caved in and let Hazel become a citizen.

It wasn't until the 1960s that Hazel joined the environmental movement, but when she did, it was with her characteristic passion and high spirits. A friend who belonged to the Audubon Society had long badgered her to join, and she eventually agreed. On an Audubon field trip to a local park, Hazel watched a small brown bird pecking and eating as it made its way up a tree. "Suddenly I realized how much we had in common," she says. "He works hard for his living, for his food. So do I. He has his lifestyle and routine. He always goes up the tree, never down. He gets up in the morning and goes through his day, just like me. I'd never paid much attention to birds before, hardly even noticed them. But I felt something in common. I liked that Audubon was committed to protecting them."

It was a revelatory moment, unleashing what would become a burning concern for the well-being of the natural world. Eager to do more than just watch birds, Hazel soon became the secretary of Audubon's Seattle chapter, a position she held for thirty-five years. Living on Social Security and a Section Eight rent subsidy, she founded twenty-one of the state's twenty-six Audubon chapters. She built alliances, drew new people into the organization, and forged links between environmental and social justice activists. I remember when she called to enlist me in a coalition concerned with the Hanford nuclear reservation's environmental impact, explaining ever so persistently why I needed to join. I've met countless activists who mention similar experiences, describing how Hazel convinced them to speak out on watersheds or old-growth forests, and how they'd been at it ever since.

"Obviously, I'm enjoying all this," Hazel told me. "When you don't get involved, you're missing something. I've learned to speak in public, which always terrified me. I've learned not to come on too hard, because no one listens when you're ranting and raving. I've met so many people I respect."

Because we're so serious about our issues, we often don't realize that humor can be an effective tool to open hearts and minds. Hazel's mischievousness was inseparable from her ability to reach out. When the state legislature proposed an innocuous bill to give free fishing licenses to all visually impaired people, Hazel convinced a friend to offer a brief amendment: "and hunting licenses." The legislators loved the idea (though wisely didn't vote for it). In her eighties Hazel repeatedly visited Nicaragua as part of her opposition to U.S. intervention. One time, a U.S. Congressman came up to her in Managua and said, in a condescending tone, "I hear you're a bird-watcher." "Yes," Hazel responded. "And there are some birds in Washington, D.C., that really need watching."

Throughout her life, Hazel worked to broaden the constituencies for her causes. She persuaded environmentalists to support the organizing of California strawberry workers, because, she said, "even if they don't care about the labor aspects, they can understand the pesticides." By the same token, she pushed unions to take on ecological issues. Middle-class environmental groups, she believed, needed to take seriously the lives of those struggling to survive as carpenters or loggers, or raising their children near toxic dumps because those were the only neighborhoods they could afford. The issues she raised and relationships she created were precursors to more recent labor-environmental coalitions: the Blue Green Alliance, founded by the Sierra Club and United Steel Workers, now includes several other major unions and the National Resources Defense Council; the Apollo Alliance, which Adam Werbach helped found, includes representatives from some of the same labor and environmental groups but also major business and community organizations. Without the work of people like Hazel, and the relationships that they built, such efforts would be inconceivable.

As Hazel said, coalitions form "when different people come together, often for different reasons. If you want to get people to respond, to do things, it also helps to make them laugh. When people see me having such a good time with all this, maybe it inspires them."

CHAPTER TEN

Pieces of a Vision

*What is hateful to you, do not to your fellow man. That is the entire Law; all
the rest is commentary.*

—RABBI HILLEL

When we work for change, what should we be working for?
The issues we address will vary according to our perspectives, backgrounds, and passions. But however we take action, it
helps to have a compass to steer by, a way to find our moral "mag-
netic north," in the words of one community activist. Although no
blueprint exists for the ideal society, there are, I believe, some overall goals worth working toward, and others that should be avoided.
I hasten to add that what I'm about to propose is not a formula for
solving all our planetary ills. No such formula exists. But I'd like to
suggest some approaches based on years of watching citizens I admire struggle to make the world a better place. Whether you agree
with them or not, think of them as another facet of our conversation
on common responsibility—an opportunity to unleash our imagi-
nations to envision the world we'd like to see.

In a troubled time like ours, much can be learned by examining
what's wrong. Writer Susan Griffin describes a "resemblance in the
look and feel of a field that has been polluted with chemical waste,
a neighborhood devastated by poverty and injustice, a battlefield."
All are products of similar dehumanization, greed, and neglect—of
an ethic of disconnection that makes people and places expendable.

They echo Carol McNulty's observation that it's hard to find inner peace when people are starving, the air is polluted, the water is filthy, and companies make money from the suffering of children.

To begin to sketch an alternative vision, we can explore what would result from an ethic of caring. We can look at all our economic, political, and cultural decisions, both individual and collective, and ask whether they respect human dignity and nurture a more sustainable relationship with the earth. "We're living in an imperfect world," says Pete Knutson. "We have to make choices and judgments that aren't always easy. But you start with basic ethics, like truthfulness, fairness, equity, reciprocity, and sharing, that are at the core of our species nature, what makes us human. You reject the PR-firm notion that truth is a disposable commodity. If powerful economic interests are backing something, you don't shy away from naming them. These are very simple things, but they've become radical concepts in today's political reality."

At the heart of the ethics Pete describes lies the principle of mutual respect. "What is hateful to you, do not to your fellow man," said Rabbi Hillel, 2,000 years ago. "That is the entire Law; all the rest is commentary." Hillel's words define a standard to live up to.

At a minimum, I'd argue, this standard calls for a world where everyone has access to food, housing, and medical care; where no one shoots, beats, tortures, or otherwise degrades their fellow human beings; and where individuals can express what they believe without fear. Though honored far too often in the breach, most of these rights were enshrined sixty years ago in the UN's Universal Declaration of Human Rights, signed by the major nations on earth.

For Virginia Ramirez, such a vision of human dignity is embodied in the ways we treat our children. "I'd like to see a world," she says, "where every child has the same opportunity. I see children suffer from hunger, sickness, cold, and lack of education. Or they're abused, humiliated, or whatever. That's the hardest thing to take, to see children suffer. To me, there would be justice if every child in this world got treated well. I don't know if that's ever going to happen. Maybe it won't. But for me that would be perfect justice."

A good society, I further believe, creates a sense of economic security for all its members—so that, in the words of songwriter Bruce Cockburn, "nobody has to scrape for honey at the bottom of the comb." It damages us all that the United States has long led the industrialized world in rates of homelessness, child poverty, lack of health care, infant mortality, inequality of wealth, and nearly every other index of desperation among the voiceless and vulnerable. Even if we still own our own homes, have decent jobs, and possess a modicum of financial comfort, we're demeaned by our society's radical economic polarization. Having to avert our eyes from those begging on the street, avoid certain neighborhoods as "too dangerous," and worry that others might take what we've got is "tacky," as preacher Will Campbell would say, and we know it. "We are going to have to develop a concept of *enough* at the top and at the bottom," Marian Wright Edelman writes, "so that the necessities of the many are not sacrificed for the luxuries of the few."

A good society gives us opportunities and resources to shape our common future. "What we're trying to do," says Ernie Cortes, the former lead organizer of COPS, "is to draw people out of their private pain, out of their cynicism and passivity, and get them connected with other people in collective action." In this sense, the very act of taking responsibility for our communities embodies the vision we seek. It makes democracy not a vague slogan masking manipulation and greed, but rather a living process that all citizens participate in to create and govern society. The public arena should be everyone's property.

A good society also helps each of us fulfill the full bloom of our uniqueness, the "acorn" of our character that James Hillman describes. It honors our individual gifts and encourages our particular callings. It gives all its inhabitants the economic, emotional, and spiritual support needed to follow their dreams. An unjust society, in contrast, starves hopes, aspirations, and possibilities. It stunts lives and potentials.

And because we realize ourselves fully only through interaction with others, a good society fosters community in all its forms. It nurtures rich and vibrant places to live, where we are surrounded by friends and acquaintances, feel a sense of belonging, look out for each other's children, and know our perspectives are welcomed. Such communities once existed in our small towns and urban neighborhoods. Efforts from COPS to Pete Knutson's engaged fishing community are an attempt to revive them. The longing most of us have for places where intimate connections are commonplace makes clear how deeply we need the company of other human beings if we are to feel at home in the world.

Whatever our situation, we'll realize neither our individual nor communal selves if we're completely consumed by our work. That points to another feature of a good society: We should be able to earn a living wage without sacrificing our psychological, spiritual, and sometimes even physical well-being by giving over our entire lives to our jobs. The bumper sticker "The Labor Movement: The Folks Who Brought You the Weekend" is more than a joke. Western European countries with a month of paid vacation still end up with productivity as high or higher than in the United States. I'd argue that a good society allows citizens time to think and reflect, be with their families and friends, and engage themselves in their communities.

Finally, if we're to have a society that promotes a greater good, we'll have to do a better job of nurturing our sense of the sacred and honoring the complex web of life that supports us. We did not create the earth, so have no right to play God by destroying its habitability. We need an ethical vision that helps us wield our awesome technological inventiveness with wisdom and humility.

WHAT DO WE VALUE?

Aristotle once said that a barbaric culture consumes all of its resources to support itself in the present, whereas a civilized culture preserves them for later generations. Many of our society's most destructive actions yield consequences whose gravest implications aren't immediately apparent. That's true of our casual destruction of the planet. It's true of our writing off entire communities of young men and women who will grow into adulthood bereft of hope and skills. It's true when we say, in one of the richest countries in the world, that we can't afford to address our most pressing common problems.

The alternative, as environmentalist David Brower said, is to act so that "the new child or the new fawn or the new baby seal pup that's born a thousand years from now . . . opens its eyes on a beautiful, livable planet." Virginia Ramirez touches on this in explaining why it's important to persist. "Maybe the things we're working on today," she says, "won't bring about changes for years. But it's just as important that we do them."

Working for the future requires a vision of accountability, which helps us hold individuals and institutions responsible for the impact of their choices, and link seemingly disconnected actions and consequences. Novelist Ken Kesey's son died when the ramshackle bus carrying him and the rest of the University of Oregon wrestling team skidded off an icy mountain road. Afterward, Kesey wrote Oregon senator Mark Hatfield, explaining that his first response was to turn the other cheek, to accept the tragedy as fate.

"But what," he continued, in a letter printed in the *Whole Earth* magazine, "if the other cheek is somebody else's kid? In some other slapdash rig? On some other ill-fated underfunded trip next wrestling season? Or next debate season? Or next volleyball season? Moreover, what if this young blood has been spilled not merely to congregate people and their feelings, but also to illuminate a thing going wrong?"

Kesey considered blaming the Oregon coach for "driving a borrowed rig over a treacherous pass without snow studs, or seatbelts, or even doors that closed properly"; or the state of Oregon for not better funding the program; or the NCAA, for devoting more energy to monitoring the ethics of a few "stars" in the sports firmament "than to the actual welfare of the untold thousands of unknown athletes traveling to their minor events all across the nation."

He mentioned other accidents on similar trips by other schools' athletic teams, then added, "But what can they do? . . . It's hard enough to pass a school budget in Oregon without asking for fancy protection. Just not enough money in the communities. Nobody wants to increase property taxes, not even for safer playgrounds, let alone for safer activity buses.

"Then, the other night, as I watched the national news, it came to me. We were lobbing those 16-inch shells into the hills of Lebanon. The Pentagon spokesman said he wasn't certain exactly which faction we were hitting, but he reassured us that we were certainly hitting *somebody*. Then he was asked what each of those shells cost. The price was something enormous. I can't remember. But the spokesman countered by saying that the price for national defense is always high, yet it must be paid.

"And I began to get mad, Senator. I had finally found where the blame must be laid; that the money we are spending for national defense is not defending us from the villains real and near, the awful villains of ignorance, and cancer, and heart disease and highway death. How many school buses could be outfitted with seatbelts with the money spent for one of those 16-inch shells?"

Expressing a similar sentiment, Congressman Ron Dellums said that we know the state of a nation's soul by looking at its budgets. In President Dwight D. Eisenhower's classic words: "Every gun that is made, every warship launched, every rocket fired, signifies in a final sense a theft from those who hunger and are not fed—those who are cold and not clothed." This statement remains truer than ever in a world where the cost overruns alone on America's contracted weapons systems total $296 billion, or more than three times the entire annual defense spending of China, our nearest military competitor.

We need to talk honestly about the human toll of such choices, asking specifically who benefits and who pays. When a nurse I know was conducting physical exams of inmates in Seattle's county jail, she discovered that a huge percentage had chronic ear infections. That prompted her to wonder about the implications of young kids with untreated earaches: It's hard to hear what the teacher is saying. Maybe they feel angry and edgy. Soon they drop out, start stealing to survive, and end up in jail. My friend wondered how many of these men might have followed a different path had their families had access to decent medical treatment.

We're often told that we can't afford to provide health care for all of our children, can't afford to ensure that they attend adequate schools or have a roof over their heads. We can't afford to fund adequate youth employment programs, though we find the money to continue building prisons. Nor, we're told, can we afford to protect our environment, the world our children, and theirs, will inherit. "We can clone animals," points out David Lewis. "We can send rockets into space. But we can't give young people anything better to believe in than worshipping the god of money. We can't even make drug treatment programs available to everybody who wants and needs them. I would like to see that same kind of effort applied to saving people's lives."

David's point hits home to me. Enough resources exist in America to meet our public needs. But only if we reform the policies and institutions that have allowed "private affluence and public squalor," in the words of economist John Kenneth Galbraith, to dominate our society. In the early 1990s, while writing my book, *Generation at the Crossroads,* on the values of students, I interviewed a group protesting tuition hikes at New York City's 200,000-student CUNY system. Most came from impoverished backgrounds. The families of nearly a third lived on combined yearly household incomes of less than $14,000. One young woman was so poor that despite working her way through school at a fast food franchise, she couldn't even afford a new toothbrush when she thought she'd lost her old one. The students went on strike and occupied campus buildings after New York State cut $92 million from the budget line that supported their colleges—in the process hiking tuition, cutting financial aid, and slashing faculty and support staff. The legislators said the state simply lacked the money.

Shortly afterward, the investment firm Goldman Sachs, headquartered in New York City, announced a good year. It paid out bonuses to its 161 partners that totaled over $800 million. Ten percent of just this tiny group's yearly bonus would have just about covered the entire CUNY budget cuts. But throughout this period and ever since, the Goldman Sachs partners—and others equally affluent—saw their federal and state taxes cut repeatedly, producing major shortfalls in government revenue. Now the legislators said they could no longer afford to maintain the right of 200,000 students to receive an education. They deemed it more important to make sure their wealthy contributors were contented.

The escalation of wealth for those at the top and cuts for those at the bottom has only continued. By 2007, as the economic crash was beginning to build, the Goldman Sachs CEO alone made $68.5 million, and the firm allocated $6.65 billion for executive compensation just in the second quarter of 2009, while the CUNY budget got slashed yet again by $51 million. Again students protested in response, as did peers nationwide, who faced similarly draconian cuts at public colleges and universities throughout the country.

Budget numbers seem abstract until we realize that they represent the common resources of our society, which could support better schools, efficient mass transit, low-income housing, community investment corporations, inspiring arts programs, universal health care, or a serious investment in repairing the environment. If the most successful attempts to heal our society's ills and promote human dignity are often local grassroots efforts, like David's Free at Last project, imagine the impact if we gave these groups enough resources to do their work as well and powerfully as they could, instead of forcing them to scramble for crumbs.

Lest you think I'm making too much of this, for less than half of the tax cuts that Congress gave corporations and wealthy individuals in the 1990s alone, we could have brought the health, nutrition, and education standards of every child in America up to European standards. Bush's $200 billion a year of regressive tax cuts then squandered potential common resources even more. But few political leaders are willing to propose reversing this trend, anymore than they're willing to examine the difference between legitimate defense spending and needless pork. A remark attributed to the late Republican senator Everett Dirksen sums up the scale of the problem: "A billion here and a billion there," Dirksen said, "and pretty soon you're talking about real money."

To borrow an environmental phrase, we need a full cost accounting of our political and economic choices. When kids grow up in poverty, many end up in jail; when the tops of Appalachian mountains are blown off to remove coal as cheaply as possible, adjoining ecosystems and neighboring towns are devastated; when people like Goldman Sachs partners get tax breaks while making tens of millions, students can't afford to go to school; when corporations lay off employees and reduce benefits, families disintegrate and communities erode. We need to think about all the deferred, denied, and unintended consequences that echo out over time, including opportunities lost and potentials unrealized. Only when we are honest about the impact of these choices can we begin to move forward.

SLOW-BURN CRISES

Understanding these consequences means looking over the horizon to recognize how buried crises become acute when we fail to address their roots. Think back to the Katrina disaster. With bodies floating in water-filled streets, families stranded on rooftops and viaducts, and desperate people trapped without food in the New Orleans convention center, Katrina was as acute an image of disaster as one could find in America's history. But this catastrophe was created by slow-burn crises that were mostly off the national radar. The wealthy and comfortable could and did evacuate New Orleans, although their lives were severely disrupted. But in one of the nation's poorest cities, vast numbers of citizens had nowhere to go, no transportation or money with which to leave, and no friends or relatives with extra space to house them. They were the people left frantically trying to get out, while a third of the Louisiana National Guard as well as its helicopters and high-water vehicles were deployed in Iraq. Many of those who left never returned and continue to constitute an invisible diaspora, scattered through America with still-wounded lives.

The Katrina disaster might well not have occurred, or not on the same scale, had the levees been properly built and repaired. But the Bush administration first reversed Clinton administration bans on development of coastal wetlands that had buffered the impact of storms. The administration then rejected the Army Corps of Engineers' request to strengthen and renovate the levees and pumping stations, instead cutting the New Orleans flood control budget by $71 million, or nearly in half. They made these latter cuts because they needed the money for the Iraq war and to give out tax cuts disproportionately benefiting a small group of wealthy Americans. There's also the role of our largest buried crisis: climate change. Although no single weather extreme event can be linked to it, Katrina fit the larger predicted pattern when blistering temperatures in the Gulf of Mexico supercharged it from a level 1 storm, the lowest, to a level 5 catastrophe.

Other disasters involve buried crises as well, like the 2008 global financial crash. The world's governments did what they could to respond to the acute challenges it posed, but the crash was rooted in the incremental, often invisible decisions of banks, mortgage companies, hedge funds, derivatives investors, and all who created the vast edifice of debt and speculation that finally came crashing down. And it was made possible, at root, by the common decision—starting with Reagan, Clinton, and Bush senior—to deregulate financial speculation, and trust that the markets would police themselves. In an overextended and distracted time, a key challenge for us is tackling our interconnected crises before they grow so immense that they overwhelm us.

AN ETHIC OF PARTICIPATION

Changing how we make our public decisions could help us tackle long-buried pressing issues. Broad-based citizen participation is itself an "antidote to cynicism," as Alison Smith says. "I'd love to see a more humane society, but to get that, we need a much greater level of involvement, across economic lines, racial lines, every line that divides us. We have this 200-and-some-year-old experiment in self-governance. I think it's a worthy experiment. But it won't work if we're passive. One of the great things about the campaign finance reforms we passed in Maine and that states like Arizona and

Vermont passed is that they require citizen participation. I want to see people running campaigns without fund-raising pressures, and serving in elected office knowing their only debt is to the voters. Imagine a political system where the worthwhile things people do in their communities count for more than the size of their wallets. Imagine people actually participating."

When people do genuinely participate, they can solve even seemingly intractable problems. In the early 1960s, some University of Nebraska economists used the university's statewide network of adult education extension offices to organize workshops, county by county, where people could discuss different ways to make Nebraska's highly regressive state tax system more fair. The existing system had long weighed disproportionately on family farmers and low-income residents, while largely exempting the huge insurance companies in Omaha. Reaching out through the extension offices and organizations such as the Farmers' Union, the Farm Bureau, and the Grange, the economists invited people to see for themselves how a range of approaches would affect them and their neighbors. "If people just really had a chance to look at the numbers," one of the faculty members recalls, "we felt they could come to an intelligent decision. But they had to have a context to analyze the system, and this seemed a perfect use of educational networks that were already in place."

The workshop's leaders pursued their task without laptops, computerized spreadsheets, interactive Web sites, or any of the other tools that would now make a comparable process far easier. But participants examined every approach to make the system more equitable, weighing the respective advantages and problems. Local and statewide media covered the debates. It took a half-dozen years of follow-up education and discussions, but Nebraska's Republican legislature finally passed a far more progressive graduated income tax.

Of course those town meetings had something our recent ones have lacked, and that's civility. I've been thinking a lot about the conservative activists who, egged on by Rush Limbaugh and Fox News, stormed town meetings on the proposed 2009 health care bill, shouting down speakers and other participants. I was disturbed by their misinformation—demanding that the government not get involved in their Medicare, despite Medicare's being a quintessential government program, or insisting that the Democratic plan had created "death panels" to decide when the elderly had to end their lives, a gross distortion of an innocuous provision to fund voluntary counseling around options like living wills. But I was most troubled by an aggressive and bullying assault on dialogue that made real citizen participation nearly impossible.

As some have pointed out, those on the political left have also shouted down speakers at times, and that's troubled me when it's happened. So how do we draw the line? The concept of civility can certainly be used to enforce false silence and counterfeit harmony. Martin Luther King didn't say "Let civility roll down like waters and politeness like a mighty stream," but challenged those who were "more devoted to 'order' than to justice." In a 1964 civil rights movement anthem, Malvina Reynolds sang: "It isn't nice to block the doorway. It isn't nice to go to jail. There are nicer ways to do it. But the nice ways always fail." Sometimes, as I've suggested, you have to stand up and be blunt. If officials whose conduct you find destructive appear in a context that excludes real dialogue, it seems legitimate to challenge them. When a political process is rolling forward where critical perspectives are simply excluded from consideration, the same is true—as when a group of doctors were willingly arrested at a Senate health reform hearing for standing up and asking why Canadian-style government health insurance was not even being considered as an option.

But if we're in a context like a town meeting, where participants will have a genuine say, shouting down others denies them their right to listen and be heard. That seems particularly dangerous when it becomes what historian Rick Pearlstein calls "manufactured incivility," with radio and cable news hosts whipping people up to shout down those who disagree with them, and insurance or fossil fuel company PR flacks promoting distorted yelling points. For all civility's limits, we need to distinguish between nonviolent civil disobedience, of whatever political stripe, and outright bullying. Inconveniencing business as usual can bring critical issues into the public eye. But physical intimidation attacks human dignity, promotes a climate of fear, and makes it harder for ordinary citizens to speak out.

Gandhi offered clues on some appropriate distinctions. As long-time nonviolent activist and theorist George Lakey points out, Gandhi believed that what protects dialogue and democracy even when millions are breaking the law is their willingness to accept the personal consequences of their actions, like being willing to go to jail. As Lakey says, "In that way they are saying 'yes' to the conditions essential for democracy even while saying 'no' to the particular thing they are defying, whether a practice of the British empire or the exclusion of the Canadian approach from the health care debate." The goal of the participants is to promote a moral force that also exercises common power—for instance by defying British tax laws or boycotting British goods. But not a force that physically intimidates opponents.

The moral and political implications reinforce each other. Had Harry Taylor simply shouted at Bush, and called him a murderer and liar, his action would have been a dismissible flicker on the news. Instead, by being respectful even toward a president whose actions completely affronted his moral sensibilities, Taylor came off as reasonable and thoughtful, and his concerns struck a nerve. The Serbian youth movement, Otpor, which led the resistance against Slobodan Milošević similarly got more traction from mocking him than screaming. Sometimes, though, if dissenters are completely denied access, all they can do is raise their raw anguished voices against the arrogance of power. But in situations with at least a chance of reaching out to those with whom we disagree—even if perspectives are as profoundly opposed as in the Boston conversations that brought together pro-choice and right-to-life activists—our responsibility is to do all we can to expand this chance of dialogue. And by fostering the antithesis of this dialogue, those who shouted down others at the town meetings ultimately undermined democracy.

A JUST ECONOMY

Challenging as it might be to make our political process more democratic and participatory, it can seem even more daunting to try and envision how we might create a genuinely just, fruitful, and sustainable economy. I hardly presume to have sure answers, but from my experience, some principles emerge. The market system has created the unparalleled standard of living that many of us in advanced industrial countries enjoy. It allows capital to organize production, encourage invention, and distribute goods to those able to buy them. It obviously has its role. But unchecked capitalism routinely destroys the environment, treats its workers as disposable commodities, and shatters lives and communities as it spurs a global race to the bottom of ever-lower wages. So from my perspective, we need to create forces that balance it.

The U.S. economy in particular has become increasingly based on speculation and debt, with financial meltdown the result. We still have a real economy, from Google and Microsoft to emerging alternative energy companies, pharmaceuticals, agriculture, and what remains of our manufacturing base, like airplanes, medical technology, and semiconductors. We also have the longtime dubious honor of being the world's largest weapons exporter, controlling over two-thirds of deals in the international arms trade. But the restless movement of capital continually undermines our real economy—as those who call the shots chase the highest possible return, even if it weakens our genuine productive capacity.

Here's a humble example. In 1992, a friend of my dentist invented a new toothbrush called a Sonicare, that used sonic waves to clean teeth. I bought one through my dentist and it lasted seventeen years until the batteries stopped taking a charge. Meanwhile, in its first five years, the Seattle-area startup that produced them became the fastest-growing private company in the United States, and the U.S. Small Business Administration named its founder as U.S. small business person of the year. Since then, Sonicare has become the top-selling rechargeable toothbrush in the country. But in

2000 the founders sold the company to the huge Dutch multinational Phillips, which later moved production from Washington State to China. A product that an American invented became a debit in the international trade balance. While the Dutch were buying up productive companies, much of the discretionary wealth in the United States was chasing speculative investments, like mortgage-based securities.

If we're going to steer our economy back toward actually creating real benefit, we need to place limits on speculation—like Nobel Prize–winning economist James Tobin's suggestion of a small tax on financial transactions, so as to favor long-term investors over those who are constantly gaming the markets. We need to limit the ability of the world's most powerful corporations to play communities, states, and countries off against each other in a vain search for stable jobs. We need to find equitable ways to fund our common expenditures, instead of making our tax system steadily less equitable, a process that has fed the greatest income inequality in America's history. Finally, we need to be honest about how deeply we've damaged our ability to produce actual goods that meet human needs.

You may disagree, but to me, a just economic order would also incorporate the advances in preserving human dignity that are now taken for granted in Western Europe, across political lines. These advances would include decent health care, child care, adequate vacations, parental leave, and retirement security. Some European economies are more affluent than ours, some less: but all provide their citizens with basics of human survival that our more individualist culture has deemed discretionary or expendable. And particularly in these uncertain times, I suspect that many of us would trade at least some of our own precarious affluence for a bit more certainty that we'll still have a place to live if we get laid off, medical care if we get sick, and a decent education for our children, whatever our economic resources. European policies that make this possible hardly guarantee universal justice and happiness, and haven't solved all the global economy's complex problems. But it's worth noting that both France and Germany emerged from the 2008 economic crash in less than a year, in part because of their strong social safety net and Germany's robust and heavily unionized manufacturing sector. We might do well to learn from them.

Another alternative model began after the Spanish Civil War, when a Basque priest who'd opposed the fascists and barely survived Franco's jails began a small cooperative stove factory in a remote Spanish town called Mondragon. Today, Mondragon's interconnected worker-owned cooperatives are the biggest employer in the Basque region, employing 92,000 people. They own, manage, and operate a highly successful community development bank; an insurance company; agricultural co-ops; Spain's largest manufacturer of refrigerators, stoves, and electrical appliances; co-ops that make buses and computer-controlled machine tools; Spain's largest chain of supermarkets; a joint co-op/government university; and a vocational school and occupational training system. The workers own and run the various co-ops, and their appointed committees make major decisions, like hiring and firing corporate managers, many of whom have themselves worked their way up from the shop floor. The company president makes no more than six times the after-tax income of the lowest-paid employee. And the cooperatives give 10 percent of profits to the cooperative bank to provide capital for new enterprises and expand existing ones.

With these successes have come new challenges. The Mondragon cooperatives have transformed the Basque region from an economic backwater to one of the most prosperous areas of Spain. But to keep up with demand, like from major auto manufacturers who buy their components, the co-op has had to open up plants in Mexico, China, Morocco, the Czech Republic, and Thailand, and hire workers there as regular (non–co-op) employees. Add in the rapid expansion of their retail stores, and non-members have grown to two-thirds of Mondragon workers. Now in the process of integrating them as full owner members, Mondragon offers a powerful alternative model that has kept people working in even the most difficult economic times in a context where they ultimately run their highly successful economic enterprises.

AMERICAN ALTERNATIVES

Although the history is mostly buried, America has its own tradition of attempting to create a more democratic economy. Thomas Jefferson believed that economic imbalances produced "so much misery to the bulk of mankind, legislators cannot invent too many devices for subdividing property." He warned: "I hope we shall crush in its birth the aristocracy of our monied corporations." Lincoln had similar reservations about the damaging effects of gross inequality of wealth. "Inasmuch as good things are produced by labor," he said, "it follows that all such things of right belong to those whose labor has produced them. But it has so happened, in all ages of the world, that some have labored and others have without labor enjoyed a larger proportion of the fruits. This is wrong and should not continue. To secure to each laborer the whole product of his labor, or as nearly as possible, is a worthy object of any good government."

The populist and socialist organizers of the late nineteenth and early twentieth century took up these themes in a context of rapid industrialization and emerging corporate monopolies. Their agendas included powerful mutual aid, whereby small farmers worked together to market their crops and challenge the stranglehold of powerful railroad and banking interests in favor of what they called "the cooperative commonwealth." Though these movements were ultimately defeated, their egalitarian philosophy led to the creation of successful institutions that persist to this day, like North Dakota's state-owned bank, Wisconsin's state-owned insurance company, and, later on, hundreds of rural electrical cooperatives and municipally owned urban utilities.

The principle of using common resources for the common good reached fruition in Roosevelt's New Deal and the policies that emerged from it. Howard Zinn recalled coming back from the Second World War and working as a waiter, a ditch-digger, and a brewery worker while trying to support two young children in a rat-infested Bedford–Stuyvesant apartment. Then he got the chance to go to New York University, with expenses paid for by his veteran's benefits. The education of Zinn and millions of other vets helped fuel the longest sustained growth period in American history. "Whenever I hear that the government *must not* get involved in helping people," wrote Zinn, "that this must be left to 'private enterprise,' I think of the G. I. Bill and its marvelous non-bureaucratic efficiency."

Our historical amnesia makes it hard to draw on such traditions. We're poorly informed about the effort that went into enacting such victories for human dignity as Social Security, Medicare, the forty-hour workweek, and our right, however constrained, to organize unions. So we're ill-equipped to comprehend the principles they represent and their relevance to our current situation. Whatever our vision of a truly just society, we need to preserve and strengthen these advances. They help answer Jefferson and Lincoln's concerns about democracy's vulnerability to unchecked economic forces.

Among the institutions that offer me hope of a more just and democratically controlled American economy are large worker-, producer-, and member-owned companies that have successfully competed with traditional corporations. These include companies as large as the Ocean Spray cranberry and Land O'Lakes dairy cooperatives, the Vanguard mutual funds, the Publix and Hy-Vee supermarkets (with 200,000 employees between them), the company that makes Gore-Tex, the 25,000-employee global engineering and consulting firm CH2M Hill, and Science Applications, a 45,000-employee scientific, engineering, and technology applications company that bought the Research & Development subsidiary of the Baby Bells.

Mondragon has recently provided inspiration for Cleveland's Evergreen Cooperatives, a new network of community- and worker-owned enterprises created by local foundations, hospitals, nursing homes, banks, a university, and City Hall. The network includes an industrial laundry, a company that installs solar panels on the roofs of government buildings and nonprofits, and a year-round urban agriculture project that will grow more than 3 million heads of fresh lettuce per year and a million pounds of basil using a hydroponic greenhouse. Participating stakeholders will purchase services and products from these co-ops, keeping the money in the local community, while co-op profits will help fund similar ventures.

Even when workers or consumers aren't also owners, they can participate more often and more directly in corporate policymaking, thereby building real democracy. Germany requires worker representation on the boards of major corporations, and Genoese longshoremen have long managed their own operations while running one of the busiest ports on the continent. According to a study by economists Lisa Lynch of Tufts University and Sandra Black of the Federal Reserve Bank, American factories that are unionized and offer such participatory programs are 20 percent more productive than the average for their industry.

Another model for economic democracy can be found in partnerships between private corporations and their surrounding communities. COPS and its sister organizations in other cities have generated commitments from major companies to invest in long-neglected neighborhoods, and to provide resources so high school students with good grades and regular attendance records will be guaranteed financial access to college. Vermont National Bank has established a Socially Responsible Banking Fund that depositors can select as a home for their accounts, while the money is lent out to support housing co-ops, environmental education centers, organic farms, an alternative energy fund, and a business that recovers methane from the Brattleboro landfill. ShoreBank, where I keep my savings account, has grown to over $2 billion in assets through investing in community development in low-to-moderate income urban neighborhoods, with a major focus on sustainability and retrofitting for energy efficiency. It has financed the purchase and renovation of over 40,000 affordable housing residences in Chicago alone, and has also restored and helped stabilize communities in Cleveland, Detroit, the Pacific Northwest, and Michigan's Upper Peninsula.

Building on Jefferson's ideas of a nation of freeholders—citizens who control their own livelihoods—economist Gar Alperovitz suggests that communities develop their own locally controlled enterprises, so their residents will be less vulnerable to the caprices of the global economy. Markets and trade would still exist. Technology would still develop. But communities would have greater control of their regional economies, and would keep as many resources as possible circulating locally. It's hard, Alperovitz says, for people to be full and active citizens unless they enjoy enough independence to speak out without fear of reprisal by powerful economic and political interests, as when factories threaten to shut down if their workers organize a union, or owners pressure their workers to lobby for pork barrel contracts. The more control we have over our local economies, Alperovitz believes, the more we can promote genuine liberty.

Similarly, Pete Knutson regards his independence as a cardinal virtue of his local fishing community, part of a way of life whose roots go back as far as human history. "We face lots of frustrations," Pete says, "like dealing with corporate domination of our markets and the destruction of the watersheds. But we also have a lot of individual autonomy. We're out there in nature, relying on a few other people, so we have a sense of camaraderie. We're doing environmentally sustainable work, harvesting a wonderful regional food source in a way we can continue, so long as people monitor the salmon runs and fight to take care of the habitat. Those are qualities of responsibility. You want them in any kind of work and any society."

I'm not suggesting that we automatically embrace every social welfare or public investment program placed before us. Whatever organizations and institutions we believe in, it's worth asking which of their approaches effectively serve a greater common good, and which do not. This applies to government projects, public schools, community development corporations, and common support systems like welfare and disability compensation. It also applies to nonprofit agencies, unions, churches, temples, the Salvation Army, and homeless shelters. And it applies to the private sector—specific companies, industries, and the market as a whole. Regardless of our political allegiances or fears about giving ammunition to hostile critics, we achieve nothing by cultivating blind loyalty to any institutions, public or private, and relinquishing our responsibility to honestly scrutinize whatever institutions we're engaged with.

We may disagree about the feasibility of any of the approaches I've suggested, or whether they're desirable. But my aim is not to convert you to specific prescriptions. Rather it's to extend our conversation on common responsibility, and suggest that alternatives exist to our current economy's most destructive aspects, and that one of our major challenges is to develop them further, drawing on the best of our traditions and ideas from other nations.

DEFENDING THE EARTH

We also possess the means to rein in the continuing destruction of the environment. Nature cannot defend itself against the damage we create. So it's up to us, as ordinary citizens, to help chart wiser paths.

"As a biblical Christian," Rich Cizik said, "I agree with Saint Francis that every square inch on Earth belongs to Christ. If we don't pay attention to global climate change, it's pretty obvious that tens and or even hundreds of millions of people are going to die. If you have a major sea-level rise then Bangladesh becomes uninhabitable. Where do you put its one hundred million people? Do you put them in India? In China? They'd have no place to go. Britain's Christian Aid talks of climate change impacting one billion people by mid-century, with drought, floods, disease, and malnutrition. I've asked African American leaders whether, as a white man, I can call climate change 'the civil rights issue of the twenty-first century.' Unanimously they say, 'You not only can, but you must.' "

Cizik believed he could still preach the gospel while also talking about these kinds of issues. "You need both. To go to bed at night and say that over a billion people live on a dollar a day and can't go to bed themselves with a full stomach, can you live as a Christian happily in your suburban home, driving your SUV? Of course you can't. Not as a real Christian. And if you happen to be a liberal, conservative, or centrist, I don't care. The gospel has priority over politics."

Climate change demands obvious steps like putting a steep price on carbon emissions, and supporting alternative technologies. But we also need to address our broader relationship to the earth. Socially responsible business executive Paul Hawken asks us to consider the "income derived from a healthy environment: clean air and water, climate stabilization, rainfall, ocean productivity, fertile soil, watersheds, and the less-appreciated functions of the environment, such as processing waste—both natural and industrial." A sustainable economy, he says, preserves and replenishes natural systems, so we can continue to live off this income indefinitely. Our current American economy, by contrast, is unsustainable. It consumes not only the income, but also the basic natural capital from which the income is derived, while passing on the consequences to future generations.

Yet examples of sustainable economic practices exist, and we can learn from them. In an essay on Peruvian mountain farmers, Wendell Berry describes agricultural traditions so rich and complex that even the least-skilled individuals do not erode the fragile land they work. Some intensively cultivated English farms have been worked for thousands of years, yet the soil has grown steadily richer. These practices are guided by cultural ethics that make accommodating nature a matter not of extraordinary skill, intelligence, or moral development, but of habits and cultural frameworks woven into the daily lives of ordinary citizens.

Hawken and others suggest that instead of subsidizing ecologically destructive activities we should be collecting "green taxes" from them, while simultaneously offering commensurate credits for businesses that restore the environment and invest in human capital. This means encouraging state-of-the-art insulation and efficient lighting instead of additional power plants, organic and bio-intensive agriculture instead of chemical-dependent monocropping, and effective public transportation systems and fuel-efficient cars instead of massive highway subsidies. It means supporting closed-loop manufacturing systems that re-use materials and energy to avoid waste and pollution in the first place, or that create durable consumer goods with repairable components: The world's largest commercial floor-covering producer, Georgia-based Interface, is moving toward doing both—dropping their greenhouse gas emissions by 71 percent since 1996 and cutting fossil fuel consumption by 60 percent, while doubling their earnings and dramatically increasing profitability. Interface did this by tackling every aspect of their environmental impact, from how they powered their factories to how they shipped their products, even manufacturing new carpet from ground-up old carpet. Sustainability means continually asking how our actions today will affect generations to come.

SAVING THE PLANET, ONE FURNACE AT A TIME

As groups like the Apollo Alliance and Blue Green Alliance have suggested, we can address multiple intertwined crises if we do it creatively enough. I stumbled into an example of this when my furnace died while I was rewriting this book. To replace it, I spent $5,000 for a high-efficiency Trane furnace, money that supported the local Seattle company that installed it, Trane's unionized factory workers in Trenton, New Jersey, and Tyler, Texas, and the beleaguered state and city governments that received my sales tax and the taxes paid by the companies involved. My thirteen-year-old furnace was down to barely 60 percent efficiency because of normal wear and tear and corrosion. My new one is 97 percent efficient and will maintain this level far longer due to improved design. Even with a modest and well-insulated house in Seattle's temperate climate, my investment will pay back in nine years, or six with federal tax rebates. If I lived in a colder climate or had a larger house it would pay back its costs sooner still. But even at the lowest figure, that's a far better return than I could get from any investment these days except the riskiest, plus I'll prevent the release of three tons of carbon dioxide every year.

So here's an expenditure that benefits my pocketbook, the American economy, and the planet. Imagine if we created a federal program to help people make such purchases nationwide, perhaps combining direct incentives like those in the 2009 economic stimulus bill with Al Gore's longtime suggestion of creating a low- or no-interest loan fund for home and business alternative energy projects. High efficiency furnaces aren't a panacea. Plugging leaks, adding insulation, and switching light bulbs produce more energy efficiency for fewer dollars. We still need solutions that eliminate use of fossil fuel altogether, like solar thermal, industrial-scale wind, advanced geothermal, ultra-efficient green buildings, and smart electrical grids. The 300,000-person Swedish city of Malmö, for instance, gets 40 percent of its residential heat and 60 percent of its electricity from a municipal incinerator plant, and is steadily extending its district heating to the suburbs. We could do the same. But switching to high-efficiency furnaces and their equivalents buys time, much like Angie De Soto did by getting Virginia Tech to turn the thermostats down and increase the efficiency of its physical plant. Efficiency takes us part of the way—and if the furnaces are American-made by union labor, does so while keeping money in our domestic economy and supporting family-wage jobs. If we could replace every furnace at least ten years old with a comparable model, and mandate high-efficiency furnaces in new construction, we'd come out far ahead.

Here's another example of how acting with enough vision can allow us to make progress on multiple fronts. Like most in the auto industry, the St. Paul, Minnesota, factory that makes Ford Ranger light trucks has been repeatedly threatened with closure. In 2004, their United Auto Workers local suggested the innovative idea of workers logging four ten-hour days each week without charging overtime for working beyond eight hours per day. The factory would schedule two shifts, working back-to-back on each of the four days, and would save money by having to fire up its paint furnaces and other energy-intensive facilities only Monday through Thursday, while selling the power from an associated hydro plant back to the grid the other three days. The employees got three-day weekends and saved time and gas through one day fewer of commuting. In the process, the plant cut the carbon footprint from its own energy use and the workers' commutes, something important to health and safety steward Lynn Hinkle, who spearheaded the idea.

The plan, Lynn said, emerged from conversations at regular workers' meetings, which the union had created over the years. Utah's Republican governor, John Huntsman, would later embrace a similar four-day plan for as many state employees as possible, with comparable cost and environmental savings. It took some persistence to convince Ford management, and to get a majority of the St. Paul plant employees to agree to it. But the approach has saved enough money to help keep the plant open, though Ford still talks of maybe closing it in another several years. Given that the facility ran on renewable hydro power, Lynn and the others also suggested converting the Rangers to run as plug-in hybrids or electrics, or on sustainable biofuels, making the factory a flagship for a greener Ford brand. Although the company strongly considered the idea, they finally passed on it, "which was a shame," Lynn said, "because if they had, they'd now be in a prime position to go after the green consumer market with a U.S. plant that treats its workers decently, instead of continuing to lose ground to the Japanese." Nonetheless, studies created for this effort helped Lynn convince a group of Minneapolis engineers to locate an innovative solar panel manufacturing startup on another Twin Cities site rather than in China as originally planned. So even the near-misses bore fruit.

WE BUILD THE ROAD AS WE TRAVEL

Examples like these may not constitute a complete road map for change, but they suggest elements of where we could usefully go. And a patchwork, continually evolving vision may strike exactly the balance between humility and boldness that's needed in these challenging times We may proceed best, as Mary Catherine Bateson writes, "by improvisation, discovering the shape of our creation along the way, rather than pursuing a vision already defined." As long as we stay open to new information, learning along the way, and relinquishing the need for absolute certainty, we can continue to work toward important goals. We can conduct what Gandhi called "experiments in truth," or as the priest who founded the Spanish Mondragon co-ops once said, "build the road as we travel."

Key to this journey is learning from the stories of our fellow citizens. This means listening to people, like Virginia Ramirez and her San Antonio neighbors, who live on crumbling streets and send their children to underfunded schools. To those who grow up unable to acknowledge their sexuality, for fear of being beaten or scorned. To those who earn decent pay and live in comfortable surroundings but are ground down by endless commutes, sixty-hour workweeks, and a sense that their jobs lack meaning. And even to those who strongly disagree with the political solutions we may offer.

As I've suggested, these stories may offer conflicting lessons, and each of us may interpret them differently. Although we may well modify our visions along the way, the more they're based on actual human experiences and not remote ideological abstractions, the more we can trust them. This requires that we pay close attention to how others live, particularly those with radically differing lives, to the specific problems that they face, and to how our society either nurtures or impedes their hopes and dreams. We can then derive our politics from what we learn from them.

Some may find this vision too gradualist, like putting a miniscule Band-Aid on a massive gaping wound. But I'm not suggesting we abandon our long-term vision of justice, only that we remember that even the most profound changes often come one step at a time. In his classic *Strategy for Labor,* French social theorist Andre Gorz distinguished between reforms that democratized power and those that masked fundamental inequities. He suggested that when working to change any institution or political situation, we ask whether our goals will increase human dignity or diminish it, embolden people's voices or stifle them, give ordinary citizens more or less of a say in shaping their world. If proposed reforms increase democratic rights, contribute to individual power and community possibility, and increase the likelihood of a sustainable future, they are worth supporting.

Even in the most difficult situations, we can construct routes toward freedom and justice. In his book, *Solidarity,* on how Poland's Solidarity movement successfully challenged the country's communist dictatorship, Lawrence Weschler describes how the Poles took on, as a new principle of action, the task of creating for themselves what they wanted for their society. They wanted free elections, so they freely elected individuals; wanted free speech, so spoke freely; wanted a trade union, so founded one. Leaders of KOR, the workers' support movement, routinely risked job loss or prison by printing their names and phone numbers on the back of each mimeographed sheet describing incidents of police harassment against then unknown activists like Lech Walesa. "It is as if," Weschler comments, "KOR were calling out to everyone else, 'Come on out! Be open. What can they do to us if we all start taking responsibility for our true dreams?' "

"We're often told that politics is the art of the possible," says Elaine Bernard, of the Harvard Trade Union Program, an intensive training school for union leaders. "But democratic politics is the art of constructing what's possible. People have been convinced that they can't hope for anything beyond their own individual mobility and the survival of their families. We need to offer an alternative."

This alternative vision may be even more important than the critiques we offer. "We have to fight what's wrong, like challenging environmental pollution," as Surfrider Foundation founder, Glenn Hening, says. "But we also have to act from more than anger or fear. We have to make clear that we can do better."

Whatever issues we address, we'll keep living with imperfect societies, imperfect human beings, and imperfect solutions, for as far into the future as we can imagine. But this doesn't justify retreat from the admittedly difficult challenges of working for a more humane world. Rather, it allows us to proceed as we are, in our existing political culture, and then open up new possibilities.

AN ETHIC OF CONNECTION

Even a patchwork vision is more than platforms and programs. It's a picture of ourselves, the world, and the relationship between the two. As a Lakota Indian activist said, "If you think you're related to the stars, you'll have a different view of your responsibility." In isolation, it's easy for our vision to fail and our heart to grow cold. When we cultivate a sense of broader connection, however, we see further, we take more of existence into account. In short, we find our place in the world. "The time has come to lower our voices," writes Thomas Berry, "to cease imposing our mechanistic patterns on the biological processes of the earth, to resist the impulse to control, to command, to force, to oppress, and to begin quite humbly to follow the guidance of the larger community on which all life depends. . . . Our human destiny is integral with the destiny of the earth."

Harry Taylor echoed this theme. "I believe we're all connected," he said, "and that when we, as a people, hurt or exploit others, we're also hurting and exploiting ourselves. My heart really does ache when I hear about all the violent, selfish, foolish things human beings do to others, and to mountains, rivers, and wildlife. It cannot continue."

This ethic of connection is integral to the destiny of our fellow human beings. In dealing with both the human and natural world, we must choose between a constricted and disconnected self and one that embraces life's richness, including moments of difficulty and sorrow. As the naturalist Terry Tempest Williams writes, "If I choose not to become attached to nouns—a person, place, or thing—then when I refuse an intimate's love or hoard my spirit, when a known landscape is bought, sold, and developed, chained or grazed to a stubble, or a hawk is shot and hung by its feet on a barbed-wire fence, my heart cannot be broken because I never risked giving it away. A man or woman whose mind reins in the heart when the body sings desperately for connection can only expect more isolation and greater ecological disease. Our lack of intimacy with each other is in direct proportion to our lack of intimacy with the land. We have taken our love inside and abandoned the wild."

When we retreat from this demanding intimacy, we lose our sense of who we are. Elie Wiesel retells the expulsion from the Garden of Eden in the words of a wise Hasidic rabbi, who explained that when God asked Adam, "Where art thou?" God knew where Adam was, but Adam did not. "Do we know where we are?" Wiesel asks, and then explains, "My place is measured by yours. . . . My place under the sun, or in the face of God, or in my own memory is measured by the distance it has from you . . . if I see a person or persons suffer, and the distance between us doesn't shrink . . . my place is not good, not enviable."

Meredith Segal was also troubled by this distance. After Obama's election she thought about pursuing a job in the administration, but instead decided to work with a Boston anti-poverty agency and run a group that advocated for children. She kept noticing the invisible lines that divided the city and our country. "I'm currently working," she says, "in an inner-city area plagued by violence, neglect, and intergenerational poverty. These are people to whom life has not been kind. As I travel to and from work, I'm struck by the worlds that silently co-exist within the city of Boston. I work in Dorchester, but when I talk with people from Harvard, even ones who are very service oriented, they wouldn't go there even to try a restaurant. If I suggested to the Dorchester people that they visit some place in Cambridge or Somerville, they wouldn't go there. They'd feel uncomfortable. There are such differences not only in money, but in life experience, expectations, how people see themselves. And because these simultaneously existing universes don't interact with each other, it makes everything else that much harder."

Our identity, as I've said throughout this book, is discovered and realized only within the context of community and connection. In *Emotional Intelligence,* Daniel Goleman talks of deriving our core moral sensibility from our ability to understand the emotions of other human beings, to sense their needs, and to care about how our choices will affect their lives. This is the essence of compassion, "to suffer with." Compassion asks us to enter places of pain, write the theologians Henri Nouwen, Donald McNeill, and Douglas Morrison, "to share in brokenness, fear, confusion, and anguish. Compassion challenges us to cry out with those in misery, to mourn with those who are lonely, to weep with those in tears. Compassion requires us to be weak with the weak, vulnerable with the vulnerable, and powerless with the powerless." Requiring "full immersion in the condition of being human," it's an ethic essential to reclaiming our souls.

If we want to create a just world, we must affirm these fundamental ties. Desmond Tutu celebrates "the rainbow people of God." "An injury to one is an injury to all," states the classic labor maxim. "We need to remind people," explains a massage therapist and children's advocate I know, "of our common humanity. That we're all in this together. When we disown a part of that humanity, when we walk on another person, it comes back to haunt us."

Whatever our particular visions, we renew our souls in the company of other human beings. "Hatred tries to cure disunion by annihilating those who are not united with us," wrote Thomas Merton. "It seeks peace by the elimination of everybody else but ourselves. But love, by its acceptance of the pain of reunion, begins to heal all wounds. . . . Consequently, we can only be happy in this world in so far as we are free to rejoice in the good of another: specifically in so far as we are free to rejoice in the good which is God's."

Essentially, Merton has described an ethic of connection. It's based on our willingness to look past our limited interests, appetites, and needs to embrace a world that will always be imperfect and contain suffering and pain, but is nonetheless worth working to redeem. If that sounds like spiritual language, so be it. In my view, any hopeful social movement has to be based in the elusive and perhaps unknowable forces that join us together. For in honoring these fundamental human bonds, we begin to embody the vision that we seek.

CHAPTER ELEVEN

Coping with Burnout

You get out of the city. You hike, run a river, or watch birds in a park. . . .
Your mind gets a rest. You come back ready to take on Exxon.

—HAZEL WOLF

In the early 1970s, when I was just out of college, I edited a small political magazine called *Liberation*. It had been around since the mid-1950s and had an inspiring history (even though it had never circulated more than 10,000 copies). Nelson Mandela had written for it, as had radical existentialist Albert Camus and leading African American novelist and essayist James Baldwin. Martin Luther King's "Letter from Birmingham Jail" had appeared in its pages. Founding editor Paul Goodman wrote one of the canonical texts of the 1960s, *Growing Up Absurd,* and was "out" when most gays were closeted. Co-founder Bayard Rustin, another gay pioneer, was a key mentor to King on Gandhian tactics and the prime organizer of the March on Washington where King gave his famed "I Have a Dream" speech. I arrived shortly after the last co-founder, veteran pacifist and Chicago Seven defendant Dave Dellinger, had left. Within six months, I'd become the senior staffer, working desperately to keep the magazine afloat.

We enlisted new financial supporters and writers including Howard Zinn, Susan Sontag, Allen Ginsberg, Noam Chomsky, Gary Snyder, and Wendell Berry. We sent out mailings and appeals—and even increased our circulation. Because I felt the magazine's survival was at stake, I put in sixty hours a week, soliciting and developing articles, designing promotions, and working to raise the $60,000 a year in grants and donations that kept us going. When a piece of junk mail arrived one day addressed to "Dear Mr. Liberation," the other staffers handed it to me, explaining with a smile, "Of course they mean Paul."

But the work and circumstances ground me down. We each earned $60 a week, in theory, but didn't always get that. Even though my rent in a shared Brooklyn house was only $85 a month, what I earned didn't cover my needs. The other staffers worked hard, too, but they logged fewer hours and could supplement their meager salaries by outside freelancing: indexing, proofreading, graphic design. They stayed financially afloat, albeit precariously, while I steadily depleted the money I'd saved from working my way through college as a bartender. Several times, I thought of asking for a bit more salary, both as compensation for my extra time and because I brought in the bulk of the magazine's budget. But I never asked. Instead, when my savings ran out after three years, I had to leave, financially and emotionally drained. Within another couple of years, the magazine had folded.

SETTING BOUNDARIES

Looking back, I see I had other options. I could have asked for more money or more help. We could have printed fewer issues. I could have found other ways to set limits on my commitment. I didn't do so because the cause seemed too important. What I didn't realize was that giving beyond what I could emotionally and financially afford left me so exhausted that I could not continue over the long haul. More important, my departure hastened the ultimate demise of the magazine I cared about so deeply.

If we are to stay involved in our causes, we must set boundaries to keep our lives from being so consumed that we're forced to withdraw from involvement entirely. For short periods—like the weeks before a key election or major event that we're organizing, or when a crisis unexpectedly emerges—we can sacrifice sleep, exercise, family relationships, and other personal aspects of our lives. But if we work only in crisis mode, with no chance to recuperate, we'll steadily erode the ties that sustain us—and perhaps our economic base as well. And sooner or later we'll collapse. For most of this book, I've been talking about the need to push beyond our comfort zones. But we also need to choose the pace and manner of our commitments, so that we don't end up too drained to continue—as happened to me at *Liberation*.

Even without unexpected crises, it's easy to stretch ourselves beyond our limits. When I visit campuses, the most active students often tell me, "Forty of us do everything. We're stretched completely thin, barely keeping up with our classes. We feel like we're driving ourselves to exhaustion." It's a familiar dilemma for all of us. There are always more causes, and more tasks to take on, than people to carry them out. But we make matters worse when we try to do too much or attempt to do everything ourselves.

Backing off often means getting help, which is critical if we're to avoid carrying an impossible load. Bringing others in to share the necessary work also helps them begin their own journeys of engagement. Angie De Soto described burning out several times by overextending herself, working too many hours, not sleeping enough, and not drawing clear boundaries. She had agreed to chair the entertainment committee for the national Powershift student climate change conference: "We were having conference calls every week, hours of e-mails every night, plus my full-time internship, and working at a café." Angie felt like she was drowning. Then she asked a student from nearby Roanoke College to be her co-chair. They divided the work, and Angie was able to stay involved.

Sometimes we need to gently refuse the tenth or twelfth invitation, however worthy, to join a committee, call a phone tree, canvass a neighborhood, draft a letter, speak at a program, or march for a cause, however worthy. Often we can do more than we think. But other times we need to draw a line, even if it means doing fewer projects.

"You can't solve all of the world's problems," environmental activist Hazel Wolf reminded me on the eve of her hundredth birthday. "You can take on one project at a time, and then another. You can do that your entire life. But you have to guard against taking on more than you can do and burning out with frustration. Sometimes you just have to say no and wish people well."

Steven Levine grew up in gangs, spent time in jail, then found a new career teaching meditation in prisons and hospices. At one of his seminars, a man who had survived family violence described his current work, counseling and playing basketball with gang kids. The kids were troubled, challenging, inspiring. "Sometimes their energy threatens to blow my head off," he told Levine. "I feel exhausted trying to keep up." He worried whether he could continue carrying the load.

Levine asked the man whether working with half the kids would be enough to fulfill him. "More than enough," the man said with a laugh. Levine suggested he find other activities that would channel the kids' creativity and slow their pace, such as creating a group garden. Maybe, he suggested, the man could also shift his workload to include some other less desperate kids. By backing off a bit, he could keep doing his important work.

To avoid a constant crisis mode, we'd do well to be as intentional as we can in our political engagement, asking what we want to accomplish at any given point. That doesn't mean getting caught in some impossible perfect standard, but rather thinking through our opportunities, challenges, and approaches, whatever the situation. That's what Rosa Parks and her compatriots explored at the Highlander Center, drawing on lessons from previous activists, and what Angie De Soto did at her climate change training. Heather Booth of the Midwest Academy, a longtime activist training center, said, "I think the most common reason people withdraw is that they don't think the strain is worth the goal. They don't think they can really win. A key way to deal with this is to have a strategic plan, developed through a common process—so your group doesn't just react from crisis to crisis or tactic to tactic. You still never know if it will work, but when you think things through together, you're stronger because different views sharpen your focus and build your community. Then when you have a plan, you can revise it as you go, but you have a sense of where you're going."

THE REVOLVING DOOR

Unfortunately, too many of us neglect the chance to bring others in, set limits on our work, and manage the pace and direction of our involvement well enough to continue for a lifetime. I've seen far too many people involve themselves in tremendously important efforts for change, but then withdraw in exhaustion or despair. Discussing burnout may seem like a detour in a book about empowerment, but it's important to understand why people burn out, because this understanding helps us continue our work. The more we know about the obstacles that lie ahead, the better equipped we'll be to surmount them.

I've described how easy it is to get overloaded and exhausted. We can get frustrated at a lack of traction when trying to challenge entrenched and powerful interests, or when we're tackling issues so deeply rooted that they seem almost impossible to solve. Our fellow activists may leave us feeling disappointed or even betrayed, as can political leaders in whom we vest our hopes. And if we neglect to develop supportive communities or to savor moments of respite, we can easily grow resentful or brittle, shattering easily at the inevitable setbacks. If all that wasn't enough, we face the pressures of everything else we need to do in our lives, such as surviving financially.

Burning out differs from temporarily pulling back due to the rhythms of our lives. If we have young children or aging parents who need care, or if we hit an acute personal or financial crisis, that may be all we can deal with for a while. And whatever our situation, taking a brief break may be precisely what we need to keep going. But many of us also withdraw more permanently, sometimes abruptly, sometimes so incrementally that we barely notice our retreat.

Those who withdraw may still watch political events from a distance, as if tracking the fortunes of a favored baseball team.

They may still click and respond to political e-mails, write modest checks to sympathetic causes, even participate in the occasional political rally or community project—all more than most people do. Yet their ambitions were once much greater. They envisioned a more generous, just, and inclusive society, and they worked long and hard to realize that vision. They once reached out to their fellow citizens. They've stopped doing that, and the more they pull back, the less they believe that their actions can make a difference, and the harder they find it to re-engage in political action.

The polarization of our time can also grind people down. As two-term Annapolis, Maryland, mayor Ellen Moyer told me, "Unless you have the hide of a rhinoceros it's hard to exist sanely as a public servant in today's climate of anger and mean-spiritedness. I have been involved in public service to my community for over fifty years. I can show my grandchildren parks, trees, art, and environmental projects I initiated or helped to implement. Yet a handful of hateful bloggers have turned this community into a negative sphere, while the local newspaper uncritically repeats their false allegations. Well-meaning citizens who once volunteered their time to enhance the quality of life on boards and commissions are now declining to participate. Efforts to promote civil dialogue fall on deaf ears, while the general public withdraws, turned off by the anger and dishonest behavior." In the face of such experiences, it can be hard to stay involved.

GETTING PAST BETRAYAL

I've described how movements bloom when they provide emotional support for their participants and encourage self-development along with social awareness. Conversely, nothing burns out activists faster than feeling that the movements we've joined or the leaders in whom we've vested our hopes have betrayed us. In the early 1970s, I worked in a bar in Queens, New York, alongside a Greek immigrant named Charley. Bitterly right-wing, he supported every military escalation by the Nixon administration, and suggested that protestors and dissenters should be shot. I cringed every time we got in a political discussion.

Then, on my last day on the job, Charley told me that he'd been a member of the Greek Communist Party. He'd resisted the brutal regime of the colonels who ran the country following the U.S.-supported coup in 1967. As a result, he was jailed and tortured. When he was released, he discovered that some of the party leaders were wealthy doctors who had survived the oppression untouched, safe in their villas on the coast. In the wake of his sacrifice, something snapped.

Charley's backlash was more extreme than that of most disillusioned activists. But when our efforts already subject us to difficult circumstances, it's profoundly damaging to see our coworkers violate our trust, for instance by espousing lofty ideals, and then treating their fellow human beings with contempt. Even when we simply treat those we work with unkindly, it can leave a trail of resentment.

"If you did exit polls of people who left after peace and justice meetings and didn't come back," said Seattle peace activist Glen Gersmehl, "most would be because they felt personally rejected. Someone talked to them in the wrong tone of voice, cut them short, failed to care about them enough to respect them."

At its most extreme, we see this disrespect for coworkers embodied in factional groups, where manipulative tactics are almost routine. Pete Knutson backed off activism for a time after his activist days at Stanford, drained by memories of a campus Maoist group whose members strutted around the quad, wearing red buttons with pictures of AK-47 rifles, and labeled those who disagreed with them as "racist sissies." Every time someone started something politically worthwhile on campus, the Maoist group would try to take control of it. The group even sent a voluptuous female member to visit Pete in his dorm room. "You know I'm very attracted to you, Pete," she said, "but I could never get involved with someone who isn't a member of a revolutionary organization." Decades later, Pete would recount their factional craziness, laugh bitterly, and shake his head in disgust. Groups like these played a major role in splintering the 1960s antiwar movement. Their successors persist to this day, selling their newspapers on city street corners and hectoring passersby with their bullhorns. While their members may be dedicated to some worthy causes, they mostly act like malevolent wind-up toys, browbeating people with their "correct" line of thinking, disrupting coalitions, and relentlessly refusing to listen to anyone else's views.

This kind of overt manipulation aside, we still can't afford to ride roughshod over the sensibilities of those we work with. Recently, a staffer at a statewide progressive organization joined with a handful of others to stop a regressive anti-tax initiative that would have paralyzed state services for decades to come. "Nobody assigned us to take on this fight," she said. "Eventually my organization played a key role, but if we had waited for someone to tell us to take the lead, it would have been too little, too late. Instead, we built a broad coalition and worked on it nearly full-time for almost a year, alongside our regular jobs. We finally won in a knock-down, drag-out fight." Then her boss blew up and screamed at her for missing a minor, unrelated newsletter deadline due to the demands of the campaign. "I thought he was calling me into his office to celebrate, but instead felt like I'd been kicked into the next county. Betrayal is too soft a word for the feeling. I knew he had been under major pressure himself, and he was usually supportive, so I eventually forgave him. But I lost my drive and haven't yet gotten it back. We were supposed to be on the same team."

We can also feel betrayed and disappointed when people fail to respond to the critical issues we raise. "I can understand why some people just wear out," said Harry Taylor. "You go to a rally about an issue that should draw three thousand people, and only three hundred, or thirty, show up. It's deflating to be part of small groups trying to do big things for so many who don't bother even to care." A lawyer who was long active in Central American human rights work remembered speaking at "all these Kiwanis and Rotary clubs. I gave my talk, showed my slides, and looked out toward a sea of blank faces. People didn't ask questions or argue. They just didn't respond. My experience was so intense, dealing with war, pain, and all of people's hopes. Then I came back and felt no one wanted to hear about it. After a while I stopped trying to reach out."

But the more we blame people who don't seem to listen to us, the less likely they are to hear what we have to say, and the more isolated we're likely to feel. Letting ourselves feel betrayed by inevitable resistance just makes it harder to keep on. Instead, we'd do well to take a certain amount of rejection as a matter of course, as Angie De Soto learned to do in her canvassing experience.

Finally, those of us who retreat from social engagement often make matters worse by blaming ourselves. Guilt may drive our overload to begin with, as we feel that we can never do enough in a world of suffering. But if we eventually decide to do nothing at all, guilt then makes it harder to become reinvolved. When we abandon citizen movements that once stirred our souls, we may believe at first that our withdrawal will only be temporary. Then inaction becomes a habit, a way of life reinforced by cultural and economic pressures. In time, we start avoiding opportunities to re-engage, because we feel inadequate to the challenge. We feel ashamed at even the prospect of explaining our withdrawal, so find it safer to stay safely distant from the movements that once stirred our hearts.

DASHED HOPES AND DISILLUSIONMENT

I've been talking about burnout as a personal experience—and will return to it shortly, as I explore strategies to help us keep going. But retreat can also be a common experience, as large groups of citizens who once worked for change withdraw en masse, from a shared sense of frustration, disappointment—or betrayal by political leaders. The presidency of Bill Clinton is a prime example. Clinton was young, charismatic, and elected on a platform of change (although with a far weaker electoral mandate than Barack Obama and with more of a history of questionable compromises). I remember how much hope his supporters had for him, and how quickly he dashed these hopes. By a couple years into his first term, I had watched countless individuals withdraw from public involvement in cynical disillusionment.

Clinton bears significant responsibility for their disappointment. Although he passed some modestly useful policies, like the Family and Medical Leave Act and a higher earned-income credit for the poor, he backed off on campaign reform, deregulated the financial industry, and proposed a baroque and compromised health care package that collapsed of its own weight. The only time he went to the mat and risked his political capital was to support the North American Free Trade Agreement (NAFTA)—a dubious victory that encouraged American factories to relocate to Mexico. Self-serving Democrats like House Majority Leader Tom Foley didn't help. The Republicans, led by Newt Gingrich, then rode in on a wave of discontent to capture both houses of Congress, helped by a near-total collapse of volunteer participation in the Democratic Party.

Suddenly facing a hostile Congress, Clinton then conceded to the Republicans on welfare, equitable taxes, and a host of other issues important to progressives. "What a disappointment," said one woman who'd been active in social causes since the 1960s. "He's bright. He's younger than I am. He plays a pretty good blues sax. I feel sad that he squandered so much hope." For many, Clinton became the personification of cynicism long before Monica Lewinsky. He left Democrats divided and demoralized, paving the way for George W. Bush.

Yet responsibility for people's withdrawal wasn't just Clinton's. As was true with a similar cycle of dashed hopes and retreat from social commitment during the Carter years, far too many Americans watched passively when Clinton first got in, waiting for him to solve our problems. As he made one disappointing move after another, they did little except gripe from the sidelines. Few worked to mobilize the sustained grassroots pressure that might have forced him to transform his presidency into an administration they could have admired.

At one national environmental meeting, grassroots representatives argued for a major campaign to reach out to the public around global climate change. "We don't need to do that," said a leader of one of the key groups. "We can just walk down the hall and get an appointment with Katie McGinty," referring to a Gore protégé who chaired the White House Office on Environmental Policy. The temptations of access prevailed and the proposed campaign never materialized. Grassroots groups were similarly silent on most other key issues. And although McGinty did her best to convince the administration to put its full weight behind the Kyoto global warming treaty, the Senate overwhelmingly voted it down, and Clinton spent little political capital in continuing the fight. A friend of Al Gore's later told me that Gore "felt cut off at the knees."

An analogous disillusionment happened among many political conservatives during the administration of George W. Bush. In contrast to Reagan (who strengthened the conservative movement), Bush squandered the loyalty of many who had voted for him through the Iraqi quagmire, the mishandling of disasters like Katrina, and his coziness with corrupt companies like Enron. Limited-government conservatives were appalled by his radical expansion of executive power. The economic crash seemed to be a final verdict. As with Clinton, disillusionment led to withdrawal from political engagement, and many formerly loyal Republicans stayed home in 2008, even as others became strongly involved once Obama took office.

Among those who opposed Bush's policies, his actions initially galvanized millions to speak out publicly for the first time, but frustration at not being able to change his course—or defeat him in the 2004 elections—then led many toward retreat and despair. "At first I needed an outlet to publicly express my outrage, bond with others who felt the same, and perhaps influence those who were undecided," said one woman. "Later, I began to feel like not one thing was being altered by millions of people protesting for years in every possible way." Many also felt betrayed by Democrats who "spinelessly capitulated" by voting for Bush's programs or failing to challenge blatant electoral abuses. It was easy to feel demoralized.

BEYOND PURISM

Building on pent-up hopes for change, the 2008 election inspired a massive wave of citizen participation. But most of those involved quickly grew silent after Obama took office. Some still responded to email appeals or called their Senators. But they weren't engaging their neighbors, rallying in the streets, or showing up at community meetings. They mostly watched and waited, first hoping Obama and the Congress would boldly address America's crises, and then becoming dispirited at the administration's compromises and retreats. Meanwhile, corporate interests, from Exxon and the coal industry to health insurance conglomerates and pharmaceutical giants, were spending hundreds of millions of dollars to block policies that might rein in their profits. Those who'd become the base of the Tea Party used support from some of these same financial interests to begin holding rallies, showing up at public meetings, writing letters, and building grassroots networks. With the community that had elected Obama largely missing from the debate, and Obama rarely going to the mat for his initiatives, they helped shift the political momentum.

When I circulated an email query in the summer of 2009, asking for stories of people who'd burned out politically, I got deluged by former Obama supporters now angry at him. He'd let them down, they said, by continuing Bush administration policies on bank bailouts and government transparency, by escalating in Afghanistan, by not investigating Bush/Cheney abuses, and by failing to fight for approaches like a strong public health care option.

Whatever the legitimacy of these critiques, and I shared some of their concerns, it seemed far too easy to put sole responsibility on Obama and the Congress. Most who felt Obama had betrayed their hopes had themselves done little to mobilize public opinion on the core issues they cared about. Instead they bailed with bitter resignation amid critical ongoing fights about energy, health care, tax policy, climate change, and the challenge of reviving America's economy. The assertion that their efforts hadn't mattered also failed to acknowledge that of the new Democratic Senators who these volunteers had helped elect in 2006 and 2008, every one backed measures like a public health care option, expanded student financial aid, and a stimulus package that would have invested considerably more in getting Americans back to work. Resistance came from Republicans and a handful of entrenched Democratic incumbents funded by the industries being challenged. So whatever you think of Obama, the last several elections have had major consequences, with seat after seat being determined by which side organized during the intervening years, and then got out to volunteer and vote. As Meredith Segal stressed, elections are critically important, but only as beginning points.

I'm not suggesting we let Obama or any other political leader off the hook on issues where we disagree. Quite the contrary. Whatever we believe, we should organize, tell the stories that convey our perspective, and join together to apply common pressure, ideally in ways that continue to open up dialogue, as opposed to shutting it off. And if we lose a particular battle or fall short in what we achieve, we should come back and build on the momentum we've created so far. But the path of purist condemnation breeds only cynical retreat.

Some of us cling to purism in part because it's easier to be in perpetual opposition than to engage a messy political reality of new possibilities and perils. "Bush was awful," said a Pennsylvania woman, "but at least we were united against him. The focused anger always brought me back. Now we're not even all on the same side." Given the depth of the problems we face, we need to ask hard questions, challenge our leaders to genuinely lead, and not settle for purely cosmetic reforms. But in the name of standing firm for radical change, we can too easily set ourselves so far above the fray that we end up changing nothing at all.

No matter how much political leaders disappoint us, we should not conclude that the whole process of engaging in democracy is futile. Advances for justice develop step by step. Even modest progress can be valuable if it lets us build further change. As an activist from the Northwest Energy Coalition put it, "Those who burn out more easily tend to be folks who don't understand the system and its problems very well. Therefore they get their hopes up too high for short-term changes and victories, and don't see the need for long-term work."

MAKE ME DO IT

So how do we create change in the face of entrenched resistance? And how do we avoid burnout, or recover from it? One model comes from a meeting between Franklin Delano Roosevelt and legendary civil rights and labor organizer A. Philip Randolph, who founded the Brotherhood of Sleeping Car Porters, the union that created an activist base for Montgomery, Alabama, NAACP-head E. D. Nixon. When Randolph asked FDR to take stronger civil rights stands, the President responded, as Eleanor Roosevelt told Harry Belafonte, "I agree with everything that you've said, including my capacity to be able to right many of these wrongs. . . . But I would ask one thing of you, Mr. Randolph, and that is go out and make me do it."

Randolph did exactly that, planning a march on Washington, D.C., to demand that FDR desegregate the military and give African Americans equal access to defense-related jobs. In response, FDR issued an executive order fulfilling the latter demand, and President Harry Truman later fulfilled the former. Roosevelt enacted his pivotal New Deal reforms only under pressure from massive grassroots organizing, like that of Hazel Wolf and her radical cohorts. Meanwhile, others challenged evictions, occupied factories, conducted strikes, marched in the streets, and organized their communities through efforts like farmers' unions and unemployment councils. Rather than waiting for an initially cautious Roosevelt to lead, these citizens fought for changes they believed in, such as unemployment insurance, the federal jobs of the Works Progress Administration, and the public pension system that became Social Security. They built enough of a political groundswell that Roosevelt responded and, with their help, got these programs through Congress.

A similar process happened with the civil rights movement, starting during the bleakest days of segregation. The movement grew as African American veterans returned from helping defeat the Nazi ethic of racial supremacy, only to face the same daily humiliations at home. Civil rights efforts then took off in the 1950s through campaigns like the Montgomery bus boycott and all that followed it. When President Kennedy took office, he and Vice President Johnson were personally sympathetic but held the movement at arm's length for fear of shattering the Democratic coalition, in which southern segregationist whites played a major role. Civil rights activists then created a political and moral force so strong that it expanded the horizon of the possible. In the wake of the March on Washington, Johnson put all his political skill and capital on the line to pass the civil rights and voting rights bills. He did this while predicting that the Democrats would, as a result, lose the South for a generation—which they did, but for nearly two generations.

After Obama's election, Princeton African American studies professor Melissa Harris-Lacefield began showing audiences a picture of Johnson and Martin Luther King smiling and shaking hands after the signing of the civil rights bill. "Which one is Obama?" she'd ask. When her audiences invariably say, "He's Martin Luther King," she'd respond, "No. He's Lyndon Johnson. He's the president. We have to be Martin Luther King. We have to be the ones to act and speak out."

CELEBRATING OUR VICTORIES

Because the fruits of our labors aren't always immediately visible, social change work can easily leave us feeling, in the words of the writer Anne Lamott, like "Sisyphus with cash-flow problems." It's understandable to grow demoralized; few of us are capable of continually taking on challenging tasks without confirmation of the value of work. We need approval, gratitude, a feeling of accomplishment, or some tangible indications of success.

Yet even when we do make real progress, we often dismiss it. Speaking about a friend who works on domestic violence issues, Virginia Ramirez said that when her friend started out no one wanted to work with her. "The issue was too controversial. Now it's changing, even on the state level. There are so many places where people can go to get help, and before there were none." But Virginia's friend, she said, felt she hadn't done enough. "She told me, 'Virginia, things are not how I wanted them to be. I only got this much change.' So I told her, 'Think about where we were seven years ago.' She wanted a hundred percent, but she got fifty percent. That's a big start. She's changed things. I don't think we'll ever get a perfect world, but we have to work the best we can."

"It's useful to be self-critical," said Julia Devin, the lawyer who helped negotiate the Salvadoran medical neutrality agreement. "But we don't stop and celebrate our victories. We don't stop and say, 'It's really amazing what we've achieved.' Perhaps that's because what we win is so often mixed. Or we feel we should already live in a just world, so when change comes it seems long overdue. But when we take major steps toward justice, we take them for granted."

We can draw strength not only from our own victories but also those of the past. I remember how bleak I felt right after the 2004 election. John Kerry's campaign was abysmal, but I felt that George W. Bush's first term had been a disaster, and that his reelection portended more of the same. Making my mood worse, I'd scheduled a conference talk the weekend after the election, followed by some college lectures. I was supposed to talk about hope, but instead wanted to hide under the covers, feeling that I'd just be passing on despair. In the end, I went only because I had committed to it previously, and it would have felt wrong to back out. When I did speak, I decided to focus on stories from difficult situations in the past, like how courageous individuals faced down South African apartheid and the Eastern European Communist dictatorships, and the uphill fight of Rosa Parks and her compatriots during the years preceding her arrest. During the question-and-answer period, many in the audience described their own demoralization and expressed gratitude for the stories I told. I had helped them connect to a deeper current of change, and in the process renewed their spirits.

The lecture also revived my morale—in part because I'd found a way to contribute. Just as it's easy to feel hopeless when we think there's nothing we can do to make a difference on issues we passionately care about, so focusing on specific, practical tasks help us carry on in tough times—even if we aren't sure precisely how these efforts will contribute to the long-term changes we seek. As I began to feel better, I started thinking about new ways to convince those on the other side and to engage those who'd stayed home in disgust. Once again, I began to see new possibilities. As the Serenity Prayer reminds us, we can't control everything that happens in the world, in our country, or our lives. But we can focus on doing what we can, as effectively and creatively as possible. As a doctor in a community health clinic, quoted in the book *Trauma Stewardship,* said, "I focus on what I was able to do that day. I focus on what went well, what changed, what moved. And the rest, the rest I leave behind."

We won't always win our battles. So no matter what happens, we need to avoid berating ourselves for what we should have done or what we did wrong. I've discussed the value of forgiving our enemies; it may be even harder to forgive ourselves for not salving every wound or instantly changing the world—or even for temporarily withdrawing. It's important to reflect on ways to make our efforts more effective, but we help neither our spirits nor our causes by perpetually beating ourselves up for our shortcomings. As writer Doris Donnelly puts it, "*Without* forgiveness, hurts grow unchecked and we recycle failures, resentments, bitterness, and mistrust in our lives. *With* forgiveness, hurts are acknowledged and healed, and we are able to break a mindless cycle of retaliation by saying that the decisions of human life, even when they turn out badly, are not beyond repair."

It's easier to forgive ourselves if we acknowledge our fallibility from the start. All of us have been wrong; we will all make mistakes again, in all domains of life. Whenever possible, we should learn from our past. And recognizing the limits of our own vision is one reason why it can be empowering to reach out to those with different views. But it doesn't help to obsess endlessly over what we should have said or done. It's better to continue forward, while doing our best to learn as we go.

FACING THE WATER CANNONS

Sometimes, as we act, we're blindsided by unexpected events or consequences of our actions. The week after a nonviolent small-boat blockade of America's first Trident submarine (whose capacities threatened to escalate an already-precarious nuclear arms race), a group of participants sat talking outside the courthouse where several others were being tried. A woman from Malibu, dripping in silver and turquoise jewelry, had come up to watch the spectacle of the blockade. Now she began a conversation with a bus driver who'd marched in Vietnam-era protests and had stopped to listen. "You get involved as you go," she explained, as if outlining a school lesson. "First sign a petition, then write a letter, do support, and the next thing you know you're blockading. You should join the next blockade."

"Right," said a listening blockader named Chris, very quietly. "And then the Coast Guard is shooting you with water cannons." Chris wasn't cynical, just shaken by the massive Coast Guard response. Expecting to go to jail, he'd given up his San Francisco apartment and left a graduate program in English. When the charges were dropped, he was free to move on with his life. But the experience left him dislocated and uncertain.

People often get deterred from acting on their beliefs by imagined costs, as when students tell me, "I'd like to get involved, but I don't want to get in trouble." After Obama was elected, I started joking, "Yes, social involvement can be really risky. You might end up getting elected president." But the downsides of commitment can be real. They're real for union organizers who are fired from their jobs; for students who were suspended for anti-apartheid sit-ins; for protestors who end up in jail.

Yet even when we pay such real costs, most of us find ways to continue our involvement, as long as we take on the risks with our eyes wide open and think through the potential consequences. The 9/11 attacks spurred Lieutenant Ehren Watada to sign up for the Army. But after he read about Iraq to prepare himself for duty, he decided that the war was based on lies and deception. As an of-

ficer, he felt a responsibility "to lead by example," and told his supe-
riors that while he'd willingly serve in Afghanistan, he couldn't in
good conscience deploy to Iraq. The Army court-martialed Watada
for this refusal, and at one point he faced up to eight years in jail.
But he refused to back off. Instead, he kept speaking out about the
reasons for his action, until charges were finally dropped due to
procedural errors. When I heard one of his talks, I felt that he was
speaking from the same Eagle Scout patriotism that had led him to
enlist in the first place. "When you are looking your children in the
eye in the future," he said, "or when you are at the end of your life,
you want to look back and know that at a very important moment,
when you had the opportunity to make the right decisions, you did
so, even knowing there were negative consequences."

Often, the costs we pay can bring new opportunities, as long as
we're flexible enough to pursue them. National Association of
Evangelicals vice president for governmental affairs Rich Cizik inadvertently gave his longtime opponents an opening by acknowledging on a radio show that he was beginning to rethink his
opposition to gay civil unions. As a result, they were finally able to
force him out of his job. But he continued to work with the evangelical community on climate change, and he later started an organization, the New Evangelicals, devoted to issues like poverty and
environmental "Creation Care." Having to leave the NAE was a
setback, but Cizik's sense of purpose remained as powerful as ever.

I experienced some more modest costs for my involvement at
Stanford. After becoming politically re-engaged through the Vietnam study group in my dorm, I made working to end the war my
prime focus. Together with Pete Knutson and several other friends,
I challenged military research on campus and confronted visiting
companies that were spearheading the war effort. After an extended
campaign culminating in a nonviolent protest against campus recruiting by Honeywell Corporation—whose cluster bombs were
maiming and killing Vietnamese civilians—Stanford suspended us
indefinitely. Although I lost the opportunity to finish a Stanford education, with all its attendant prestige, my life didn't end. It simply
changed. I transferred to the New School for Social Research in

New York City; although it was far less well-known than Stanford, I got a first-rate education from the school—and the city. I discovered *Liberation* magazine and learned much there. Given the stakes of the carnage we were fighting to stop, I still believe that I did the right thing. If my choices closed off some possibilities, they opened up others at least as rich.

MULTIPLE SOURCES OF SUPPORT

Sometimes the difference between staying in a movement and dropping out can be as simple as finding people who believe in us. When Saddam Hussein first invaded Kuwait, my friend Glen Gersmehl had just taken on the job of directing Washington State SANE/Freeze, the state's largest peace organization. He'd grown up poor, and worked in low-level jobs until he got a master's degree at Harvard's Kennedy School of Government. After running the peace studies program of a Massachusetts college, he took the position at SANE/Freeze. As the buildup to the First Gulf War escalated, Glen threw himself into coordinating volunteers, bringing in new members, forming new coalitions, and organizing press conferences and rallies. He did a terrific job.

But the war severely strained the organization. Staffers who were supposed to be raising money took off to protest at the federal building. The board members, suddenly panicked by the organization's chronic financial crisis, targeted Glen's leadership as the source of the problem. In a rushed and contentious meeting, they forced him out of the job.

Glen was already exhausted from eighty-hour weeks spent in crisis mode. Being scapegoated made him feel worse still. For a while, he retreated to the books that had always sustained him. He read about how people had acted for change in the past, and what kept them going in difficult times. He spent time expanding what had been a side project—a Peace and Justice Resource Center where he consulted with libraries and sold books about social change. Despite his wounded feelings, he also stayed active in SANE/Freeze,

developing a project to challenge the U.S.'s role as the world's leading arms trader.

Most important, Glen found encouragement to persist from the
woman who later became his wife, as well as a loyal circle of friends.
Along with the stories he read about from past movements, he also
drew strength from his Christian faith, "Which if you take it seriously isn't about trying to minimize the difficult moments in your
life, the painful aspects, but about engaging them, making them
sources of strength—making a priority out of our relationships, our
compassion, and using our intelligence and skill to challenge what's
destructive." In other words, Glen had multiple sources of support as
he overcame his hurt. Eventually, he found a job he loved, coordinating the national Lutheran Peace Fellowship, and returned full-time
to work on the issues he passionately cared about.

SHARING THE JOURNEY

At a discussion group on sustaining commitment, Glen stressed that
those who are just beginning to get involved in social change say
that "they're in it for the issues: the environment, homelessness,
Iraq, whatever. But the long runners talk about finding a supportive
and caring community." That's why he worries about the tendency
of social activists to turn on each other, or even just to take each
other for granted. Another participant amplified his sentiments.
"When someone quietly drops out," she said, "we rarely take time to
find out why. But we need to see whether it was something personal,
or if they were feeling underappreciated, or whether we might be
able to help them be involved in a different way, perhaps at a less
demanding level of commitment."

"When I work with churches," said Glen, "I'll tell them that I've
been wrestling with forgiveness. 'I'd like to be able to love my enemies,' I'll say, 'but as an intermediate step I've decided to try to act
lovingly toward everyone I serve on a committee with.' They'll break
up laughing when I say this, because they know how rarely it happens. Maybe we should invest just two percent of our organizational

budgets in finding the best people possible to teach us how to work together and express legitimate disagreements without backbiting and blaming. We'd spend it in a minute on mailings or phone bills. But we're afraid to invest it in ourselves."

Sometimes, to maintain a supportive community, we need to draw difficult lines. At Seattle Central Community College, members of a sectarian organization joined the highly active Students Against War group. When they said things like, "We need to support the Iraqi resistance," the vets in the group would respond, "Are you fucking nuts? Those are the people who've been blowing up my buddies." The sect was so disruptive that the group finally told its members that they were no longer welcome. This community needed to set boundaries precisely so participants could feel welcomed and supported, not ambushed and assaulted.

In his book *Why Marriages Succeed or Fail,* University of Washington psychology professor John Gottman observed that in successful relationships, daily words and deeds that affirm the fundamental bond outnumber those that erode it by at least five to one. I'm skeptical of attempts to reduce love to mathematics, but the principle holds: The more relationships are nurtured, the stronger they become; the more they're neglected or undermined, the more likely they'll collapse.

The way people participate in social movements may follow a similar pattern. We act not only out of altruism or a sense of duty but because of what we get back—both the sense that our efforts can matter and the feeling of shared purpose with others who struggle alongside us. As sociologist-turned-comedian Bertrice Berry puts it, "You want to make your movements so good they're like a party where people want to come and join in, and feel left out if they're not taking part." Our ability to keep on may well depend on the balance we can create between these moments of affirmation, and those of frustration and despair. Dave Hall, the former president of Physicians for Social Responsibility, echoes this link, explaining, "I have friends who'll say 'I don't go to church, I go to PSR meetings.' We've developed a common vision. But we also really like each other. The work matters, but also the chance to do it together."

Sometimes, the community we rely on is more diffuse. Meredith Segal recalls "nights during hectic periods when I was sitting in a computer lab trying to research and write a class paper due the next morning. My phone would periodically ring, and I'd step out to answer. I'll never forget those calls when a student whose voice I'd never heard before shared their story. One woman from an Indiana community college had no political experience, but wanted to know how she could help Obama so her family would receive the health care they needed. Another young woman had convinced her grand-mother to become an American citizen so she could vote in this election, and she wanted to help other children of immigrants do the same. An African American student from Virginia was going to have to leave college due to lack of money, but she asked what role she could play so that other students would have the opportunities she was about to lose. Hearing the awakening, urgency, and hope expressed by students from all over the country renewed my com-mitment, and I'd head back and attend to more campaign e-mails."

THE STRENGTHS OF VULNERABILITY

Community doesn't only help prevent burnout. It also helps us re-cover from it. We often speak of burnout in physical terms, as a deep exhaustion. But physical exhaustion can be remedied by sleep, exercise, vacation, or the passage of time. Much harder to overcome are memories of feeling isolated, overextended, unappreciated, and betrayed. Indeed, a sure gauge of the seriousness of our burnout is what happens when, months or years later, we so much as think about resuming social activism. If we once again feel overwhelmed by apprehension, weariness, and powerlessness—by the feeling that we have no more to give—then the burnout is severe.

These kinds of negative feelings have some similarities to the experience of veterans with post-traumatic stress disorder. The visible scars heal, but the invisible ones don't. As our mental and emotional circuits short out, the pain of the past overwhelms the possibilities of the present. Evolutionary biologists have suggested that human beings may well be hardwired to relive painful memories. Our brain replays trauma so authentically that it triggers a full response from our involuntary nervous system. Fortunately, we're not completely at the mercy of this brain chemistry. Studies of abused children have shown that strong interpersonal bonds and intense positive emotional experiences can overcome the handicaps caused by violence. Recovery from political burnout is vastly easier than from war or abuse, but it, too, depends on acknowledging our unseen injuries, building supportive relationships, and allowing ourselves to be challenged by new possibilities.

To be truly supportive, our communities must also let us acknowledge our doubts about particular approaches or causes. If we're not permitted to do this, the gap between our internal psychological state and our outward allegiances can actually erode our will to act. Former Vietnam-era activists interviewed by sociologists Jack Whalen and Richard Flacks consistently cited ways that the movements they'd joined had discouraged them from expressing fears, misgivings, or feelings of inadequacy. "If one's collective embarked on an organizing project," write Whalen and Flacks, "members expected each other to become instant organizers, free of anxiety about talking to strangers, confidently able to argue a position publicly, perfectly at ease in roles that most people would find intimidating . . . Activists who had belonged to such collectives are likely to recall the experience as painful because of the unacknowledged gap between public profession and private feeling—and the shame and guilt that resulted." If movements don't allow hesitation, uncertainty, ambivalence, they make it almost impossible for many of their most dedicated participants to continue.

Opening ourselves up to take on the troubles of the world can leave us emotionally vulnerable. This vulnerability can ultimately strengthen us, but not if we keep it to ourselves. As psychologist Joanna Macy writes, "Many peace and environmental advocates, exposed to terrifying information by the nature of their work, carry a heavy burden of knowledge. It is compounded by feelings of frustration, as they fight an uphill battle to arouse the public. Yet they view their own despair as a sign of weakness that would be counterproductive to their efforts. In their roles as mobilizers for the public will, they don't feel they can 'let their hair down' and expose the extent of their distress about the future. The consequent and continual repression of this despair takes a toll on their energies that leaves them especially vulnerable to bitterness and exhaustion."

Macy explores how engagement with the critical issues of our time requires opening ourselves up to human suffering and pain. But if we try to do this entirely on our own we can easily get overwhelmed. In their studies of therapists who counsel abuse survivors, the psychologists Laurie Anne Pearlman and Lisa McCann have developed the concept of secondary or vicarious trauma. Therapists working in such situations hear story after story of human suffering. At first, the stories inspire sympathy, generosity, and a passionate commitment to reducing human violence and destructiveness. But if the therapists witness too much pain for too long, they can themselves become hopeless and despairing. We've all met burned out social workers, teachers, and counselors whose work has left them hollow-eyed and listless, just going through the motions even in situations of the gravest human consequence.

Yet Pearlman and McCann discovered an alternative. When practitioners meet regularly to talk together, complain together, even shed a few tears together—as well as to share their successes—they usually feel stronger. The support participants receive from such communities isn't technical. The very act of discussion transforms interactions that would otherwise be draining and overwhelming into experiences that feed participants' souls. In her work with physicians who attend dying patients, Rachel Naomi Remen notes a similar process. She concludes that "burnout only really begins to heal when people learn how to grieve."

Those who've spent years serving or working for change in their communities rely on such intimate conversations to keep themselves and others going. If people do nothing but work in shelters and soup kitchens day after day, or fight protracted, piecemeal battles with entrenched institutions, they can easily be overwhelmed. But if they have the chance to talk with each other and process what they experience, they tend to maintain their confidence and hope.

They pass on stories and jokes, reminisce about why they got involved to begin with, reflect on how they've changed along the way. It's no accident that most of my friends and I have found our true loves through social involvement. Creating this kind of community not only re-energizes activists, it's also a central satisfaction of joining social movements—or it should be. Working for social change in solitude is a contradiction in terms.

We all need opportunities to share our concerns and apprehensions, our hopes and desires. When I organized discussion circles among people who'd pulled back from public engagement, something surprising happened. The very act of talking over a potluck meal and reflecting on the process of withdrawal made people want to get involved again. When I asked one group what drew them in to begin with, they answered with specific stories, recounted with a passion: "It made me furious that we were dropping bombs on innocent people in Vietnam." "I had a black friend and she got treated so badly." "I knew someone who had an illegal abortion and nearly died." "When I lived in a Guatemalan Indian village, I learned what it's like to haul water by hand every day." Without exception, their initial commitments had been sparked by examples of strength or of suffering. As they described people they'd worked with, and their sense of common purpose, my friends became more animated. They stopped slouching. Their faces lit up. Exploring the taproots of their commitment gave them a renewed sense of hope and possibility. They began to shake the despair that had cast such a cloud over their souls.

NURTURING OUR SOULS

The more we appreciate what's worth savoring in life, the easier it is to keep on. I recently met a student who was involved in climate change issues. One of his favorite musicians, singer Ani DiFranco, was playing 75 miles away. He wanted to go see her but hesitated because he'd have to burn up gas and emit carbon dioxide to get there. "Go," I said. "Carpool and bring friends, but you have to go. You love Ani Di Franco. She's going to charge you up to do great work for weeks afterward." We can't afford to be so pure that we leave no room to renew our souls.

The trick to surmounting any difficult and protracted challenge is to find ways to foster this renewal, even as we maintain our commitment. This is how Susan Butcher repeatedly won the 1,200-mile Alaskan dogsled race, the Iditarod. In an intensely competitive situation, Butcher won, in part, by caring for her dogs. At every rest stop in one race, her prime rival left early, while Butcher attended to her dogs for the full four hours allotted. By the end of each lap, Butcher's dogs were forging ahead of his. "My dogs just kept getting stronger and stronger," she told the *Boston Globe*. "They gained in power the further along we got." By the last stop, her lead became unbeatable.

We need similar moments of respite in the midst of our political commitments—to keep from getting so overloaded that we drop out or, as an Arizona environmental activist said, "end up using the same words as ten or twenty years ago, going through the same motions, fighting the same battles with no end in sight." It can also help to vary the work that we do, or take on different facets of interconnected issues. At some points, we may need to withdraw from particular organizations or ways of acting that seem not to work, and re-engage ourselves through fresh angles of approach—like switching from the national to the local stage, or bringing global issues into our home communities. But the goal should always be to allow ourselves to keep on with as fresh a vision as possible.

Creativity and humor are important as well, both to revive our souls and to make our points in effective and unexpected ways. When a student group was trying to get the University of Washington to allow its janitors to unionize, they began by publicly delivering a series of meticulously crafted letters with student signatures to the president's office. On Valentine's Day, however, they switched tactics, presenting huge paper hearts made of butcher paper with more signatures and the message "Show some love for your janitors." As part of another successful campaign, the same group leafleted wearing trash bags and handwritten signs saying "I'd rather wear a trash bag than UW's sweatshop apparel."

Acting with a sense of balance requires letting go of the assumption that we have to do everything, or fight every battle. It means leaving the computer and phone to play with our children, read a book, go to a movie or baseball game, exercise, dance to good music, savor good food, hang out with friends, get a massage, or soak in the bathtub and do nothing. "There are days," says Pete Knutson, "when you just have to drop everything, take the dog down to the woods or the beach, and simply take a break."

Think again about the difference between physical and psychological exhaustion. "Classical physics has taught us that energy is finite and conserved," writes Mary Catherine Bateson, "but when we use terms like 'energy' in speaking about human potential, we are into another area entirely. . . . One person can 'energize' or 'empower' another without any transfer of physical qualities. The energy to write this page is released by metabolizing food—it comes from my breakfast. But the 'energy' to write this page depends on my state of mind, and such 'energy' can come from a sunset or a remembered smile. During the worst periods at Amherst [where Bateson was a dean trying to challenge a resistant old-boy culture] . . . I learned to keep books of art and poetry in my office, giving myself three- and five-minute breaks to look at an African mask or linger over a verse and be refreshed. . . . An activity that affects vitality is not directly competitive or subtractive from other activities—on the contrary, it may enhance them."

If we save enough time for contemplation and rejuvenation, we can continue our work throughout our lives. "You get out of the city," said Hazel Wolf. "You hike, run a river, or watch birds in a park. With all the things to observe, there's less room for worry. Your mind gets a rest. You come back ready to take on Exxon."

Such moments of beauty and respite can help build engaged community—and lift the souls of those of us who participate. I once found myself weighing whether to attend Seattle's Hiroshima Day commemoration, an annual event coordinated by local religious, peace, and environmental organizations. I was feeling very down that day. Years of social reforms were being steadily dismantled. The movements that should have offered an alternative seemed silent.

At first, I thought I'd stay home. I knew more than enough about the horror of the bombs. Why depress myself further?

At the last moment, however, I decided to go, hoping that seeing friends would cheer me up. When I arrived, hundreds of people were gathered by a lake to float paper lanterns with candles inside. Calligraphers decorated the lanterns, and people folded paper cranes to attach to them. Musicians played taiko drums and shakuhachi flutes. A children's peace choir sang, accompanied by young dancers. A Buddhist minister gave a benediction and spoke of a world in which children would no longer be killed by weapons of war. People filed slowly down to the lake and launched their lanterns, which floated across the water, creating glowing trails of light.

As I listened to the music and visited with people I knew, I felt cleansed and calmed. The ceremony melded spirit and politics. It reminded me that isolation amplifies our impulses toward fear, resignation, and despair; whereas community helps us overcome them.

CHAPTER TWELVE

The Fullness of Time

It is not up to you to complete the task. Nonetheless, you are not free to desist from it.

—*RABBI TARFON*

However we promote social change, we act in our own historical time, while at the same time linking past, present, and future in our attempts to create a better world. Some historical eras, however, seem more pregnant with possibility than others. Sergei Eisenstein was the great Soviet director who in the 1920s and 1930s made films like *Battleship Potemkin* and *Alexander Nevsky*. A British art exhibit I once saw surveyed his work, his times, the history he helped shape. It conveyed the atmosphere of a period when everything seemed to be breaking loose—politically, technologically, and artistically. One room of the exhibit re-created Eisenstein's office, spilling over with artifacts given to him by such artist friends as Pablo Picasso, Georges Braque, Fernand Leger, the muralist Jose Clemente Orozco, and the photographer Edward Weston. There was a bust of the composer Prokofiev (Eisenstein's frequent collaborator), and signed photos of James Joyce, Albert Einstein, Charlie Chaplin, Walt Disney, Harpo Marx—and Lenin. The exhibit was a metaphor for a time of dramatic promise, when people believed they could reinvent the world. Whatever their illusions—and the brutal Soviet system would soon shatter many—they rode an exhilarating wave of hope.

The 1960s were marked by a similar sense of political and cultural ferment. Ordinary people worldwide challenged entrenched institutions and policies. Artists staked out new ground. People talked of creating a more humane and generous future and worked together to move toward it. Their movements eventually collapsed because of powerful opposition, participant exhaustion, and some dangerous moments of arrogance. But for a time, they unleashed a powerful sense that the world could change for the better.

Our lives today are hardly stagnant. If anything, the world seems to be shifting too quickly, from the uncertainties of a rollercoaster economy to the unparalleled threats of global warming. Technology opens up new opportunities. Political hopes rise and fall. One moment we feel that our nation will finally grapple with its most deeply rooted problems, and the next we decide that the interests of unaccountable wealth and power are so entrenched and all-corrupting that they'll inevitably prevail. The startling pace of change around us can easily leave us shell-shocked, feeling that all we can do is retreat to our private lives. Yet these profound challenges combined with genuine reasons for hope offer powerful opportunities for change. If much of our common future is indeed up for grabs, then our actions now matter as much as in any other time.

It's tempting to gaze back longingly at historical periods where progress seemed clear, at least in retrospect. "People seem so uncertain these days," says battered women's advocate Ginny NiCarthy, "so quick to despair. But things looked far more grim and immovable in the late 1950s, when I first got involved. A dozen of us would picket nuclear bomb shelters or stores that wouldn't hire black people, and bystanders would yell at us, tell us to 'Go back to Russia,' 'Go back to your kitchen, where you belong.' There were no clear reasons to believe that we could change things, but somehow we did. We leaped forward, started the ball rolling, and built enough political momentum that it kept going. We need to do that again."

HOPE AND HISTORY

We can never predict when a historical mood will suddenly shift and new hopes and possibilities emerge. As Vaclav Havel wrote before the epochal Eastern European revolutions, "Hope is not prognostication." Sociologist Richard Flacks remembers visiting Berkeley in September 1964 and hearing members of the activist student group Students for a Democratic Society (SDS) complain that their fellow students were almost terminally apathetic, uncaring, and passive. A few weeks later, the Free Speech Movement erupted, ushering in a decade of political ferment.

However unexpected these changes are, they occur only when courageous individuals take action. Recall the struggle of Susan B. Anthony. She labored her entire life for women's suffrage, then died fourteen years before it was achieved. Few could have imagined that the Soviet bloc would crumble as it did, thanks in part to the persistence of individuals from Havel to Lech Walesa and Andrei Sakharov, who voiced prophetic truths for decades despite immense personal costs. Few would have thought that South Africa would become a multiracial democracy, with Nelson Mandela its president. Major victories for human dignity rarely come easily or quickly. But they do come.

"When nothing seems to help," said early-twentieth-century reformer Jacob Riis, "I go and look at a stonecutter hammering away at his rock perhaps a hundred times without as much as a crack showing in it. Yet at the hundred and first blow it will split in two, and I know it was not that blow that did it—but all that had gone before."

If we want a more humane society, we need to risk partial steps, failed experiments, and ambiguous results. We work and work, and then "once in a lifetime," as poet Seamus Heaney writes, "the longed-for tidal wave of justice can rise up, and hope and history rhyme." Howard Zinn marveled at how often in the past century we have been surprised: "By the sudden emergence of a people's movement, the sudden overthrow of a tyranny, the sudden coming to life of a flame we thought extinguished. We are surprised because we have not taken notice of the quiet simmerings of indignation, of the first faint sounds of protest, of the scattered signs of resistance that, in the midst of our despair, portend the excitement of change."

RADICAL PATIENCE

For most of human existence, the world changed at a glacial pace. People were born, grew up, worked, loved, and died much as their parents and grandparents had before them. They believed society was governed by external forces. The purpose of life was to fulfill tradition, not overturn it.

Now, circumstances are almost the opposite. Our society makes speed an ultimate virtue, as if simply by moving faster we can overcome all obstacles, including our own mortality. And too often we don't pause to reflect on the pace of our lives. Writing in the *Whole Earth* magazine, poet Anne Herbert examines the cycle of frenetic motion and rapid burnout so common among activists, and asks how our choices might differ if we cultivated the view that we have a hundred years to change the world, instead of constantly scrambling to stave off immense collapse. She describes experiences with "organizations, campaigns, whole movements, [all run with] everybody feeling behind, feeling there isn't enough time, feeling important because every little thing is urgent because it hasn't been well planned."

As Milan Kundera writes, "there is a secret bond between slowness and memory, between speed and forgetting." We need to challenge the all-leveling pace of vast institutions, global markets especially, to give human communities time to sort through what is wise and unwise in the cornucopia of new choices. We also need to slow our lives down enough to determine what we want to fight for in the first place. This means taking time to reflect and listen closely. It means finding what T. S. Eliot called "a still point in a turning world," and returning to a slower rhythm of life that might even presage the kind of future we'd like to fight for. It means developing radical patience.

Writing from a Christian social justice tradition, *Sojourners* editor Jim Wallis explains the need for meditative respite: "Action without reflection can easily become barren and even bitter," he says. "Without the space for self-examination and the capacity for rejuvenation, the danger of exhaustion and despair is too great. At an even deeper level, contemplation confronts us with the questions of our identity and power. Who are we: To whom do we belong? Is there a power that is greater than ours? How can we know it?"

Those who are able to sustain their activism for a lifetime know how to create this perspective. Longtime civil rights activist Ysaye Barnwell, of the singing group Sweet Honey in the Rock, has compared social involvement to the process of making music. You can't rush things in either form, she says: "Music has its rhythm and pace. You have to keep up with it and not go too slow or too fast, or the song won't work. You need to take all the time you need. You want to breathe, savor each note, feel the spaces between the words that you sing."

Granted, the crises we face demand our urgent attention. And some efforts, like electoral campaigns or union organizing drives, have finite deadlines, where everything may hinge on our last-minute push. But even in our most overextended moments, when we're running on adrenaline and fumes, we still work best when we're as calm and deliberate as possible, rather than harried and desperate. It still helps to breathe deeply, slow down, and ground ourselves as much as we can. Finding the right pace is easier if we bear in mind that producing the social changes we desire will take time, which makes activism a lifelong endeavor. As Billie Holiday sang, "The difficult—I'll do right now. The impossible will take a little while."

So how do we deal with issues like global climate change, where time is running out? The fight for justice is an intergenerational march, but if we start melting the frozen Arctic methane beds and releasing the potent greenhouse gases now locked into the tundra, disaster may become impossible to avoid. So we may not have the dozen years between Rosa Parks's first NAACP meeting and her stand on the bus, much less the twenty-seven years of Nelson Mandela's Robben Island imprisonment. We need concerted national and international action, and we need it without delay. Yet even on climate change, where delay can be catastrophic, we can't afford to burn out in frantic motion.

Here's a cautionary example from an earlier global crisis. The nuclear arms race of the early 1980s now seems remote, but we came dismayingly close to global cataclysm. Top Reagan administration officials suggested that nuclear wars could be winnable. The United States was deploying nuclear missiles in Europe, so close to those of the Soviets that both countries planned for hair-trigger retaliation, for fear of otherwise losing their missiles to a massive unexpected strike. By September 1983, tensions had been steadily escalating for several years. A few weeks before, the Soviets shot down a Korean airliner that wandered into prohibited airspace over secret military facilities. NATO was preparing a highly provocative exercise that simulated how they would respond in a limited nuclear war. An ill and paranoid Yuri Andropov, the Soviet leader, had ordered the KGB to look specifically for any advance signs that the United States was planning a surprise nuclear strike. Then, shortly after midnight on September 26, alarms went off in the bunker where the Soviets monitored their early-warning systems, while lights flashed and computer screens showed a succession of incoming U.S. nuclear missiles. The officer in charge, Lieutenant Colonel Stanislav Petrov, had five agonizing minutes to decide what to do while his monitors showed the missiles speeding toward their targets. Petrov finally made a judgment that it was likely a false alarm, and called the generals in charge of retaliatory strikes to offer this judgment. They had automatically received the same alert and similarly had just a few minutes to make a decision. Had Petrov responded differently, we might not be here today.

This story came out a decade after the end of the Cold War, was covered briefly in the U.S. media, and then disappeared from common memory. But according to analysts like the Center for Defense Information's Bruce Blair, we may have come as close to catastrophe as this rushed midnight judgment of a single human being. What brought humanity back from the brink was a global citizens' movement that pressured Ronald Reagan to shift toward de-escalating the arms race, and encouraged Soviet dissenters, including Mikhail Gorbachev. No person inspired more citizens to join this movement than Australian physician Helen Caldicott. Speaking in city after city across the globe, Caldicott described in grim detail what the specific local results would be of a nuclear attack, mapping concentric circles of distance within which people would be incinerated, burned beyond recognition, and poisoned by radiation. By doing so, she helped her audiences imagine the unimaginable, and galvanized them to speak out. Yet Caldicott let herself become so overwhelmed by the possibility of annihilation and the foreshortened time to act on it, that her talks became more and more desperate and apocalyptic. She began to give her audiences the impression that unless they acted at that very instant, and with impossibly perfect eloquence and skill, whatever they could do would be too late. Before the 1984 election, she pronounced "a mathematical certainty" of nuclear war if Reagan were re-elected to office. Shortly afterward Caldicott withdrew from active political involvement for nearly a decade.

Just as the nuclear arms race presented us with the possibility of species-level catastrophe, we face a similarly catastrophic potential at the far extremes of climate change. So when I call for "patience," I don't mean tolerance or acceptance of human destructiveness, whether in addressing climate change or any other critical issue. As Martin Luther King said, we need "to be saved from that patience that makes us patient with anything less than freedom and justice." Yet frantic desperation gains us nothing, only reinforcing the sense that these crises are so out of control that it's futile to try to address them.

Activists who practice radical patience continually address urgent issues, while at the same time recognizing that success depends not only on changing specific policies but also on broadening the stream of those who are involved in social change, developing new political relationships and creating new opportunities for citizens to take a stand. If we do our work well, our efforts will help regardless of the short-term outcome of particular battles. Jim Forest, of the international religious pacifist group Fellowship of Reconciliation, compares the labors of social activists to those of the artisans who built the great medieval cathedrals, working generation after generation on projects whose completion few would live to see. We may not have multiple generations worth of time on every issue, but if we work with all our energy, imagination, and courage, history suggests we have at least a chance to turn the tide.

Not getting too attached to the results of our actions isn't only a strategy to avoid burnout, then. It's also the approach that's most likely to yield significant social change. "There are moments when things go well and one feels encouraged," wrote Danilo Dolci, the great Italian pacifist who challenged the Mafia in Sicily and helped empower poor peasant communities. "There are difficult moments and one feels overwhelmed. But it's senseless to speak of optimism or pessimism. The only important thing is to know that if one works well in a potato field, the potatoes will grow. If one works well among men, they will grow—that's reality. The rest is smoke. It's important to know that words don't move mountains. Work, exacting work, moves mountains."

SAVORING THE JOURNEY

As Dolci implies, if we're going to keep working to create a better world, we must find ways to savor the work itself, as well as the everyday richness of life. Approached in desperation, social activism can erode our souls, causing us to treat the world as nothing more than a vehicle for our causes. That's why activists who endure balance their demanding work with pursuits that nourish their spirit and bring joy into their lives. I've talked of the renewed strength we can get from community, beauty, humor, and creativity. When Hazel Wolf visited the Soviet Union in her mid-eighties, she stayed up half the night dancing and drinking. The son of longtime peace activist and Pentagon Papers leaker Dan Ellsberg once described watching his father bodysurf at a beach in northern California. "It was a clear, beautiful day. The water was cold. On that afternoon, he seemed like he didn't have a political thought in his mind. He just kept riding the waves. He probably spends more time thinking about the awful things in the world and how to stop them than anyone else I know. But that day I was so glad he was just doing something he enjoyed."

I remember Catholic peace activist Philip Berrigan drinking red wine and talking passionately with an old friend about Sophia Loren's beauty and prowess as an actress. Berrigan's willingness to spend much of his life in jail for protesting war stemmed directly from his profound gratitude, from how much he prized the richness of God's gifts, including Loren's abundant talent.

Among the riches that deserve savoring are life's absurdities. As I've mentioned, humor can be a powerful way to reach out to others. It also helps us stay the course, preventing us from taking ourselves too seriously, helps us put life's bruises in perspective, and enlarges our vision. Humor gives us ways to come to terms with pain, loss, and failure, yet also look beyond it.

Because of the Chinese occupation of Tibet, the Dalai Lama has experienced years of exile, the deaths of many close friends, and the systematic ravaging of his culture. He has every reason to despair. Yet whenever I've heard him talk, he's been mischievous and playful. Giving a scarf to Seattle's mayor, he joked, "It's made in China." When someone asked about the occupation, he said, "The fourteenth Dalai Lama is very popular. Without the Chinese, he probably wouldn't be." When asked what he did for fun, he flapped his hands like chattering mouths and said with a giggle, "I gossip."

Desmond Tutu has a similar mischievous sense of humor. I can think of no one who has addressed more difficult issues. He spoke out courageously for South African freedom, saw friends imprisoned, tortured, and murdered, and then chaired the Truth and Reconciliation commission—where people told the stories of abuses they'd committed to help maintain apartheid. Later Tutu worked in Rwanda to bring healing to that scarred land after over a half million people were massacred. And he refused to be airlifted out when riots followed a stolen Haitian election—instead he helped encourage more peaceful protests, which ultimately succeeded. He challenged the Iraq war, both before it started and afterward. Recently he said the 3 billion poorest people in the world (those who would be the most vulnerable and had the fewest resources to adapt) give us 3 billion reasons to act on global climate change. From all this, you might think he'd be exhausted or despairing from engaging with so much human blindness and callousness. But when he speaks, he dances, talks, and teases, clearly having a good time. I've seen him three times and each time he repeated the phrase, "God has a sense of humor," and then told a joke. "Who would think the world would learn anything from South Africa?" he asked, in the one I remember. "We're not the brightest country. Our scientists said they'd built a rocket to the sun, and when people pointed out that it would burn up, they said it would be fine. They'd launch it at night." Then he continued to talk about the Truth and Reconciliation commission.

I laughed with everyone else, then wondered why, with all the amazing stories Tutu could recount, he took time to tell this relatively silly joke. Then I realized he was reminding us to keep laughing, even in the most difficult situations. And that this was as important as any other lesson he could teach. Both Tutu and the Dalai Lama clearly savor life, in all of its delight and all of its sorrow.

In *Zen and the Art of Motorcycle Maintenance*, Robert Pirsig offered a similar judgment on savoring our journeys. "Mountains should be climbed with as little effort as possible and without desire," he wrote. "Then, when you're no longer thinking ahead, each footstep isn't just a means to an end but a unique event in itself. . . . To live only for some future goal is shallow. It's the sides of the mountain which sustain life, not the top. Here's where things grow." Those most committed to their communities similarly value the journey of working for change. For all the obstacles they face, and all the times where their efforts fail, they derive satisfaction from the people they meet, the challenges they engage, and the knowledge that they're staying true to their beliefs.

"There's always something to do, no matter what [your] age, as long as you can get up and walk and talk," Jessie de la Cruz, a seventy-four-year-old farmworker organizer, told Studs Terkel. "There's always hope. We have a saying: '*La esperanza muere al ultimo.*' Hope dies last. Hope for whatever you want to do. If you can't do it today, there's always tomorrow or the next year."

Those who work most steadfastly learn to gain strength from the struggle for justice and from the world they'd like to create. At her Columbia, South Carolina, house, eighty-four-year-old African American activist Modjesca Simkins pointed out the dining room table where a young NAACP lawyer named Thurgood Marshall had composed his early briefs, long before he became a legendary Supreme Court Justice. Modjeska co-founded her state NAACP in 1939, and the two worked together for years. She showed me a faded handbill from the late 1950s, at the top of which were these words: "Main Street in Columbia Is Off Limits To Seekers After Freedom." The flier advised black participants in an Easter boycott to trade with friendly merchants or "wear old clothes in real dignity," rather than patronize Woolworth's, McCrory's, and other stores "where you are most welcome to stand on your 'dogs' and gnaw on a Hot Dog while a simple request for a 'SITTING DOWN' lunch will mean insults and arrest."

Modjesca helped win that fight, just as she helped break the state's all-white Democratic primary and desegregate South Carolina's public schools. Though the movement won much, she said, the poor were still poor, the powerful and wealthy still on top. People need to keep their eyes on the light, she said, for "the betterment of mankind," and "not let the chintzy things get in the way." Faith came from "exposure to suffering," and if you had as much faith as you could put in a mustard seed, she believed you could move the world.

Along with her civil rights involvements, Modjesca also took stands on issues like the environment. She thought most blacks felt that "the white man got the world messed up. Let him straighten it out himself." The black community, used to being excluded from public decision-making, was fatalistic even about getting holes in the streets fixed. Like most Americans, Modjesca said, they had "a disease where they run along like a feather in the breeze till they come up against something they didn't see." But if the nearby Savannah River atomic complex ever blew, they'd "be pinched up just like pork skins, along with everyone else."

It was hard raising these kinds of questions, Modjesca went on, because most people cared only about "what song's on the radio or what they're going to buy, not about what kind of world they're going to leave for their children." But Modjesca persevered. The Saturday after my last visit to her house, she planned to get up at 5:30 a.m. and drive 170 miles in her battered tan Chevy to address an environmental rally in Savannah, Georgia. "I never turn down requests from young people," she said. "So as the song says, I'm 'gonna put on my high-heeled sneakers,' and go. Take two of my friends who like things like that. I hope I can get some good fish down there on the wharf."

THE POWER OF STUBBORNNESS

I've mentioned the need to be patient and to savor the journey as we go. Less obvious, perhaps, is the virtue of sheer stubbornness, placed in service of higher ideals. We need to be open to learning, to change, and to compromise. But sometimes we just have to dig in our heels and resist the fine-sounding rationalizations that would appease our conscience and silence our voice. If we don't, we might forget what we wanted to fight for in the first place.

Modjesca embodied this kind of stubbornness. Besides her passion, fiery spirit, and strong sense of humor, she simply refused to give up. When I think about people who continue their involvements for years, whatever the odds, they remind me of farmers who replant when hail destroys their crops. They keep on because work needs to be done. If this work is sometimes frustrating, that's part of the bargain.

Besides, as John Kenneth Galbraith wrote, "There is something personally satisfying about being disagreeable by advancing the truth." Stanford's Stephen Schneider, one of the world's leading climate scientists, had a similar response when I asked if he got worn down by the ability of corporations like Exxon and the coal companies to distort public discussion of global climate change. "My reaction was just the opposite of burnout," Schneider said. "It was hot pursuit of their phony claims and immoral agendas. They motivated me to go after these world wreckers even harder."

Bob Zellner was an Alabama organizer whose father was a Klansman and a preacher. Zellner eventually became the first white field secretary of the Student Nonviolent Coordinating Committee (SNCC). When a Klan mob tried to lynch him, Zellner wrapped his arms around a tree, holding on with all his strength. It took so many men to pry him off that at last a Klan leader looked down and said, "Anybody who wants to live this much, we're going to let you." Zellner has inspired other activists who knew him to fight for what's right with the same determination.

Such stubbornness can give us that extra measure of strength we may need to address the morally urgent but potentially overwhelming issues of our time. A friend of Pete Knutson's was crewing on a boat through a treacherous passage in Canada's Queen Charlotte Sound when they entered a fog bank. All around, the waves pounded the rocks. People couldn't see past their faces. The skipper panicked, abandoned the helm, and exclaimed, "It's all over, boys. We're done for." Then he went below to lie down on his bunk, smoke a cigarette, and wait for the boat to hit the rocks. "Well, you may be done for," said Pete's friend and the other crew members, "but we're not." They steered themselves through the passage and out of danger. Pete likes to tell this story. Many who set our society's course have given up on creating a just world, or never had any interest to begin with. If we follow their lead, we may founder on cynicism and despair. But that doesn't mean we're powerless. It's in our hands to steer society toward a better outcome, no matter how thick the fog or how dark the night.

Pete feels far better, he says, trying to change things, even if doing so means battling powerful institutions. "They're not going to get rid of me," he says with a smile. "I take some perverse satisfaction in giving them grief."

"We could have given up during Initiative 640," he explains, "when the aluminum industry, the timber companies, and the sport fishing interests all came after us. We could have said, 'It's all over, boys.' But we managed to translate what was important about saving the commercial fishing economy to people who cared about the environment. You never know if you're going to win or not, but if you don't sell out to expediency, it's amazing what a handful of people can do.

"We often underestimate our power," Pete believes. "We fall into a trap of intellectually convincing ourselves that there's no way we can change things. We get paralyzed by the enormity of the problems and the apparent strength of our opponents. But in a weird way, that magnifies our helplessness. We think of ourselves as beleaguered and isolated. Yet lots of other people share our sentiments about the difference between greed and human respect. We need to help give them a voice."

Maybe, Pete wonders, the forces we challenge recognize the power of an engaged citizenry better than do those of us who are involved. "When the major industrial interests behind Initiative 640 were meeting, they had a copy of the article I wrote for the local Sierra Club newsletter exposing their environmental duplicity. They read it aloud, and were just livid. They referred to me as 'the eco-gillnetter.' You just have to laugh when you realize that you're some multibillion-dollar corporation's worst nightmare. It's like Richard Nixon being totally obsessed by the antiwar movement, while he denied he was even paying attention. We just can't predict the impact we'll have." We can't predict our impact, which is why we should persist.

We can view the stubbornness that Pete exemplifies as the deepest kind of patriotism, standing up for the well-being of the planet and saying, in effect, "We aren't just visiting. We live here. And we intend to pass on a better world."

I saw this attitude in a seventy-eight-year-old grandmother, Ruth Youngdahl Nelson. One of her brothers had been a two-term Minnesota governor, another a Congressman. Ruth herself was a nationally prominent Lutheran laywoman whom the organization that sponsors Mother's Day had named National Mother of the Year. Ruth had always charted her own path: meeting her minister husband after defeating him in a 3-mile swimming race; helping integrate their Washington, D.C., church at a time when that seemed unthinkable; consistently speaking her mind. But her life remained relatively "respectable" until the early 1980s, when her minister son, Jon, committed civil disobedience at the Seattle-area Trident submarine base.

Ruth visited Jon in jail. When he made plans to participate in the small-boat blockade of the first Trident submarine, Ruth announced that she'd also join in. She considered it "very obnoxious that we should threaten to obliterate thousands of people who we've never even met." On the day of the Trident's arrival, the Coast Guard brought in an armada, using the high-powered water cannons to scatter the protestors' boats and dump their occupants in the water. When a young sailor aimed his water cannon at the motorboat containing Jon, Ruth, a suburban nurse, a former priest, and a Lutheran deaconess, Ruth mustered up all her prairie-bred courage and integrity, and in her most grandmotherly style shook her finger at him.

"No, no, young man," she commanded, kindly but firmly. "Not in my America. Please. You wouldn't do that." The young sailor looked at her, froze, and backed down.

SLOW-BURNING FIRE

Like Pete Knutson responding to the destruction of Northwest salmon runs and Ruth Nelson to the "very obnoxious" nuclear weapons, we often become involved because we get outraged. We see lives and hopes damaged by distant institutional powers. We see the gap between the world that is and the world that should be. We watch human beings turned into expendable abstractions. We feel we have to do something.

Mastered and honed, the resulting anger can help us keep going for the long haul. Without "a capacity for anger," argued longtime peace activist Reverend William Sloane Coffin, we begin "to tolerate the intolerable. . . . If you are not angry, you are probably a cynic. And if you lower your quotient of anger at oppression, you lower your quotient of compassion for the oppressed. I see anger and love as very related."

Yet political anger can also devour us. Anyone who's been around social movements has met people so consumed by their fury that they scarcely remember what they're fighting for. Some of these activists are fueled by personal resentments, using their causes as an outlet for their every complaint against family, friends, and a world that fails to properly appreciate them. Others have adopted the stereotype of the shouting protester as a political tactic, on the assumption that only the greatest militancy can force the powers that be to pay heed. For most of us, however, the danger lies in being overwhelmed by the gravity of the injustices we see yet feel inadequate to address. Images of suffering and destruction become our sole focus, our obsession. Necessary indignation turns into rage. We risk giving up in frustration or losing sight of the world we'd like to create.

How do we transmute our anger so that, in Gandhi's words, "as heat conserved is transmuted into energy," it becomes "a power that can move the world"? How do we use this volatile fuel to help us challenge injustice without succumbing to it ourselves?

First, we can remember the sense of human connection that underpins our commitment. Second, we can practice radical patience. When the old woman in her neighborhood died in the cold, remembers Virginia Ramirez, "I didn't know what to do. It was very hard to control my anger. I'd kept it quiet for so many years that when I began to let it out, it consumed me. When I first spoke out, I bit people's heads off. I had to do role-playing to learn how to have an impact without attacking people. You lose control when you feel there's nothing you can do. When you feel you can stop these bad situations, you do it in a different way. I'll always be angry about the situation of my community. But if I can work for the long run, I'll have better results."

"I had to turn my anger into a slow-burning fire instead of a consuming fire," explained Myles Horton, founder of Highlander Center, where Rosa Parks attended workshops before her epochal protest. "You don't want the fire to go out—you never let it go out—and if it ever gets weak, you stoke it. But you don't want it to burn you up. It keeps you going, but you subdue it because you don't want to be destroyed by it."

Meditation teacher Steven Levine, who's done powerful work with teenage prisoners and with the dying, agrees that we may need to be angry in the process of working for change. He urges, however, that we accompany this anger "with a soft belly," so we stay rooted, flexible, and receptive. Beneath our anger, Levine says, lies "an ocean of sadness," which we need to acknowledge if we are to act effectively. We can't do that if our gut is clenched with rage.

MOMENTS THAT INSPIRE US

When we do achieve successes, they can sustain us long after the events have passed. Alison Smith talked of working with electoral reform activists throughout the country to help them follow in Maine's footsteps. "I always felt we were doing good work," she said. "But it's amazing to realize that people are watching us and getting inspired. I'd like to make this enough of a success so my children can live in a country where regular people feel proud of their democracy, know people running for office, maybe even run for office themselves. But it won't happen unless people participate. The longer I do this work, the harder it feels to stop."

Rich Cizik was sustained by his faith, and by shifts in the evangelical community. "In 1972," he said, "when the Lord called me to Himself, evangelicals were nearly completely silent on any public witness. There was a call for conversion of the lost, as in the preaching of Billy Graham. But the Gospel was truncated by the failure of evangelicals to speak to issues of that day such as racism. In 1970, the first Earth Day had no one from the evangelical community involved. Back then the evangelicals would have shunned the event, were they invited. But we're changing that." Cizik had just come back from Morocco, "where we're planning the first Earth Day in a Muslim country." He called his fellow evangelicals "a slow-moving earthquake. They don't quite understand themselves how they're changing, but they are."

Successes don't have to play on a grand stage to boost our spirits. During one of my visits to San Antonio, Virginia Ramirez described a celebration she'd just attended. For forty years people had prodded the city to rebuild an old street that flooded every time it rained. Officials said repeatedly they didn't have the money, although they'd spent plenty on wealthier neighborhoods. Finally COPS mustered the support to pass a bond issue. "The other day the engineers came by to start construction," Virginia said, "and we had a party to celebrate. It will be a real street, with sidewalks and storm drains. People were so excited, talking about how their sidewalks would look and their little yards, and how much they'd take pride in it. It's a small thing, but it gives hope to the community."

One of those celebrating, Virginia said, was a young woman with a three-month-old baby. "My grandmother always wanted to see them fix the street," the woman told Virginia. "She fought so hard to get a bond passed, but they always said it was too expensive, and now she's dead. I wish she could have lived to see it."

"But you're here," Virginia responded, "and so's your child. Now when your child walks to school someday, she won't have to walk through all the mud and water. It's for you now, and for her." "These are the kinds of victories," Virginia told me, "that keep me going."

Even in the face of apparent defeat, we can take heart from the victories of others—examples we might call miracles of hope. Nobel Peace Prize–winner Jose Ramos-Horta saw his country, East Timor, brutalized by Indonesian rule. More than 200,000 people were killed, including members of his family and many of his closest friends. Ramos-Horta maintained his hope during the most horrific times, he said, by drawing strength from the courage of those who kept working for his country's freedom despite all the violence and intimidation. But he also drew strength from all the others who'd acted for justice around the world. Ramos-Horta felt particularly inspired by times "when the human spirit has triumphed over force," with little help from those in power, like "the practitioners of realpolitik in Washington, London, and Bonn. According to them, Vaclav Havel should have continued to accept the irreversibility of Soviet rule in Eastern Europe. The Armenians shouldn't have a country. South Africa shouldn't be free. Pinochet should still be ruling Chile. But all this has been changed by human courage."

America has its own legacies of inspiring engagement, even during inhospitable times. It's tempting to give up on campaign reform—until people like Alison challenge the cynicism that insists politicians have to be bought and paid for. Urban violence seems inevitable—until people like David Lewis and Deborah Prothrow-Stith create innovative programs to limit its reach. Climate change seems overwhelming—until people like Angie Do Soto, Rich Cizik, Bill McKibben, and innovative mayors and green entrepreneurs begin shifting the tide.

These people and others whose journeys I've described have transformed untapped aspirations for change into powerful social progress. Who could have imagined that Glenn Hening and his circle of friends could mobilize surfers to protect the environment, or that Pete Knutson would do the same with his fellow fishermen? Could anyone anticipate that Virginia and her fellow COPS members would bring a billion dollars of public and private investment into San Antonio's poorest neighborhoods? When unions are being dismissed as anachronisms, people like Jorge Rivera and campaigns like Justice for Janitors are helping revive them as vital social movements. In all these cases, and more, individuals acted despite their uncertainties. They didn't have all the answers and their victories haven't ushered some ultimate kingdom of justice. But they're legitimate causes for hope.

Harry Taylor felt this hope when reflecting on the unexpected impact of his own actions, explaining, "As one who has seen, firsthand, how powerful we can be when we're in the right place, at the right time, and with a message that resonates, I know that we can alter the future—hard as that is to believe at times. I've learned that if you can stand up and speak, you'd better do it."

We can draw inspiration from both past and future. Meredith Segal recalled her family's long tradition of service, and how, "in times of skepticism or discouragement," the determination, courage, and tenacity of her parents and grandparents inspired her to keep working for justice. When things got tough, Angie De Soto helped sustain herself by thinking about the children she hoped to have ten years down the line and how "all those yet to be born are relying on us to not give up."

YOU CAN'T HELP BUT BE INSPIRED

Whether looking back on how other citizens created change against impossible odds, or forward toward the world we'd like to create, we're locating ourselves in the river of social justice that historian Vincent Harding described. This stream of courage and solidarity allows an action fifty years ago or halfway around the world to inspire and sustain us here and now. The people I've described in this book have their moments of bleakness. They don't win every battle. But they continue, despite the obstacles. And if we take their lives seriously, we'll know that our actions can matter. "You can't help but be inspired," said one longtime activist, "simply knowing people who've been involved all their life and always will be."

Just as we draw hope from common leaps of progress, we can also be inspired by changes in particular lives. This is why, when we work to transform the world, we can make an impact in two ways. If we win our immediate battles, we can reform specific institutions, shift specific policies, and open up future possibilities for change. So we need to act as effectively as we can. Yet even if we lose seemingly critical fights, our actions may still help open minds and change hearts. They may inspire people to rethink their values and choices, raise questions they'd kept to themselves, move from silence and accommodation to engagement—and in the process set the stage for their next round of involvement. Given the stakes, our first priority is achieving our specific goals of change. But it's also a victory each time we bring a new participant into a culture of engagement.

Few things are as heartening as watching this process. "You see this big iceberg out there," says Carol McNulty's husband, Bill. "It's hard to see how to shift its direction. But locally, you see this person on board who wasn't before, this person writing letters, another person who's going to fundraise. It's progress."

Pioneering gay activist Harry Hay described the sense of accomplishment he got when he traveled around the country and young men told him, "Thank you for my life." "Every time," Hay said, "every time, it wipes me out. For me, that's the greatest gift of all."

One change nurtures another, personally and politically. Having toyed with Islam while in prison, David Lewis now makes it a mainstay of his life. He draws strength from going to AA meetings, reading the Koran, and attending a mosque, where, he says, "I can see the power of people gathering, and devoting themselves to God." He also feels inspired by people whose lives he's helped turn around, like an African American prisoner who felt hopeless until he heard David speak, then got out and became Free at Last's lead outreach worker. Another, a Latino man, had swum across the Rio Grande five years before, knowing not a word of English. Now he has graduated from college with honors and helps run the organization's health education efforts.

David recently attended the graduation of Free at Last's women's residential treatment program. "You look in a woman's eyes," he says, "as she's walking out of our facility to an apartment and a job. Six months ago she was standing on the side of a freeway with a sign that said 'I'll do anything for a sandwich.' Those are the kind of things that keep me going. They're sometimes far between. You can go for a while when you don't see any hope, just groan and doom. But then when change happens, all the money in the world can't pay for looking in another human being's eyes and knowing that God gave you the ability to help them change. When I see the uplifting of another human being out of the jaws of destruction and calculated bullshit, it just affects me profoundly."

GROWING AS A PERSON

Earlier I noted that effective social activism builds upon our existing belief structures, giving us opportunities to apply our innermost notions of justice to new causes and circumstances. As we continue in our commitments, we can grow even more rooted in these values, and, in the process, nourish our soul.

"When I joined the PTA, I was so timid," says Virginia Ramirez. "All I could do was make the punch and cookies. Then I started being challenged when I joined COPS. I became hungry for learning. I had so many wonderful mentors who taught me, and helped me think through what I believed. They taught me to listen to the pain in our poor community, but also hear the good stuff, because there's lots of that, too. You can learn a lot from the smile of a child, or watching a mother's face. I just went to a graduation of our new job-training program, the one I testified before Congress about. I felt good that I worked on it. After twenty-five years, I'm still growing as a person."

Virginia takes particular pride in being able to stand up for her own views. "When I was growing up, women weren't equal. It wasn't nice to talk to a man, other than your husband. When I joined the organization, I saw more equality, and learned to speak when I had an opinion. As a Hispanic woman, that was a very important step, for me to learn to deal with men as an equal."

COPS also constantly helped members evaluate their actions, so they could continue learning. The organization had succeeded, she believes, because it stressed developing individual skills. "The issues are important," she says. "But what happens with the people is more important. I was watching one of our new leaders today. She chairs our committee on streets and drainage. I've seen her grow so much in the past year. Now she's training others and holding all these meetings. It's a wonderful transition."

COPS doesn't lose many battles, Virginia says, but even when it does, the group's emphasis on personal development helps members maintain their commitment. After every campaign, successful or not, they ask themselves how they might have proceeded differently, enlisted more support, conveyed their message more clearly, built a broader coalition. "Even when we lose," Virginia explains, "we still gain something."

When times get hard, Virginia relies on her community. "Sometimes you have to say, 'I've just had enough,'" she says. "You go home and take a week off. But then you see someone, and they say, 'Oh, Mrs. Ramirez, I'm so happy to see you. I'm so happy you were out there representing us.' Or they remind me how much fun we had working together. Or you see an injustice and get mad all over again. These are the things that make me go back, and think that whatever's going on, I want to be part of it."

FAITH AND HOPE

As Virginia says, nothing is more hopeful than watching people grow. But the paths we follow in our engagement are rarely fixed or linear. Social activists often shift course, addressing successive issues with different approaches, all the while trying to realize a larger vision of justice. Cornel West writes of African American music as a model for an approach where the path we take evolves continually. "When you look closely at jazz, or the blues, for example, we see a sense of the tragic, a profound sense of the tragic linked to human agency. . . . [The music] does not wallow in a cynicism or a paralyzing pessimism, but it also is realistic enough not to project excessive utopia. It's a matter of responding in an improvisational, undogmatic, creative way to circumstances, in such a way that people still survive and thrive."

Rachel Naomi Remen offers a parallel metaphor on finding our particular paths to involvement, learning and improvising as we go. We each heal from physical illness in our own way, she reminds us. "Some people heal because they have work to do. Others heal because they have been released from their work and the pressures and expectations that others place on them. Some people need music, others need silence, some need people around them, others heal alone." Similarly, we each need our own approach to healing the world.

Even as we're pursuing these unique paths we need to continue nurturing our hope—so it can enable us to persevere despite all obstacles. Vaclav Havel calls hope "an orientation of the heart," explaining, "Hope is definitely not the same thing as optimism. It is not the conviction that something will turn out well, but the certainty that something makes sense, regardless of how it turns out." Given the profound problems we've inherited and the deep-rooted obstacles to addressing them, we can't guarantee that the future will get better, at least not soon. So optimism may not get us through. But hope allows us to stand up for what we believe even in the most difficult circumstances, whatever the immediate results.

In this view, hope rarely springs from certainty. Instead, it begins and ends in what stirs our hearts, where we place our trust, how we conduct our lives. As writer Norman Cousins explained: "The case for hope has never rested on provable facts or rational assessment. Hope by its very nature is independent of the apparatus of logic. What gives hope its power is not the accumulation of demonstrable facts, but the release of human energies generated by the longing for something better."

The more we voice our beliefs and speak to these longings, the more hope has a chance to emerge. We talk with new people, hear inspirational stories, build bonds with new communities. We no longer sit passively, immobilized by despair.

My friend Robert Gordon spent years teaching writing in the Washington State prison system, until the legislature cut the budget for his and other education programs, even though these programs dramatically lowered the rates of inmates reoffending. At a talk to a group of fellow prison teachers, he explained, "Some of the people we work with will already have redeemed their lives. Others, no matter what we do, will be back in here again. And for some, our efforts will make all the difference." The challenge, he said, is that we'll never know which group is which, but that shouldn't deter our efforts. It seems an apt metaphor not only for any context of teaching, but for any social change work.

Those willing to live with such uncertainty still experience frustrations and disappointments, but they're better equipped to withstand them and thus persist for the long haul. As the Reverend Carla Berkedal, of Earth Ministry, says, "Hope isn't about the things that we can see—all the problems. It's about the things that we can't see, and having faith in them." Like Berkedal, many of us draw our hope from strong religious traditions. At the core of these traditions is belief in a divine spirit that's present to support us, and in a promise that acts of courage, faith, and compassion will sooner or later make an impact—that, as Martin Luther King said during the Montgomery bus boycott, "the universe bends toward justice." Novelist David Bradley describes this faith as a fundamental trust that "somewhere, never mind exactly where, something good and right and fair is happening which someday, never mind exactly when, will make itself apparent; that in some distant constellation a star has flamed to unaccustomed brilliance, and what we must do is wait for the arrival of the light." Because this light is always and everywhere imminent, ready to reveal itself, our religious traditions remind us that we're never completely alone and forsaken. However much human destructiveness can ravage individual lives, communities, and even ecosystems, it cannot destroy the fundamental source of life and, thus, of hope.

Rosalie Bertell, a Catholic nun with a PhD in mathematics who has become an outspoken expert on radiation and human health, compares our situation with that of the Israelites during their wilderness sojourn. After their exodus from Egypt, the tribes wandered the desert for years; many soon longed for the familiar security of their previous bondage. Even when manna fell from heaven, many held back from accepting it. We need to know how to take in new nourishment, new manna, Bertell says, from the community we create, and from our sense of faith. It's inevitable, she believes, that sometimes we will long for the comforts of our own familiar bondage, our accustomed political silence. Inevitably, we'll mistrust the prospects for change. Maybe, like Moses, we will only glimpse the promised land that we seek. But we have to take the first steps to leave Egypt.

Activists like Bertell draw heart from a God who gives strength to the weary and powerless, who comforts the oppressed. "When things go real bad," says Virginia Ramirez, "and sometimes they do, I'll pray. If I'm on the road and I'm having a bad day, like I made a jackass of myself, I'll say, 'Oh Lord, it's been a bad day. Please be with me.' We want to win so things can get better. But if we lose, we lose. It's not going to tear us apart. Even if we lose, God will give us more strength, because then we have to fight even harder."

David Lewis also relies on a spiritual source of support, during good times and bad. "I was in a real low place," he says, "driving from Oregon to California after a workshop. But I had a feeling of this presence next to me, comforting and soothing me, reviving and engaging me. We like to be certain about what we count on. If we can't touch it, see it, kick it in the ass, we don't consider it real. But there's a deeper force that helps me cut through the garbage and remember the truth."

In an essay he wrote in a Nazi prison cell while awaiting execution for his participation in a plot to kill Hitler, Lutheran theologian Dietrich Bonhoeffer explored the link between faith and moral strength. In a world where evil approaches us in "so many respectable and seductive disguises that [our] conscience becomes nervous and vacillating," he wrote, and where we're taught to trust duty, reasonableness, or private virtue, keeping ourselves "pure from the contamination arising from responsible action," we can easily accommodate the worst moral ills. The courage to challenge them, Bonhoeffer said, resides in "the man whose final standard is not his reason, his principles, his conscience, his freedom or his virtue, but who is ready to sacrifice all this when he is called to obedient and responsible action in faith and in exclusive allegiance to God."

Bonhoeffer counseled a highly demanding faith. While we may want to trust the wisdom of the self, he argued, it can't be an isolated self, the one-dimensional creation of a shallow or destructive culture. Instead, we need to listen to that voice of conscience that represents the deeper wisdom of God, and be loyal to it, embracing what he called "the cost of discipleship." Many of Bonhoeffer's writings and speeches, as he worked to organize German churches against Hitler, challenged what he called "religionless Christianity," which adapted far too easily to the terrible crimes being committed in Europe at the time. We challenge injustice, wrote Bonhoeffer, by trying to make our whole life "an answer to the question and call of God."

Most religious traditions consciously address hope, placing it within a larger spiritual framework. For those of us who don't believe in a transcendent force or being, the ultimate sources of hope may be less apparent. I've seen many secular activists take it for granted that issues alone will motivate people to act, that if we promote strong alternative perspectives, and articulate them well, our fellow citizens will necessarily respond. We tend to underestimate or ignore the spiritual and psychological reasons why people take public stands. Yet since the eighteenth-century intellectual movement known as the Enlightenment, citizens who've fought for liberty, justice, and democracy have, I believe, embraced a particular implicit philosophy of hope, rooted in assumptions about historical progress.

Some of these activists viewed their efforts as part of the civic republican tradition that was embodied by people like Thomas Jefferson, whose intellectual roots go back to Aristotle. Others acted on behalf of a vision of economic democracy, as conceived in the labor and socialist traditions. And others staked their reform efforts on the mix of technical invention, economic growth, and modest redistribution of resources at the heart of the post–Second World War social welfare state. In all these cases, people acted in the belief that history was moving toward a time of greater justice. That future wasn't automatic, but conscientious human effort could help bring it about. Together with people's direct outrage at insults to human dignity, and a more general longing for a better world, their belief in this promise helped many to stand up for their beliefs.

Now, for all the reasons I've described, that promise is less certain. As biologist Stephen Jay Gould has pointed out, Darwinian evolution is irreversible, but social evolution can roll backward. Whatever our immediate political context, people are likely to feel themselves at the mercy of distant and unaccountable global forces for at least the immediate future. Concentrated wealth will continue to threaten the democratic process. Climate change and ecological limits will pose stark new challenges. Economic opportunities long taken for granted may well continue to be threatened. Given all this, those of us on the more secular side can hardly take our political hope for granted. We have to reclaim it actively, maybe even cobble it together.

To do so often involves developing a sense of larger connection similar to that of the religious activists, though expressed in nontheological terms. For instance, from the complex majesty of the natural world, a shifting dance of creation that existed long before humans inhabited the earth, and will exist long afterward. As Rabindranath Tagore wrote: "The same stream of life that runs through the world runs through my veins night and day and dances in rhythmic measure. It is the same life that shoots in joy through the dust of the earth into numberless blades of grass and breaks into tumultuous waves of flowers."

When I despair of our culture's greed and short-sightedness, I often go for a run on my favorite Seattle beach. It's a long, arching cove, with red-barked madrona trees growing on the tall bluffs that rise behind it. Across the water are the snowcapped Olympic Mountains. The sun sparkles on the waves. Ferries and freighters go by, and sometimes seals or sea lions. The run itself pumps blood through my veins. After a short time, my mind begins to quiet. I feel calmer, less frenetic, connected with something larger and more enduring. By the end, my soul feels cleansed and I remember that we inherit a rich and generous planet, which, if we treat it well, should offer enough to sustain us all.

How else can the more secular among us find and sustain hope? Glenn Hening is motivated by a connection with his children. "When you put them to bed at night," he says, "you want to be able to look at yourself and ask, 'What did I do to make the world a better place for them?' You can't depend on anyone else to ask that question for you. You have to take responsibility for the life you brought into the world. You have to decide if you've lived up to your responsibility."

Even if the past holds no guarantees for the future, we can still take heart, as I've suggested, from previous examples of courage and vision. We can remember that history unfolds in ways we can never predict, but that again and again brings astounding transformations, often against the longest of odds. Strength can also come, as we've explored, from a radical stubbornness, from savoring the richness of our journey, and from the victories we win, lives that we change, and community we build.

More than anything, activists—religious and secular—keep going because participation is essential to their dignity, to their very identity, to the person they see in the mirror. To grow silent, they say, would be self-betrayal, a violation of their soul. "That's why we were put here on this earth," they stress again and again. "What better thing can you do with your life?" "There'll be nobody like you ever again," said veteran environmentalist David Brower. "Make the most of every molecule you've got, as long as you've got a second to go. That's your charge." "We do not do justice work to 'change the world,'" says Unitarian minister Merilyn Sewell, "We do the work because we must."

"I don't feel I have a choice," says a friend who works long unpaid hours to host an alternative local cable show. "For instance, once you understand the reality of climate destabilization it's not possible to go back to sleep. I know people who take the position that we've had it and there is nothing we can do, so why knock ourselves out. They tell me, 'You have to be optimistic, you're an activist.' But I can't comprehend that attitude at all. Actually I'm not that optimistic either, but what's the point of your existence if you take a position like theirs? So I'm resolved to keep working for change no matter what."

We want to respond to the ills of our time with what Rabbi Abraham Heschel once called "a persistent effort to be worthy of the name human." A technical editor who chaired her local Amnesty International chapter felt demeaned just by knowing about incidents of torture. To do something about it helped her recover her spirit. "When you stand in front of the Creator," says Carol McNulty, "you want to say, 'I tried to make a difference.' It isn't going to be what kind of car I had or how big a house. I'd like to think I tried."

Being true to oneself in this fashion doesn't eradicate human destructiveness. We need to live, as Albert Camus suggested, with a "double memory—a memory of the best and the worst" of human existence. We can't deny the cynicism and callousness of which we are capable. We also can't deny the courage and compassion that offer us hope. It's our choice which characteristics we'll steer our lives by.

PICKING YOUR TEAM

Cynicism or hope? That's the real question, the choice all of us face, as individuals, families, neighborhoods, communities, nations, and members of a species whose continued survival is by no means guaranteed.

Howard Zinn explored the tension between our best and our worst in terms of how we view America's past. "What we choose to emphasize in this complex history," he wrote, "will determine our lives. If we only see the worst, it destroys our capacity to do something. If we remember those times and places—and there are so many—where people have behaved magnificently, this gives us the energy to act, and at least the possibility of sending this spinning top of a world in a different direction." Zinn continued, "History is full of instances where people, against enormous odds, have come together to struggle for liberty and justice, and have won—not often enough, of course, but enough to suggest how much more is possible."

By deciding which side of history we want to be on, we also decide what kind of community we want to be part of. "Every day presents infinite reasons to believe that change can't happen," says Sonya Vetra Tinsley, "infinite reasons to give up. But I always tell myself, 'Sonya, you have to pick your team.' It seems to me that there are two teams in this world. And that you can find evidence to support the arguments of both. The trademark of one team is cynicism. They'll tell you why what you're doing doesn't matter, why nothing is going to change, why no matter how hard you work, you're going to fail. They seem to get satisfaction out of explaining how we'll always have injustice. You can't change human nature, they say. It's foolish to try. From their experience, they might be right."

Then there's another group of people, Sonya believes, "who admit that they don't know how things will turn out, but have decided to work for change. I see Martin Luther King on that team, Alice Walker, Howard Zinn. I see my chaplain from college and my activist friends. They're always telling stories of faith being rewarded, of ways things could be different, of how their own lives have changed.

They'll give you reasons why you shouldn't give up; testimonials why we've yet to see our full potential as a species. They believe we're partners in God's creation, and that change is really possible.

"There are times when both teams seem right. Both have evidence. We'll never know who's really going to prevail. So I just have to decide which team seems happier, which side I'd rather be on. And for me that means choosing the side of faith. Because on the side of cynicism, even if they're right, who wants to win that argument anyway? If I'm going to stick with somebody, I'd rather stick with people who have a sense of possibility and hope. I just know that's the side I want to be on."

COMMITTED TO EACH OTHER

No one I know has persisted longer or influenced more people than Hazel Wolf did. Six hundred and fifty people filled a hall to celebrate her hundredth birthday. Hundreds more were turned away. In characteristic fashion, Wolf used the occasion to establish an endowment for Junior Audubon clubs in middle school classrooms, just as her ninetieth birthday party raised money for a women's and children's hospital in Nicaragua. The event mixed birdwatchers, labor activists, Native American leaders, environmentalists, a former Washington governor, and an array of ordinary citizens, old and young, all inspired by her life. "Hazel has touched hundreds of people," said the president of Audubon's local chapter. "Thousands," people corrected spontaneously. "Not hundreds. Thousands." The president laughed and agreed.

The ceremony opened with slides of Hazel as an activist in her thirties, with her determined eyes and half-smile, and in her mid-nineties, kayaking on Washington's Puget Sound. People laughed at testimonies to her style of "endless pressure, endlessly applied." A Native American friend of hers drummed and chanted, then offered a prayer for "this beloved elder" who'd walked on the planet and left tracks for others to follow. Someone described how Hazel founded Audubon chapters statewide, and got fired three times during the Roosevelt era for starting unions. "She came to my middle school fifteen years ago, and I've been an environmental activist ever since," said one activist. Another described retiring at sixty-five and Hazel giving him a call to say, "Hey youngster. You're just getting started. Have I got a great committee for you." The president of the National Congress of American Indians, Ron Allen, recalled how he scraped through college with no money, no role models, and no support systems, and would have dropped out a dozen times or more, except for Hazel knocking on the door of his basement apartment "to tell me how I was going to make a difference, and how I wasn't just doing this for myself, but for my community."

At one hundred, as Hazel told Earth Day founding coordinator Denis Hayes, she woke up each morning and rubbed her eyes, delighted to be on "the right side of the grass." Quoting poet Samuel Ullman, Hayes described Hazel's quality of youth as the presence of courage over timidity, and an appetite for adventure rather than for a life of ease. "People grow old," in Ullman's words, "by deserting their ideals. Years may wrinkle our skin, but to give up our enthusiasm wrinkles the soul." By that standard, said Hayes, no one in the room was younger than Hazel.

People stood and applauded, as they did again and again throughout the ceremony. The applause wasn't perfunctory. For years, Hazel had stirred all of our souls as a model of how to spend a lifetime working for change, and doing so with passion and joy. She walked more slowly than she had a decade earlier, and talked more slowly, too. But she remained as quick-witted as ever—joking that she'd have to negotiate with the beavers that built five dams in a nearby marsh now bearing her name, "because we all know that dams without fish ladders are a problem." Hazel still savored the world she fought to save, and would savor it until her death two years later.

Near the evening's end, she noticed that no one had taken some fliers that had been left on a table to advertise a book on women environmental pioneers. So she excused herself from the parade of people who were congratulating her, grabbed a sheaf, and moved through the crowd with long-practiced style, greeting old friends and asking each, "Did you get one yet?" She kept talking, joking, and teasing, handing out fliers all the while.

Long runners like Hazel sustain their involvement less through an accumulation of knowledge than through a steady development of personal relationships; as time goes by, they become tied to more and more people who are struggling for justice. "I was describing to someone the solidarity we felt in trying to change Inland Steel," says Scharlene Hurston. "It was like war buddies, pulling people out of the trenches, and knowing you'll be friends for life. There were moments when we were tired or felt defeated. But we energized each other. When one person was tired, others picked them up. We were committed not just to the cause, but to our group."

Sonya Vetra Tinsley finds the same camaraderie with the activists she works with. As she says, "The relationships you build are so important. Rarely does everyone lose faith at the same time. It's nice that it works that way. I've come to realize that faith is not what you have because everything's going well. It's what keeps you going when you continue to believe and persist even when things are hard."

We inspire each other simply through our participation. We lift our coworkers' morale by showing up and sharing our humor, passion, and desire to act together for a common cause. We do this most easily when we have specific organizational structures to plug into—unions, churches, COPS, the Sierra Club, the League of Women Voters, local MoveOn or NRA groups, Democratic or Republican Party chapters. And when those organizations nurture the kinds of approaches that help keep people involved: visions that link long- and short-term goals; opportunities for citizens to make various commitments of time and energy; a willingness to listen and learn; forgiveness of our own shortcomings and the shortcomings of others; and a recognition that the most important fruits of our labors may not be evident for years. But whether through formal or informal communities, we're more likely to continue when working with people whose company we enjoy and whose lifelong commitment helps strengthen our resolve.

As Howard Zinn wrote, "The reward for participating in a

movement for social justice is not the prospect of future victory. It is the exhilaration of standing together with other people, taking risks together, enjoying small triumphs, and enduring disheartening setbacks—together.

"These years," wrote Zinn, "when I attend reunions of SNCC people, and we sing and talk, everyone says, in various ways, the same thing: how awful they were, those days in the South, in the movement, and how they were the greatest days of our lives." This isn't nostalgia, so long as those who look back remain engaged in the present. But it recognizes the unique satisfaction of fighting together for what's right.

Engaged community builds a sense of loyalty to others similarly struggling for a better world, and to all who've moved democracy forward in the past. Virginia Ramirez often recalls her sixty-eight-year-old fellow COPS activist who spoke no English but so inspired her that "whenever I got tired, and began to say, 'This is too much,' I'd think, 'If she can do it, what's holding me back?'" Even temporary communities can nurture our spirits, like the sense of excitement and possibility at the student Powershift global warming conference.

"I've thought about quitting," says a young Nebraska activist who organizes his fellow small farmers, "especially at times when I don't see results. But I've seen so many people in harder situations who keep on and don't give up. A friend of mine who works with the League of Rural Voters had a tornado hit their farm. He was injured with his wife in an auto accident. He has the responsibilities of two kids. But he's kept on staying active throughout."

Our communities don't have to be rooted in a specific time and place. They can extend to all those who fight for human dignity. Jose Ramos-Horta talks of being sustained by others who'd worked for justice before him. He singles out the Dalai Lama and Chinese human rights activist Harry Wu; Nelson Mandela, sitting in jail for twenty-seven years; Aristedes Mendes, the Portuguese consul-general in Bordeaux, France, who issued false Portuguese passports during World War II to save thousands of Jewish lives. "If those people had the courage to do what they did," says Ramos-Horta, "how can I give up? If I give in because of the difficulties, and simply sit back, I'm betraying all those who have died, all those who are fighting or in prison." He feels emboldened, he says, by all these acts of courage.

THE FULLNESS OF TIME

No matter how dedicated we are, social change never happens overnight. "Lots of people believe that it does," Virginia Ramirez told me, "but it always takes time. You get a few scars in the process. You never make these kinds of changes in one day." Think of my friend Lisa Peattie, who helped prompt famed baby doctor Benjamin Spock to speak out for peace just by standing with her kids— ragged, wet, and holding a sign in the rain. Think of the Columbia University students whom Desmond Tutu thanked for helping to end apartheid, and the students who helped engage a young Barack Obama. Think of the thousands inspired by Hazel Wolf. "All you can do," says Sonya Vetra Tinsley, "is keep on the best you can, and stay ready for the possibilities that come. The picture's always going to be bigger than you can see."

The poet Rainer Maria Rilke said much the same thing in the following eloquent lines:

My eyes already touch the sunny hill,
going far ahead of the road I have begun.
So we are grasped by what we cannot grasp;
it has its inner light, even from a distance—

and changes us, even if we do not reach it,
into something else, which, hardly sensing it, we already are . . .

As Rilke seems to be suggesting, although the future is unknowable, it nonetheless pulls us forward, toward what we might become. Whether citizen activists are just starting out or have been involved for years, those who persist learn to view this as a contingent world, whose future depends on the choices we make today. The Berlin Wall didn't fall by itself; people dismantled it, politically and physically. Lyndon Johnson didn't desegregate the South; it took the courage of those who risked their lives in Selma, Nashville, Greenville, Birmingham, and hundreds of places that never made the headlines. Similarly, our current social crises won't be solved unless far more of us participate. James Baldwin put it this way: "Everything now, we must assume, is in our hands. We have no right to assume otherwise." We are grasped, as Rilke said, by what we cannot grasp.

You may recall psychiatrist Robert Jay Lifton's concept of the "broken connection," the severed link between our convictions and our conduct. One way to repair this breach is to cultivate a sense of history. If we see our efforts as isolated acts, we're almost certainly going to grow desperate and disheartened. By contrast, viewing them as part of an ongoing historical narrative helps us feel we have all the time we need to act, even given the urgencies of the moment. It lets us concentrate on the work we have at hand, and trust that if we follow our most generous impulses, our labors will bear fruit. It shifts us from thinking solely about current crises, to asking how our efforts can best shape the world for generations to come.

However we work for change, we need this perspective. Perhaps we need it more than ever given the mix of hope and uncertainty of our time. Think of some of the diverse events that inspired or facilitated the civil rights movement: Gandhi's nonviolent protests in India; the anti-colonial rebellions in Africa; the labor struggles that led to the formation of supportive unions from the United Auto Workers to the Brotherhood of Sleeping Car Porters; the long and patient work of people like Modjesca Simkins and of groups such as local NAACP chapters. Brought about by a tremendous upwelling of courage, vision, and commitment, the movement's triumphs came later. But like all advances for freedom and justice, they would have been impossible without a rich legacy of struggle and resistance.

I've mentioned a student named Winston Willis, who joined

Columbia University's pivotal anti-apartheid campaign and later headed the school's Black Students Association. After Winston left Columbia, he taught eighth grade in Harlem, then returned to school to get a doctorate in history from Atlanta's once all-white Emory University. In a talk to Emory's black students association, Winston explained that he'd followed the example of his civil rights activist parents and of the black student leaders who'd preceded him at Columbia. "We're here not just because we're good students, or on our intrinsic merits," he said. "We're literally here by the blood of our people."

"I'm only twenty-seven," he told me, shortly afterward, "but I'm beginning to come to grips with the reality that I probably won't see the fundamental changes I want when I'm still around. It helps to know there are many folks before us—and many more who will follow."

As Winston says, each of us builds on the work of others. We can take the stories of people who've struggled for justice in the past as a challenge to do the same. Others have risked and persevered. Now it's our turn. As Rabbi Tarfon wrote, 1,900 years ago, "It is not up to you to complete the task. Nonetheless, you are not free to desist from it."

The cynics will continue to smirk, insisting that our efforts are futile. But when we act with courage and vision we never know what we might be able to achieve. To fail even to try is to reduce the potential of our soul. It's to diminish the spark that burns within us.

We all have our own distinct gifts, strengths, and opportunities to make our lives count. We all have our particular fears, flaws, and constraints. But no one kind of person is responsible for healing all the wounds of the world. That has to be a common task. The challenge is to ask what we want to stand for, and to do our best to act on our beliefs. For our choices will create the world that we pass on.

I began this book by quoting Rabbi Hillel; "If I am not for myself, who will be for me? And if I am only for myself, what am I?" Hillel asks a final question: "If not now, when?" I take his words to mean the moment of commitment cannot be deferred. It must become a lifelong process, one that links our lives to the lives of others, our souls to the souls of others, in a chain of being that reaches both backward and forward, connecting us with all that makes us human.

Postscript: The Ten Suggestions

An activist rabbi I know suggested I do a postscript of the Ten Commandments for effective citizen engagement. Calling them Commandments seems a bit presumptuous, but here are ten suggestions that can make engagement more fruitful:

Suggestion #1: Start where you are. You don't need to know everything, and you certainly don't need to be perfect.

Suggestion #2: Take things step by step. You set the pace of your engagement. Don't worry about being swallowed up, because you'll determine how much you get involved.

Suggestion #3: Build supportive community. You can accomplish far more with even a small group of good people than you can alone.

Suggestion #4: Be strategic. Ask what you're trying to accomplish, where you can find allies, and how to best communicate the urgencies you feel.

Suggestion #5: Enlist the uninvolved. They have their own fears and doubts, so they won't participate automatically; you have to work actively to engage them. If you do, there's no telling what they'll go on to achieve.

Suggestion #6: Seek out unlikely allies. The more you widen the circle, the more you'll have a chance of breaking through the entrenched barriers to change.

Suggestion #7: Persevere. Change most often takes time. The longer you continue working, the more you'll accomplish.

Suggestion #8: Savor the journey. Changing the world shouldn't be grim work. Take time to enjoy nature, good music, good conversation, and whatever else lifts your soul. Savor the company of good people working for change.

Suggestion #9: Think large. Don't be afraid to tackle the deepest-rooted injustices, and to tackle them on a national or global scale. Remember that many small actions can shift the course of history.

Suggestion #10: Listen to your heart. It's why you're involved to begin with. It's what will keep you going...

Continuing the Journey

I f you haven't already been involved in your community, I hope *Soul of a Citizen* will be your entry point. If you've taken on critical public issues for years, I hope it will help keep you going. Either way, please view this book is the beginning of a conversation, not the end. Here are some ways to continue exploring the themes it addresses:

The main Web site for *Soul of a Citizen* is www.soulofacitizen .org and for my work in general www.paulloeb.org. These sites include information on classroom use, my lectures at colleges and conferences, and my articles and other books, as well as links to more general resources on social involvement. Here are some specific pages:

Classroom Use: Includes classroom study questions derived from faculty already using the book, from all-campus first-year adoptions to graduate seminars, descriptions of their accompanying service learning projects, and suggestions on using the book if you have time to only assign part of it: www.soulofacitizen.org/classroom .htm.

Reading Group Guide: Soul of a Citizen has also been used in every imaginable kind of common reading context from church social justice groups to activist trainings to regular reading groups. You can find questions for these discussions at www.soulofacitizen.org/ bookgroups.htm.

Loeb Lectures: I've lectured and done workshops and residencies at more than 400 colleges and universities and many national conferences. See www.paulloeb.org/lectures.htm for information including my lecture schedule.

Bulk Discounts: Soul of a Citizen is available at a 50 percent discount for fifteen or more copies. See www.paulloeb.org/buy.htm or call (800) 221-7945 ext. 64.

Articles and Other Loeb Books: For my other books, including my award-winning political hope anthology *The Impossible Will Take a Little While,* see www.paulloeb.org. I also write articles on social involvement for outlets from *The New York Times* and *USA Today* to *Huffington Post.* See www.paulloeb.org/articles.htm for these articles, and to receive them directly see www.paulloeb.org/subscribe.htm.

We'll also be setting up an online discussion site. See www.paulloeb.org/discuss.htm. This page will also have links to my Facebook, Twitter, and any other social media sites.

Resource Guide: These are books on citizen involvement that I've found useful, as well as alternative media links and national organizations (most with local chapters) that offer ways to get involved: www.paulloeb.org/weblinks.htm.

INDEX

ACKNOWLEDGMENTS

It takes a village to write a book, and many villages to make it a success. *Soul of a Citizen*'s initial creation and impact over the past decade would have been impossible without a broad community that offered intellectual brainstorming, financial support, emotional sustenance, places to stay, collaboration in key projects, and a wealth of other kinds of assistance. Thank you RuthAlice Anderson, Allison Barlow, Harriet Barlow, Abby Brown, Susan Burmeister-Brown, Rabbi Leonard Beerman (who's inspired my journey from the beginning), David Bergholz, Mark and Sharon Bloome, Kyle Bohland, Brainerd Foundation, Leslie Brockelbank, Campus Compact, Don Carlson, Paul Cate, Center for Ethical Leadership, Laura and Richard Chasin, Cynthia Cohen, Martin Collier, Craig Comstock, Jim Compton and Compton Foundation, Sue Cook, Theresa Cusimano, Maureen Curley, Lenny Dee, Jonathan Dolger, Gary Dreiblatt and Nancy Sinkoff, Jim Driscoll, Kathy Engelken, Marge Fasman, Gary Ferdman, Ellen Ferguson, Carol Ferry, Jorge Garcia and Barbara Schinzinger, Giraffe Project, Adelaide Gomer, Bill Grace, The George Gund Foundation, Wade Greene, Wayne Grytting and Kevin Castle, Andy Himes, Tresa Hughes, Susan Hussey, Pamela Johnson, Robert Karlsrud, Hildy Karp, Alan Kay, Corrine Dee Kelly, Dick Kinsley, Ann Krumboltz, Lisa Keyne, Maria Monteiro, Dale Neinow, Liza Newman, Pete Knutson and Hing Lau Ng, Martha Kongsgaard, Jenny Ladd, Leland Larson, Ruth-Ann Larson, Karen Partridge, Gladys and Perry Rosenstein and Puffin Foundation, Rochelle Lefkowitz and ProMedia, Stanley Sheinbaum, Rodney Loeb and Carol Summer, Suzy and Wally Marks, Sue and Dan May, Dick and Nancy Mayo-Smith, Nan McMurray, Michael Minks, Ken Mountcastle, Jean Moshofsky and Brian Butler, Neal and Donna Mayerson and the Mayerson Foundation, Joan Palevsky, Bill Patz, the Peacemaking: Power of Nonviolence Conference, Ruth Pelz, Dan Petegorsky, Drumond Pike, Puffin Foundation, Alan and Andrea Rabinowitz, Bernard, Ron, and Abby Rapoport, Samuel Rubin Foundation, Marshall Saunders, Stanley Sheinbaum, John Sherer, John and Janet McKee Silard, Jodi Solomon, Norman Solomon, Paul and Ann Sperry, Steve Stapleton, Jerry Starr, Marcia Thompson, Tibet House, Tides Foundation, Sonya Tinsley, Bill Vandercook and Betsy Elich Vandercook, Magda and Fred Waingrow, Joan Warburg, Doug Ward and Frances Beula, John Weeks and Jeana Kimball, Marion Weber, Cora Weiss, the Western States Center, Jaki Williams Florsheim, Henry Florsheim, and the late Ron Williams, Bob and Blaikie Worth, Youth Service America, and David Zupan.

Soul of a Citizen has also benefited from the comments of Ron Aronson, Elaine Bernard, Kim Fellner, Dick Flacks, Glen Gersmehl, Jorge Garcia, Wayne Grytting, Jean Houston, Erica Kay, Pete Knutson, George Lakey, Joanna Macy, William Martin (my wonderful stepson, and a fine emerging writer in his own right), Gideon Rosenblatt, Peggy Taylor, Sam Tucker, Magda Waingrow (my eagle-eyed mother), John Weeks, and Howard Zinn. Lane Gerber connected me with key psychological research. Mark Powelson helped me give questions of faith the weight they deserved.

Harry Levinson has done a great job redesigning my Web site, building on an earlier design by Michael Stein. Gideon Rosenblatt, Jon Stahl, and Dean Ericksen from One Northwest give wonderful technical assistance to the Northwest environmental community and have long hosted my e-mail listserv. Gail Duff, the most patient travel agent I know, puts up with my endless changes to my travel itineraries. Katherine Oldfield, Laura Zanieski, Jerry Chroman, Corrine Dee Kelly, Barbara Kidder, Patrick Kintner, and Dan Lewis keep me physically and mentally healthy through all the stresses, external and self-imposed.

At St. Martin's Press, I've had two generations of helpful people to work with. Becky Koh convinced her colleagues to give the book a shot and edited the initial edition with the help of Jolanta Benal. After she left, I continued to work with the wonderful Nichole Argyres, who began as an editor's assistant and has been steadily promoted as the company wisely recognized her gifts. Nichole has done a great job shepherding and editing the book through its second round, with the help of her own smart, creative, and wonderfully organized assistant, Kylah McNeill. As *Soul*'s new edition goes to press, I've begun an excellent working relationship with publicist Rachel Ekstrom. But the person at the press who's done the most to make *Soul* a success in the marketplace is Macmillan Vice President of academic marketing Peter Janssen. Soon after *Soul*'s release, Peter noticed how powerfully students were responding to it in the classroom. When my friend, the brilliant progressive marketer Harvey McKinnon, convinced me to invest my own funds in mailing thousands of faculty who might assign the book in their courses, Peter became my wonderfully creative collaborator, sticking his own neck out to give away an exceptional number of books, and as a result making it possible for *Soul* to inspire students on campuses throughout the country.

Some key individuals were so closely woven with *Soul*'s genesis and fruition, it's hard to imagine it without them. Jean Tarbox and JoAnn Miller gave me the original idea for this project, and John Weeks cracked the whip to get me writing. My agent, Geri Thoma, of the Markson/Thoma Agency, first sold the book in the marketplace (as well as its successor, *The Impossible Will Take a Little While*), and has since become as staunch a friend, ally, and literary counselor as I could imagine. My friends Liz Gjelten and Edwin Dobb helped edit my very first book in 1982. They've now worked on every book of mine since, doing amazing work on both editions of *Soul*, to cut and reorder my initial and subsequent drafts, hone my arguments, and make sure that each word, sentence, paragraph, and story conveyed precisely what I meant to say. Hiring my part-time assistant, biochemist turned community organizer Erica Kay, was one of the best choices I've ever made, and Erica's proved tireless in tracking down every bit of research to make the book completely up-to-date and accurate. My wife, Rebecca Hughes, has brought me the gift of caring for the past fifteen years. She put the final touches on editing the manuscript when it first appeared, then spent her busman's holiday editing it once more to make it work for this round. Thank you Rebecca, for all your love, presence, patience, and humor.

Lastly, a final thank you to all the citizen activists I've interviewed for this book, and to all the others who share their courage and commitment.

ABOUT THE AUTHOR

Photo by Peter Lindstrom

Paul Loeb has spent forty years researching and writing about citizen responsibility and empowerment—asking what makes some people choose lives of social commitment, while others abstain. Born in California in 1952, Loeb attended Stanford University and New York's New School for Social Research, and worked in both places to end the Vietnam War. Loeb has written for a range of publications including *The New York Times, Washington Post, USA Today, Los Angeles Times, Huffington Post, Redbook, Psychology Today, Chronicle of Higher Education, Boston Globe, Christian Science Monitor, The Nation, Utne Reader, Salon, Parents, Mother Jones, Technology Review, Atlanta Journal-Constitution, Baltimore Sun, San Francisco Chronicle, Cleveland Plain Dealer, Detroit News, San Jose Mercury, St. Louis Post Dispatch, Tampa Tribune, Academe, Sojourners, National Catholic Reporter, Teaching Tolerance, Inside Higher Ed*, and the *International Herald-Tribune*.

Loeb's first book, *Nuclear Culture* (Coward, McCann, and Geoghegan, 1982; New Society Publishers, 1986), explored the daily world of atomic weapons workers in Hanford, Washington. *Hope in Hard Times* (Lexington Books, 1987) examined the lives and visions of ordinary Americans involved in grass roots peace activism. *Generation at the Crossroads: Apathy and Action on the American Campus* (Rutgers University Press, 1994) explored the values and choices of American college students. *Soul of a Citizen* (St. Martin's

Press 1999, second edition 2010) looks at what it takes to lead lives of social commitment despite all the obstacles. Including this wholly updated edition, *Soul* has over 150,000 copies in print between them. Paul's anthology on political hope, *The Impossible Will Take A Little While: A Citizen's Guide to Hope in a Time of Fear* (Basic Books, 2004), was named the #3 political book of 2004 by the History Channel and American Book Association, and won the Nautilus Award for best social change book.

Because it offers uniquely intimate perspectives on the fundamental questions of our time, Loeb's work has sparked widespread attention. His writing has been covered by the Associated Press, cited in Congressional debates, and praised, quoted, and discussed in an array of publications including *The New York Times, Washington Post, Time, Newsweek, The Economist, Modern Maturity/ AARP Magazine, Los Angeles Times, Harper's, New York Review of Books, Christian Science Monitor, Psychology Today, Parents Magazine, Chicago Tribune, Chicago Sun-Times, London Sunday Times, Manchester Guardian, Family Circle, Chronicle of Higher Education, USA Weekend, Newsday, Atlanta Journal Constitution, Detroit Free Press, Dallas Morning News, San Francisco Chronicle, Boston Globe, New Age, Christian Century, Commonweal, Teacher Magazine, Sojourners, Houston Chronicle, Cleveland Plain Dealer, Philadelphia Inquirer, Pittsburgh Post-Gazette, Orlando Sentinel, Charlotte Observer, Seattle Times, Greenpeace, NEA Today, Toronto Globe and Mail, Daily Age* (of Melbourne, Australia), the major German paper *Süddeutsche Zeitung, Baltimore Sun, Minneapolis Star-Tribune, Mother Jones, Academe, Contemporary Sociology, National Catholic Reporter,* and the *Atlantic.*

Loeb has also given over 1,000 TV and radio interviews, including nationwide appearances on TV networks like CNN, PBS, C-Span, the NBC Nightly News, Fox News, National Public Radio, the BBC, the ABC, NBC, and CBS radio networks, American Urban Radio, Voice of America, and national German, Australian, and Canadian radio.

Loeb has also lectured to enthusiastic responses at over 400 colleges and universities around the country—including Harvard,

Stanford, Chicago, Michigan, MIT, Yale, Duke, and Wisconsin—
and been a lead speaker at numerous conferences including the
National Education Association, American Society on Aging, Education Commission of the States, National Youth Leadership Council, National Association of Student Personnel Administrators,
Campus Compact's Presidential Summit, the American Bar Association's Equal Justice Conference, a national conference on race and
ethnicity on campus, the company meeting of Patagonia Corporation, the Unitarian General Assembly, and the annual provost's
conference of the American Association of State Colleges & Universities. In 2008, he founded the Campus Election Engagement Project,
which worked with 750 colleges and universities in 2012 to engage
their students in the election.

Contact Loeb for speaking at lecture@paulloeb.org or c/o Paul
Loeb, Campus Election Management Project, 3232 41st Ave. SW,
Seattle, WA 98116. To receive Loeb's articles regularly (about once
a month), or for all other information, visit www.Paulloeb.org.